PORTFOLIO

FINDING THE NEXT STARBUCKS

Michael Moe, CFA, is the cofounder, chairman, and CEO of ThinkEquity Partners L.L.C., and was formerly director of global growth stock research at Merrill Lynch. He has been named to Institutional Investor's All American research team and has been awarded "Best on the Street" by the *Wall Street Journal*. Quoted regularly by national publications, he is a frequent guest on CNBC and CNN. He lives in San Francisco.

FINDING THE NEXT STARBUCKS

How to Identify

and Invest

in the Hot Stocks

of Tomorrow

MICHAEL MOE

Portfolio

PORTFOLIO

Published by the Penguin Group

Penguin Group (USA) Inc., 375 Hudson Street, New York, New York 10014, U.S.A. • Penguin Group (Canada), 90 Eglinton Avenue East, Suite 700, Toronto, Ontario, Canada M4P 2Y3 (a division of Pearson Penguin Canada Inc.) • Penguin Books Ltd, 80 Strand, London WC2R 0RL, England • Penguin Ireland, 25 St Stephen's Green, Dublin 2, Ireland (a division of Penguin Books Ltd) • Penguin Group (Australia), 250 Camberwell Road, Camberwell, Victoria 3124, Australia (a division of Pearson Australia Group Pty Ltd) • Penguin Books India Pvt Ltd, 11 Community Centre, Panchsheel Park, New Delhi – 110 017, India • Penguin Group (NZ), 67 Apollo Drive, Rosedale, North Shore 0632, New Zealand (a division of Pearson New Zealand Ltd) • Penguin Books (South Africa) (Pty) Ltd, 24 Sturdee Avenue, Rosebank, Johannesburg 2196, South Africa

Penguin Books Ltd, Registered Offices:
80 Strand, London WC2R 0RL, England

First published in the United States of America by Portfolio, a member of Penguin Group (USA) Inc. 2006
This paperback edition published 2007

10 9 8 7 6 5 4 3 2 1

Publisher's Note:
This publication is designed to provide accurate and authoritative information in regard to the subject matter covered. It is sold with the understanding that the publisher is not engaged in rendering legal, accounting or other professional services. If you require financial advice or other expert assistance, you should seek the services of a competent professional.

THE LIBRARY OF CONGRESS CATALOGED THE HARDCOVER EDITION AS FOLLOWS:
Moe, Michael.

Finding the next Starbucks: how to identify and invest in the hot stocks of tomorrow / Michael Moe.
p. cm.
Includes index.
ISBN 1-59184-134-8 (hc.)
ISBN 978-1-59184-189-0 (pbk.)
1. Stocks—United States.   2. Investments—United States.   3. Investment analysis—United
States.   I. Title.
HG4910.M64 2006
332.63'220973—dc22   2006049814

Printed in the United States of America
Set in Minion
Designed by Katy Riegel

To my wonderful and loving family: my wife, Bonnie; my girls, Maggie and Caroline; my mother, Marcia; my father, Tom; my stepmother, Karen; my brothers, Mark and Tommy; my sisters, Laura, Jamie, Jennie, Aimee, and Jackie; and to my extended family at ThinkEquity Partners, all of whom have contributed to this effort in immeasurable ways.

CONTENTS

GROWING UP, I was obsessed with sports—both playing and watching. I knew every obscure fact and statistic for "my teams"—the Vikings, the Twins, and especially the University of Minnesota Golden Gophers.

As a kid, I was around business a lot because my dad was a successful corporate attorney who constantly had clients coming over to our house to work on deals at our kitchen table and calling at all hours of the night. Additionally, both my grandfathers, whom I adored, were accomplished senior business executives and active investors. But business and investing were of little interest to me—give me the sports page.

In life you have these Aha! moments that are extremely impactful, maybe like the first time you met your spouse. You remember the time, place, and date as if it was yesterday, even if it was twenty years ago. An Aha! moment happened for me at the University of Minnesota, where I majored in political science and economics, thinking I would be a lawyer like my dad, but my real "major" was as a very backup quarterback for the football team.

When I was a senior, a friend of my dad's took me to lunch and asked me if I ever thought of working on Wall Street. At the time, I thought the Federal Reserve was an Indian reservation. He gave me examples of how very small investments in companies like Control Data,

Medtronic, and 3M turned into very large sums of money based on the success of those companies.

Seeing I was interested, he explained how the magic of compound interest works over time and the Rule of 72. I couldn't believe how amazing it was. I was hooked and found a new passion. Out with *Sports Illustrated,* in with the *Wall Street Journal.*

I wrote this book to share what I have learned over the past 20 years about how to identify and invest in the small companies that can become big companies—what I call the stars of tomorrow. The hunt for these companies has the greatest potential for reward, but can also be very dangerous for the ill-prepared.

In reality, finding the best stocks is really finding the best companies— over time a stock's performance will be aligned with how the company does. Great companies and investors are both systematic and strategic to achieve their obejectives. The framework I provide in this book with our growth-investing 10 commandments, the four Ps for every great growth company (people, product, potential, and predictability), and sources to use to spot these companies early is a guide to finding tomorrow's ten baggers.

I am honored that one of my investment heroes, Peter Lynch, reviewed *Finding the Next Starbucks* and gave me some practical input to making it clearer and better. An analogy he used to describe the purpose of the book is that of a ski instructor. With a couple of lessons, you can't expect to be an expert, but you will learn some important fundamentals and also some strategy for not getting hurt. This book is meant to be a guide that will help you with both.

You don't have to be the next Warren Buffett or Peter Lynch to find the next Starbucks, Google, or Amgen, but you do need the right fundamentals, which I hope you'll find here.

Star Search—Finding the Supernovas

"Personally, I hope to find the next Siegfried and Roy."

—SIMON COWELL, *AMERICAN IDOL*

I WAS FORTUNATE to be one of the first research analysts to identify Starbucks Coffee as a huge opportunity following its IPO in 1992, when its market cap (share price multiplied by number of shares outstanding) was $220 million. Today, its market cap is $23 billion.

I was also one of the first research analysts to follow and recommend Apollo Group after it went public in December 1994, with a $110 million market cap. Apollo was the top-performing stock out of all U.S. publicly traded companies from 1994 to 2004. A dollar invested in APOL at its initial public offering (IPO) is worth $83 today.

My firm was the first to recommend the purchase of Google the day it went public at $85 a share. When the shares hit $200, I was on CNBC saying Google was "cheap" and the most important growth company in the world. CNBC *Squawk Box* host Mark Haines made an offhand remark that only somebody in San Francisco could be that nuts. As of December 31, 2005, it was $415.

Lucky? Maybe a little. Art or science? Both. Hard work? Absolutely. Let me tell you a story.

It was a Thursday afternoon after a long week on the road visiting companies. I was in Seattle with one meeting to go before I flew home. My friends told me about this coffee company—named after a *Moby-Dick* character—that had a cult following. I almost canceled my meeting on the way to the airport because I just wanted to get home and the company sounded ridiculous.

Maybe people in Seattle would embrace a coffee house as a great business, but I couldn't imagine this concept traveling beyond the Puget Sound. I didn't even drink coffee! But, Starbucks headquarters was just off Interstate 5 on the way to the airport and I figured, "Why not, I'll make it quick."

The minute I walked into the reception area, I knew something was going on there. The receptionist made me feel like we'd been friends for 100 years. The level of energy in the air was electric.

When I sat down with the CEO, Howard Schultz, he crystallized how Starbucks was going to become the most important coffee company in the world. He talked about the importance of his employees and how he was creating a partnership with them. He was passionate about the quality of the product and the customer experience. He painted a picture of how Starbucks was going to develop one of the most respected brands in the world. After our first meeting, I was convinced. I started to drink coffee!

An investor who looked at opportunities based on price to earnings (stock price divided by the company's earnings), price to book (stock price divided by book value of the company's net assets), or price to comparables (valuation relative to other restaurant companies) would have wondered what Howard had in his coffee. I left that believing that I had just met the next Ray Kroc—the man who turned McDonald's into a billion-dollar hamburger business.

What gave me that impression? Read on.

→ STARS OF TOMORROW, TODAY

"Don't bunt. Aim out of the park. Aim for the company of immortals."
— DAVID OGILVY

One dollar invested in Microsoft when it went public in 1986 is worth $374 today. One dollar invested in Cisco Systems when it went public in 1990 is worth $274. One dollar invested in Home Depot at its IPO in 1981 is worth $1,153, and a dollar invested in Yahoo! at its IPO in 1996 is worth $72.

				VALUE OF $1 INVESTED AT IPO			
COMPANY	IPO	MARKET CAP AT IPO	MARKET CAP TODAY	VALUE OF $1 TODAY
Wal-Mart (WMT)	1970	$25 million	$195 billion	$5,809
Home Depot (HD)	1981	$34 million	$86 billion	$1,153
Microsoft (MSFT)	1986	$519 million	$278 billion	$374
Dell (DELL)	1988	$212 million	$71 billion	$338
Southwest (LUV)	1971	$11 million	$13 billion	$299
Cisco (CSCO)	1990	$226 million	$105 billion	$274
Oracle (ORCL)	1986	$228 million	$63 billion	$264
Amgen (AMGN)	1983	$463 million	$97 billion	$210
Genentech (DNA)	1980	$263 million	$98 billion	$133
QUALCOMM (QCOM)	1991	$314 million	$71 billion	$86
Apollo Group (APOL)	1994	$118 million	$11 billion	$83
Yahoo! (YHOO)	1996	$334 million	$55 billion	$72
eBay (EBAY)	1998	$715 million	$59 billion	$58
Starbucks (SBUX)	1992	$216 million	$23 billion	$56
Schwab (SCHW)	1987	$419 million	$19 billion	$41
Guidant (GDT)	1994	$247 million	$21 billion	$18

Source: FactSet, ThinkEquity Partners.

The stocks that generate the most spectacular returns are small companies that become big companies. My objective is to identify and invest in what I call the stars of tomorrow—the fastest-growing, most innovative companies in the world.

In the long run, a company's share price will be nearly 100% correlated with its earnings growth. Earnings growth drives stock price. Accordingly, over time, the companies that have the highest returns will be the ones that have the highest earnings growth rates. But, as economist John Maynard Keynes wrote, "In the long run, we are all dead." Hence, we need to analyze short-term pitfalls as well.

Earnings Growth Drives Stock Price

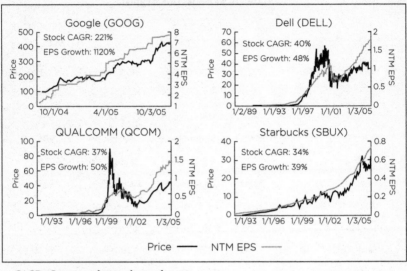

CAGR=Compound annual growth rate
EPS=Earnings per share
NTM=Next 12 months
Source: FactSet, ThinkEquity Partners.

The reason why Google, Starbucks, QUALCOMM, and Dell have had spectacular stock performance is that they have had spectacular earnings growth. Unfortunately, in growth investing, often what seems like the next Starbucks turns out to be the next Boston Chicken. Our objective is to provide a process to identify the stars of tomorrow and avoid the roman candles.

The highway of emerging growth companies is littered with the remains of once high-flying stocks. The reality is that when you are going 80 miles per hour along the highway and hit a speed bump, it causes a much greater problem than if you encountered the same bump at 15 miles per hour.

Boston Chicken was once thought to be a huge growth story, but hypergrowth combined with aggressive financing and a flawed business model resulted in a spectacular crash when Boston Chicken's market value went from $3 billion to zero. I know; I used to follow it. A Silicon Valley truism is that you can learn more from your losses than from your winners. I've learned a lot.

Hall of Shame: High Flyers to Zero

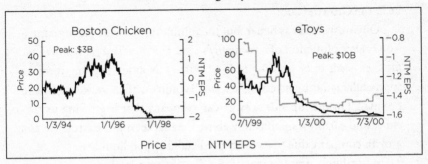

Source: FactSet, ThinkEquity Partners.

→ WHY GROWTH?

"The race is not always to the swift, nor the battle to the strong, but that's the way to bet."
                                                          —DAMON RUNYON

To get things started, we need to have a common understanding of what a growth company is (and isn't). At its most fundamental level a growth company is a business that is growing its sales and earnings at a much higher rate than the average company. I think revenue growth, unit growth, and earnings growth are a start, but not the finish.

Some would say, "Since gross domestic product (GDP) is growing at 3 or 4% per year, a company that is growing faster than that is a growth company." I think that's rubbish!

Others look at the long-term earnings per share (EPS) growth of the U.S. stock market of 7% and say that if a company is growing faster than that, it's a growth company. While we are getting closer, we're not there yet.

I had a very sophisticated investment consulting firm tell me a growth company is "a company with a higher price to earnings ratio (P/E) than the market"—the logic being that growing companies would have higher P/E multiples. While this was interesting, it was ABSURD! It's like saying that the definition of a home-run hitter is a batter who strikes out the most. The point being, while home-run hitters often strike out a lot, and growth companies often have higher P/Es than the market average, to identify the home-run hitters you should count not the strikeouts, but the home runs!

So, what is the right hurdle rate of revenue and earnings growth to be in the Growth Club?

Obviously faster is better, but the minimum growth rate for admission is also a function of a company's size. *The smaller a company is, the faster it needs to be growing to be of interest.* Nobody is going to make spectacular gains by investing in a small company that is always going to be small. On the flip side, a large-cap company that is growing its revenues and earnings significantly above the market may be attractive as a growth company due to its likely predictability and liquidity.

Accordingly, my framework for classifying a business as a growth company takes the company's market cap into account. For a company with a market cap below $250 million, revenues need to be growing at a rate of at least 25% and earnings at a rate of at least 30%. For a company with a market cap between $250 million and $1 billion, the minimum revenue growth is 20%, and the minimum EPS growth is 25%. For a company with a market cap between $1 billion and $5 billion, the minimum revenue growth is 15%, and the minimum earnings growth is 20%. At a market cap above $5 billion, the minimum revenue growth is 10%, and the minimum EPS growth is 15%.

GROWTH CLUB QUALIFICATIONS		
MARKET CAP	REVENUE GROWTH	EARNINGS GROWTH
<$250 million	25%	30%
$250 million–$1 billion	20%	25%
$1 billion–$5 billion	15%	20%
>$5 billion	10%	15%

The story goes that when infamous thief Willie Sutton was asked why he robbed banks, he replied, "Because that's where the money is." Similarly, the reason I focus on growth companies is because that is where the greatest potential investment returns are. In the short term, a variety of factors influence stock prices—geopolitical events, fund flows, interest rates, oil prices, and so on. In the long term, one thing influences stock prices—earnings growth!

As I will continue to say, over time there is nearly a 100% correlation between a company's earnings growth and its stock performance. Or as Peter Lynch once said, "People may bet on the hourly wiggles of the market, but it's the earnings that waggle the wiggles long term."

→ GROWTH AND RISK

"Worldly wisdom teaches that it is better for a reputation to fail conventionally than to succeed unconventionally."

—JOHN MAYNARD KEYNES

One of the golden truths of high finance is the relationship between risk and reward: the greater the potential reward, the higher the *perception* of potential risk. This truth, when applied to just about any activity—whether it's sports, education and career choice, gambling, or investing—provides for many possible combinations of risk and potential reward. Before conceding this truth then, it is important to understand what is at risk.

At one extreme of the risk–reward spectrum is the combination of paying a premium for quality in exchange for greater confidence in a potentially winning outcome. The P/E multiple on QUALCOMM, a blue-chip growth company, is approximately 50% higher than the overall market's, but the likelihood of its having superior earnings growth justifies that multiple. At the other extreme is the goal of maximizing potential gain by buying cheap, with the hope of hitting it big. There are numerous examples of buying inexpensive fallen angels that find new wings for turnarounds and actually turn. This strategy obviously has the appearance of carrying with it a high degree of risk, not only from the potential for permanent loss, but also from the *appearance* of foolishness if it fails.

Given that people are by nature risk-averse, the avoid-looking-foolish principle compels many investors to pay a premium in order to hide behind the averages of their peers if the chosen strategy falls short of succeeding.

Unfortunately, history shows that investors fall into this "quality trap" all too frequently. With well more than half of all portfolio managers underperforming the market each year, the most common source of the quality trap is extrapolating past success into the future. Ultimately, this leads to paying a hefty premium for those phantom successes.

Somehow, it is accepted as conventional wisdom that it's more conservative to buy Wal-Mart or General Electric at any price than to buy a lesser-known emerging growth company at a low price. However, if we look at investing from a different perspective, this conventional wisdom falls short of making sense.

Consider, for example, the following two companies: first, a large, well-established, 50-year-old company trading at $40, with $2 per share in earnings, that is expected to grow future earnings at the rate of 8% per year; and second, a small, emerging growth company, trading at $50, with $1 in EPS, that is expected to grow earnings at 50% per year.

If we look at P/E multiples for what they are—the number of years before we realize in today's earnings what we paid for in share price—then the large, established company looks more attractive at 20 times earnings, versus the growth company's 50 times (in other words, 30 fewer years until we are repaid in earnings what we paid for the stock).

However, when the rate of earnings growth is accounted for, the results change dramatically. At the large company's annual growth of 8%, we would be repaid in earnings in just over 12 years, while at the emerging company's 50% growth rate, we would be repaid in just over seven years. By year 12, we could receive $387 in earnings versus the $50 we paid for the stock. (See the charts on pages 10 and 11.)

Even if we assume that the emerging company's growth slows by 10% each year, so that in year 10 growth has slowed to "just" 16%, we would have been repaid in 9½ years, or 2½ years sooner than the conservative investor. Of course, as our top-performer study highlights in chapter 3, we would also expect to be compensated handsomely for our

P/E to Growth for Growth Stocks

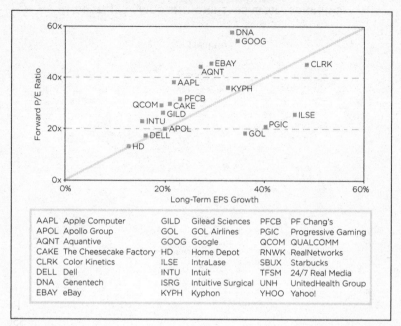

AAPL	Apple Computer	GILD	Gilead Sciences	PFCB	PF Chang's
APOL	Apollo Group	GOL	GOL Airlines	PGIC	Progressive Gaming
AQNT	Aquantive	GOOG	Google	QCOM	QUALCOMM
CAKE	The Cheesecake Factory	HD	Home Depot	RNWK	RealNetworks
CLRK	Color Kinetics	ILSE	IntraLase	SBUX	Starbucks
DELL	Dell	INTU	Intuit	TFSM	24/7 Real Media
DNA	Genentech	ISRG	Intuitive Surgical	UNH	UnitedHealth Group
EBAY	eBay	KYPH	Kyphon	YHOO	Yahoo!

efforts, with sizable appreciation in share price consistent with growth in earnings.

Ultimately, in sports, gambling, investing, and life, there is little value in knowing what happened yesterday. The largest rewards come from anticipating what will occur in the future. As Warren Buffett once said, "If history books were the key to riches, the Forbes 400 would consist of librarians."

Fundamental in our pursuit of attractive investment opportunities is my philosophy of risk and reward. I view risk as measuring the potential for permanent capital loss, not short-term quotational loss, and assess the probability of that against what we think the value of a business will be in the future.

EARNINGS ARE EVERYTHING—THE POWER OF GROWTH

Annual EPS

YEAR	BLUE CHIP: 8% EPS GROWTH	GROWTH COMPANY: 50% EPS GROWTH	GROWTH COMPANY: DECELERATING EPS GROWTH
0	$2.00	$1.00	$1.00
1	$2.16	$1.50	$1.50
2	$2.33	$2.25	$2.18
3	$2.52	$3.38	$3.06
4	$2.72	$5.06	$4.17
5	$2.94	$7.59	$5.54
6	$3.17	$11.39	$7.17
7	$3.43	$17.09	$9.08
8	$3.70	$25.63	$11.25
9	$4.00	$38.44	$13.67
10	$4.32	$57.67	$16.32
11	$4.66	$86.50	$19.16
12	$5.04	$129.75	$22.17

	CUMULATIVE EARNINGS		
YEAR	BLUE CHIP: 8% EPS GROWTH	GROWTH COMPANY: 50% EPS GROWTH	GROWTH COMPANY: DECELERATING EPS GROWTH
0	$2.00	$1.00	$1.00
1	$4.16	$2.50	$2.50
2	$6.49	$4.75	$4.68
3	$9.01	$8.13	$7.74
4	$11.73	$13.19	$11.91
5	$14.67	$20.78	$17.45
6	$17.85	$32.17	$24.62
7	$21.27	$49.26	$33.70
8	$24.98	$74.89	$44.95
9	$28.97	$113.33	$58.62
10	$33.29	$171.00	$74.94
11	$37.95	$257.49	$94.10
12	$42.99	$387.24	$116.27

It is with this perspective that I fly right in the face of conventional wisdom, which suggests that the bigger the return, the more risk one has to assume. From my point of view, large returns will occur when we find an opportunity where the upside is substantial, yet the price we pay for it is not. My goal is to find a stock whose price is below what I think the appraised value should be, not what the quotational value is as indicated by the current stock price. I also want to find the stock in the "right neighborhood," an industry where there is tremendous market growth potential. This heaven-on-earth company is not an easy one to find, but that is my mission.

→ THE GROWTH OPPORTUNITY—
FINDING THE SWEET SPOT

"Great stocks are extremely hard to find. If they weren't, then everyone would own them."
— PHILIP A. FISHER

In searching for the fastest-growing companies with the greatest potential, the best pond to be fishing in is the small-cap pond. Not only does the small-cap pond have the most fast-swimming fish, it's typically the least expensive relative to growth opportunities.

For purposes of this book, I will define size relative to market capitalization in this way:

Nanocap stocks	Below $50 million
Microcap stocks	$50–$250 million
Small-cap stocks	$250 million–$1 billion
Midcap stocks	$1 billion–$5 billion
Large-cap stocks	Over $5 billion

Ironically, while the opportunities for outsized returns for investors lie in identifying early-stage growth companies, large investment banks are driven by the economics of trading volume and therefore generally ignore the stars of tomorrow today. In fact, analyst coverage for small companies (nano-, micro-, and small caps) is proportional to a company's size. For example, while 75% of NASDAQ companies have a market cap below $1 billion, 85% of research from the seven largest firms on Wall Street is on companies with market caps above $1 billion. Moreover, the big winners over time almost always start with a market value below $1 billion—and often under $200 million—which is microcap territory.

Wall Street Research Focuses on Big Companies—
Tomorrow's Winners Are Small-Cap Today

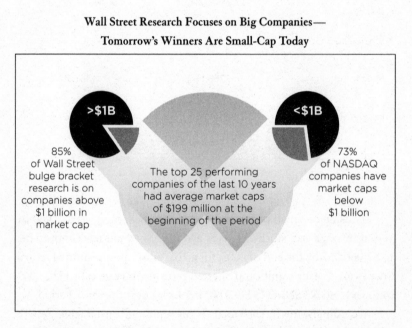

>$1B

85% of Wall Street bulge bracket research is on companies above $1 billion in market cap

The top 25 performing companies of the last 10 years had average market caps of $199 million at the beginning of the period

<$1B

73% of NASDAQ companies have market caps below $1 billion

The reason I point this out—and, for that matter, the reason I'm writing this book—is that if you are looking to invest in tomorrow's winners, it's unlikely you will find them by reading Wall Street research. Mainly, Wall Street is focused on reporting on companies everybody already knows about. Consequently, to identify and invest in tomorrow's stars, you are unlikely to be battling Wall Street's finest—they aren't there.

As proof of the inefficient analysis of smaller companies, of the 767 publicly traded nanocap companies in the United States, only 126 (just 16%) have analyst coverage. For microcaps, the percentage covered by analysts rises to 58%, which still leaves nearly 650 microcaps uncovered.

Combined, the total number of nano- and microcap companies without analyst coverage is nearly 1,300, or 20% of all equities. Even for those that do have coverage, often only a single analyst provides research.

$10,000 INVESTED IN 1973		
	VALUE IN 2005	ANNUAL RETURN
Small-Cap Stocks	$1,066,057	16.3%
Midcap Stocks	$756,864	15.0%
Large-Cap Stocks	$127,963	8.6%
Inflation	$44,060	$4.9%

Focusing on small companies has proven rewarding, as $10,000 invested in small-cap stocks 33 years ago (1973) would have appreciated to $1,066,057 by the end of 2005, for a 16.3% compound annual return. Small-cap returns significantly bested returns on large caps ($127,963, or 8.6%) and NASDAQ ($239,214, or 10.8%) over the same period.

Accordingly, my intense focus is on rapid and sustainable growth, and I believe that size forges an anchor to sustaining rapid growth in sales and earnings. In my view, if I can identify a young, unknown company with a lot of growth potential, then I stand to benefit not only from the long-term earnings potential, but also from the herd nature of investors as the opportunity becomes more widely recognized.

We have conducted a number of studies over various periods of time to determine characteristics of top-performing stocks. The punch line is always the same. Of the 25 best-performing companies over 5 and 10 years' time, the average market capitalization at the beginning of each period is always very small—between $100 million and $200 million (microcaps). Now, many of these companies are well recognized as the stars of today's equity market, with much larger market capitalizations (some well into large-cap territory) and, of course, widely followed by analysts.

With the right framework, I believe the heightened perception of greater risk with growth stocks leads to greater opportunities for growth investors. As analyst coverage of underfollowed companies increases, and the information gap narrows, the potential return is driven not only by the underlying potential being reflected in share prices, but also by the reduced risk aversion from the broader group of investors.

You may think, "Great, unloved for sure, but most are small and forgotten for a reason." And perhaps you think I'm biased. After all, just as you don't ask a barber if you need a haircut, don't ask a small-cap growth guy where you should invest.

While this may be true, the fact is that just as trees don't start as trees, they start as acorns; big companies don't start as big companies, they start as small companies. Behind every one of today's bellwethers and blue chips was an entrepreneur who had the foresight to identify a market opportunity and build a company around a vision, product, and customers.

It is easy to forget that even large-cap stalwarts such as UnitedHealth Group and Nike had market caps of just $29 million and $418 million, respectively, when they went public in 1980. In both instances, the companies were founded by an entrepreneur who saw an opportunity to do something better than it had been done before.

What characteristics do I look for in a small company that can become a big company? I call them the four Ps: *people, product, potential,* and *predictability.* The four Ps are key ingredients for the secret sauce of investing in the stars of tomorrow, and I will discuss them in more detail in chapter 6. In the meantime, the facts support my affection. Small companies with great growth potential are the brightest stars of tomorrow. The goal of investing should be to get the highest return for acceptable risk.

WHERE DO BIG COMPANIES COME FROM?

COMPANY	YEAR OF IPO	MARKET CAP (MILLIONS)		STOCK CAGR	EPS GROWTH
		IPO	TODAY		
UnitedHealth Group	1984	$29	$79,002	33%	33%
Apple	1980	$810	$59,662	12%	18%
ADP	1961	$10	$26,737	15%	15%
Gilead Sciences	1992	$208	$24,173	27%	30%
Nike	1980	$418	$22,660	15%	20%
Boston Scientific	1992	$1,692	$20,274	13%	15%
XTO Energy	1993	$192	$15,964	35%	38%
Electronic Arts	1989	$59	$15,834	34%	30%
Biogen	1991	$109	$15,030	21%	21%
Paychex	1983	$61	$14,732	27%	23%
Coach	2000	$884	$12,775	70%	50%
Express Scripts	1992	$82	$12,296	44%	27%
VeriSign	1998	$437	$5,633	20%	23%
Dollar Tree Stores	1995	$294	$2,571	22%	27%

Source: FactSet, ThinkEquity Partners.

2

The Power of Growth—The Magic of Compound Interest

"Compound interest is the eighth wonder of the world."

—ALBERT EINSTEIN

SINCE MY PHILOSOPHY is that earnings growth is what drives stock price over time, it seems that the simple solution would be to find companies with high earnings growth, take a deep breath, and then hang on for the ride. While that's true, investing in high-growth enterprises is even better than that due to the way compound interest works. Understanding the magic of compound interest and the power of earnings is critical to appreciating why growth investing has such huge potential rewards.

Compound interest, high earnings growth rates, and time create a potent combination that leads to spectacular returns. Even slight differences in short-term returns can produce dramatic results over a meaningful time period when aided by compounding.

To understand the magic of compound interest, let me tell you another story. In 1626, Dutchman Peter Minuit purchased the entire island of Manhattan for $24 worth of trinkets from the Wappinger Indians. In other words, for what it would cost to order a bagel and café latte at a midtown hotel today, Monsieur Minuit owned the *entire* Big Apple.

While there are many outside of Gotham who would look at neither as a bargain, my point is to demonstrate the power of compound interest. Albert Einstein called compound interest the eighth wonder of the world, and with the help of the ninth wonder of the world, the HP 12C, we can calculate whether Peter Minuit got a good deal.

Obviously, the key variable to determine the answer is the interest rate that we apply to the $24. In other words, what could we have earned in an alternative investment?

The difference between a 5% return and a 10% return isn't a simple doubling but a compounding that becomes staggering over time. If the $24 had been invested at 5% interest over the past 380 years, it would have grown to $2.6 billion today, implying a good price given that Rockefeller Center alone sold for $1.85 billion in 2000.

At a 10% return, however, the $24 doesn't just double the 5% return to $5.4 billion. With compounding it magnifies it to $129 quadrillion, 45 million times greater!

Purchase price for Manhattan Island in 1626	$24
Value today if invested at 5% annual yield	$2.7 billion
Value today if invested at 7.5% annual yield	$20.7 trillion
Value today if invested at 10% annual yield	$128.7 quadrillion
Rockefeller Center sale price in 2000	$1.9 billion
U.S. market capitalization	$15.5 trillion

As you're going to hear once or twice more, the foundation of my investment philosophy is that over time, share prices are nearly 100% correlated with earnings. Hence, my objective is to identify companies whose earnings grow at a high and sustainable rate and benefit from the magic of compound interest.

In the world of investing, few stocks have accomplished the returns of Peter Minuit's land purchase, yet consider that Microsoft went from a $500 million market cap company at the time of its IPO to nearly $300 billion today by increasing its earnings at an approximately 40% compound annual growth rate over the past 20 years.

The trick, of course, is that it is almost impossible to grow at a rate that high for so long a period, as the laws of compounding cause growth to diminish with size. Only six companies managed to grow their earnings in excess of 20% each year during the past 10 years—out of a universe of more than 12,000 companies!

	20/10 CLUB									
COMPANY	EPS GROWTH									
	1996	1997	1998	1999	2000	2001	2002	2003	2004	2005
Apollo Group	66%	61%	51%	33%	28%	30%	40%	55%	45%	25%
Bed Bath & Beyond	30%	37%	32%	31%	32%	32%	26%	37%	28%	29%
Capital One	32%	22%	21%	41%	31%	30%	30%	35%	25%	27%
NVR	95%	63%	31%	126%	81%	70%	63%	44%	34%	37%
Ryland Group	148%	59%	107%	54%	37%	57%	44%	37%	39%	42%
Starbucks	67%	20%	33%	25%	30%	29%	37%	20%	22%	42%

Source: Company SEC filings, ThinkEquity Partners.

→ **RULE OF 72**

A useful tool for comprehending the impact of compound interest and the doubling effect, but something they don't teach at Harvard Business School, is the Rule of 72. While in my view the HP 12C is magic for math tricks, all you need for the Rule of 72 is simple arithmetic. The rule says that if you divide an interest rate into 72, it will tell you how many years it will take to double your investment. At 9% interest, a dollar would double in 8 years ($72 \div 9 = 8$). At 12% interest, a dollar will double in 6 years. Another way to look at it is that a company growing its earnings at 15% a year, with a constant P/E, will double its share price in roughly 5 years; a company growing its earnings at 25% per year with a constant P/E will double its value in roughly 3 years.

RULE OF 72		
INTEREST RATE	NUMBER OF YEARS TO DOUBLE	VALUE OF $1 IN 30 YEARS
3%	24	$2.43
6%	12	$5.74
9%	8	$13.27
12%	6	$29.96
15%	5	$66.21
25%	3	$807.79

To illustrate the dramatic impact compounding has over time, if you earned 3% on your funds for 30 years (a decent after-tax bond return) versus 12% (the average return of small-cap stock over the past 80 years), you would have more than 12 times more money with a 12% return in 30 years.

In other words, if we invest in a company that grows its earnings at 25% for 10 years, and we have a constant P/E multiple, the stock price will go up nearly tenfold.

→ **ONE CENT DOUBLING EVERY DAY OR $10,000 PER WEEK?**

To illustrate the power of the doubling effect, suppose you were offered a job as a consultant for a month and you had your choice of being paid $10,000 per week or a penny the first day, and having it double every day for the remainder of the month. Easy choice, right?

At $10,000 per week, you would make $40,000 for the month. On the other hand, making a penny the first day, two cents the second, four cents the third, eight cents the fourth, and so on, you actually end up making more than $20 million by the 31st day! That is the power of growth!

The Doubling Effect:

Would you take $.01 doubling each day or $10,000 per week?

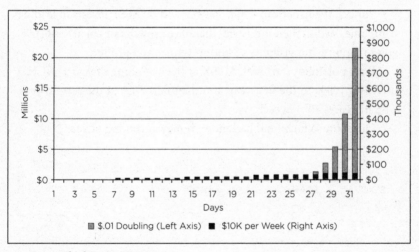

Source: ThinkEquity Partners.

→ **MATH OF NEGATIVE RETURNS—**
   THE OTHER SIDE OF THE SWORD

"There are old pilots and there are bold pilots, but there aren't many old-bold pilots."   —UNKNOWN

Just as compounding geometrically increases the value of positive returns, it also exacerbates the impact of negative returns. To illustrate this point, consider two imaginary portfolios.

Fund 1 is the New Century High Octane Fund (NCHO). Its average P/E is N/M (not meaningful), and annual turnover of the portfolio is 2,000%. Figuring out the top 10 holdings is difficult because this changes so often, but a reasonable proxy is to look at the stocks that are making new daily highs.

Fund 2, the American Eagle Stalwart Fund (AES), invests in leading companies within their industries that have growth rates of at least 20%, good margins, and visibility of both revenues and profits.

Both portfolios start with $100K at the beginning of year 1. NCHO increases 100% in the first year, and then falls 30% in the second year. AES increases 20% in each year.

Question: Which fund had more money at the end of year 2?

| FUND | START | YEAR 1 | | YEAR 2 | |
	PORTFOLIO VALUE	RETURN	PORTFOLIO VALUE	RETURN	PORTFOLIO VALUE
NCHO	$100,000	100%	$200,000	−30%	$140,000
AES	$100,000	20%	$120,000	20%	$144,000

Answer: the American Eagle Stalwart Fund ($144,000 versus $140,000).

Part of the secret of successful investing is the compounding of returns over a period of time. Sadly, negative returns drastically undermine the magic of compounding. For example, if you are down 50%, to get back to even you don't need a simple 50% rebound, but a 100% gain.

Think for a second of the return you would need to get back to even if you bought shares in WorldCom at $43 in March 2000 and held it through the end of 2002, when the share price was only 12 cents! The return to get back to even is 35,733%! Investors who purchased shares in Lucent at $50 in March 2000 and are still holding them today at $2.66 currently require a return of 1,780% to get back to even.

CUTTING YOUR LOSSES EARLY— RETURN NEEDED TO BREAK EVEN	
DOWN	TO BREAK EVEN
−10%	11%
−20%	25%
−30%	43%
−40%	67%
−50%	100%
−60%	150%
−70%	233%
−80%	400%
−90%	900%

The cold, hard fact of investing in growth stocks is that volatility is the norm and living with short-term negative returns is part of the game. The way to win long-term is to focus on fundamentals with earnings growth and price performance running in tandem over time, and, when wrong, to be intellectually honest and admit it. The five baggers and the ten baggers (terms coined by Peter Lynch to reflect investments that pay off fivefold and tenfold, respectively) more than offset the -10% and -20% mistakes, but the -90% nuclear bombs are next to impossible to overcome.

→ THE PIONEERS GET ALL THE ARROWS . . . BUT THE SURVIVORS GET ALL THE LAND

"Trust, but verify."   — RONALD REAGAN

Investing in emerging companies requires a strong stomach and a lot of self-confidence. Often, conventional wisdom is against the company, and the "smart guys" think the stock is ridiculous. (Side note: for some reason, on Wall Street cynics are thought to be brilliant.)

Here are some typical comments you hear: "Nobody has ever done that before." "It's too risky." "If it's such a good idea, why doesn't [the gorilla in the industry] do it?" "The stock is too expensive. The P/E is three times the market." "Competition is going to wipe them out." "It's a fad." "The stock has doubled in the past six months—trees don't grow to the sky."

When I was aggressively recommending that investors buy Starbucks shares when its market cap was well below $1 billion, I was ridiculed for being a fool: "No barriers to entry." "Nobody is going to pay more than $.50 for a cup of coffee in NYC." "Wait until Maxwell House gets into the business!"

Furthermore, when an emerging star stumbles, and most of them will, the chorus will be unmerciful. The "I told you so's" will be out in full force, and true believers will be as quiet as Peter in Jerusalem.

The pitfalls are many, the risks are real, but the rewards are staggering.

How do you distinguish between the Starbucks and the Krispy Kremes? The Dells and the Gateways? The Apollos and the Edison Schools?

→ **THE RISK OF CONSENSUS**

Zebras have the same problem as institutional portfolio managers like myself.

First, both have quite specific, often difficult-to-obtain goals: for portfolio managers, above-average performance; for zebras, fresh grass.

Second, both dislike risk. Portfolio managers can get fired; zebras can get eaten by lions.

Third, both move in herds. They look alike, think alike, and stick close together.

If you are a zebra and live in a herd, your key decision is where to stand in relation to the rest of the herd. When you think that conditions are safe, the outside of the herd is the best, for there the grass is fresh, while those in the middle see only grass that is half-eaten or trampled down. The aggressive zebras, on the outside of the herd, eat much better.

On the other hand—or hoof—there comes a time when lions approach. The outside zebras end up as lion lunch. The skinny zebras in the middle of the pack may eat less well but they are alive.

A portfolio manager for an institution such as a bank trust department, insurance company or mutual fund cannot afford to be an Outside Zebra. For him, the optimal strategy is simple: stay in the center of the herd at all times. As long as he continues to buy the popular stocks, he cannot be faulted. On the other hand, he cannot afford to try for large gains on unfamiliar stocks that would leave him open to criticism if the idea failed.

—RALPH WANGER, *Zebras in Lion Country*

The term *groupthink* was popularized during the Vietnam era. Essentially it describes how smart people, when together, make really dumb decisions. Groupthink typically occurs when people become preoccupied with what the group consensus is, and that obsession overrides the motivation to assess situations objectively. Groupthink, while in the same family as conventional wisdom, is driven by group dynamics, whereas conventional wisdom is an aggregate collection of the seemingly obvious.

Take, for example, the concept of investment risk. As individuals, most people would define risk as the chance of permanent investment loss, the degree of volatility, uncertainty, and so on. In a group setting, risk becomes defined as deviating from what the consensus thinks. Not looking stupid is a very powerful influence on how people look at risk.

As it applies to investing, groupthink results in it being riskier to buy a lesser-known company with above-average growth potential and a reasonable valuation than it is to buy shares in a well-known company with perfection already reflected in its price. Yet "the group" knows the company, loves its history of success, and considers it a blue chip. This is the investment equivalent of the old saying "You can't get fired for hiring IBM."

STAR GAZER

HOWARD SCHULTZ
founder and CEO of Starbucks Corporation

Howard Schultz is the visionary who turned an obscure coffee company in Seattle into a dominant global leader and one of the most admired and respected brands. When Schultz's company, Il Giornale, bought Starbucks and changed the chain name to Starbucks Corp. in 1987, there were only 17 stores; today Starbucks is a $24 billion market cap company that operates its stores worldwide.

Michael Moe: *What were some of the key things that you were able to do that made Starbucks what it is today?*

Howard Schultz: When I look back to the earliest part of the growth and development of the company, there was a constant theme that we had then, that we have today, and it was linked to consistently investing ahead of the growth curve in almost every discipline. From the earliest days, we saw ourselves bigger and broader than a local company in Seattle. That's not to say we ever imagined there would be 11,000 stores all over the world, but we saw and dreamed and had the vision to build a bigger company. We had our sights on the needs and the requirements to accomplish that, whether it was systems, infrastructure, people, or manufacturing—all these things that lead us to hire and invest ahead of the growth curve. If you are not investing ahead of the growth curve, that is going to catch up to you.

We were in the business of really building the equity of the brand from within. That meant that the culture, the values, and the guiding principles of how we were going to build the company were going to be the way we communicated the essence of the Starbucks experience first to our people and then to our customers. We said early on that we wanted to exceed the expectations of our customers, but in order to do that we recognized we had to exceed the expectations of our people first. One of the ongoing reasons that Starbucks has such a strong foundation of trust with our customers is that we have built an emotional relationship around human connection with both our people and our customers and that has defined the brand. The facts that we are in the coffee business and that it's such a social and romantic beverage have given us the platform to create a sense of community in our business and in the company, and we have been able to do that around the world.

As employees, we want to be valued and respected, and as customers, we want to walk into a place that feels safe and that is not trying to get money out of our pockets but is trying to touch our hearts and give us something back, and that has given us the runway to expand the company well beyond what we ever thought.

MM: *Bill Campbell, chairman of Intuit, tells a great story of being on a panel with you. When someone asked who would be the first hire at a new company, he said VP of sales and you said VP of HR. And then he said he was wrong and agreed with you!*

HS: It is true that I was asked, if I were starting a business today, who would I hire first, and I said head of Human Resources. I think that in most growth companies, people recognize almost too late that the most important function in a company is human resources, and they get to that too late because they are hiring for sales or marketing or finance or whatever. I would invert that model and say that HR has to be right at the beginning of the core competency at the very highest level and then over time you have to make sure the HR function not only has a seat at both the leadership table of the company and the boardroom, but that that seat is valued and respected and their opinions are going to be heard. When I think back about why we have succeeded, almost without hesitation I'd say it's because we have been able to attract and retain great people. We've almost always been able to attract the right person at the right time, and I think it's because we've invested so heavily in the HR function and have put it in a position to always be at the leadership table of the company. I sit back today looking at what we're doing in China. We're replicating that exact same model now in China, where we continue to make significant investments well, well ahead of what the business is today. We couldn't succeed at the level we are dreaming about unless we were going to do that as we did in the United States.

MM: *How do you create the brands of the future, and what are they going to represent?*

HS: I don't think there's one formula for success, but I think there are consistent aspects in most enduring brands. I hate to use words that have been used before, but there has to be great authenticity and truth to the story. Building a brand on the foundation of a 30-second or 60-second Super Bowl commercial without any substance is not going to work—it's more noise. In today's world, in one way success is much more difficult than ever before, but in another way it's easier because there aren't many companies that stand for these things since they are looking for the short-term results and the short-term solution—and there is none. Think about the great brands of today. Think about what Apple has done and what the iPod represents, the emotional engagement that that device has to the customer. Think about Nike, IKEA, and Google. These are companies whose products transcend the experience the customer is having. It's much more meaningful than just the experience. They have a level of emotional engagement from the customer that is very, very different than, say, buying a box of Tide.

MM: *What do you think about international opportunities for Starbucks as well as for other businesses?*

HS: Whether you read Tom Friedman's book *The World Is Flat* or you pick up any business or consumer newspaper, you can't escape the fact that China and the rest of Asia are going to be at the center of the world. What's going on in India or Russia, in all of these countries, speaks to the fact that the Internet in many ways has been the death of distance. I don't look at customers or markets as where they live or what country they're in;

I look at one marketplace. Now I realize that in order to succeed in these multiple marketplaces, you have to be as relevant and as local as possible, but I think that from the beginning you have to see that the marketplace and the opportunities are well beyond the borders of the United States. We probably did go to Japan earlier than we had the capacity to do so. We learned as we went, we made some mistakes, but if we hadn't done that, we wouldn't be in a position to have more than 3,000 stores in 37 countries now and we never would be in a position to take advantage of the opportunity in China. You want to balance going after new opportunities with not sacrificing the core, but you have to dream big and be able to seize opportunities, and sometimes you're not prepared for it.

MM: *Talk about protecting the core and what you think about growth.*

HS: Growth can be intoxicating and very seductive and you have to make sure that someone is looking in the rearview mirror because it does reveal mistakes. You have to keep looking back as well as forward.

Great retailers are very adept at preserving the core business while enhancing the experience. We've done that around music, the Starbucks card, and the WiFi network that we've created. All of these things have enhanced the experience but have been very complementary to the core coffee business. I think that as a retailer and as a merchant, you want to make sure that you aren't doing anything that would in any way dilute the integrity of why people come in. In terms of the corporate aspect of growing the company, I think if I've learned one thing over the years, it's that you have to make sure that you're not chasing too many rabbits, that the core business is really the foundation of what you do and that you don't go off half-cocked and constantly get seduced by every opportunity that comes in the door, because most growth companies are consistently going to have more opportunities than they have capacity. The road is paved with companies that have done so well along the way, but then they embrace some level of arrogance and they start doing things that over time erode either the equity of the brand or trust with the customer or else in some cases are fatal to the company's ability to sustain itself.

MM: *How do you think about competition?*

HS: I think many companies become paranoid about competitors and what competitors are doing, and that takes them in directions in which they are trying to offset competitive pressure. Another thing we have learned over the years is that our best competitive defense is what we do as a company in our stores with our people and obviously how we create wonderful moments with our customers.

MM: *When you look to the future, either for Starbucks or just in the marketplace, what are you most excited about?*

HS: Like everyone else in the world, I am amazed and stunned by what is going on in China. I'm spending a week every quarter in China. Having said that, I want to share with you that I think a lot of people are going into China perhaps the way they went to the Gold Rush. Not unlike the Internet, there's going to be a burst, and people are going to fail.

MM: *What else are you bullish on?*

HS: There's going to be a new evolution of retail players that create spaces of comfort for people. One of the things Starbucks has benefited from significantly is the fact that we have not only become the third place, but, more than that, the environment has become as important as the coffee itself. Retailers and merchants that create environments where people enjoy themselves amid the merchants trying to sell products are going to win. Not enough people have figured that out. Another dynamic that fascinates me is the adoption rate of things. It took us 20-plus years to build the Starbucks brand. When things are positioned properly in today's environment because of quick, free information flows, there's an unbelievable rate of adoption that is dynamically quicker and stronger than in years past.

MM: *Anything you want to say about music?*

HS: Even though Starbucks is in the coffee business and the bricks-and-mortar business, no business today can ignore the way in which your customers are acting during the day outside of your stores. You have to be a chameleon and really get underneath all this so that you maintain your relevance.

Another example of how groupthink infects thoughtful evaluation is in portfolio diversification. A group generally considers it less risky to own a broad, diverse portfolio than to own a relative handful of stocks that they follow closely and whose business and fundamentals they fully understand. Ironically, investors that tend to underperform the market do as the group does to avoid having all their eggs in one basket. In contrast, investors that demonstrate superior performance over time maintain more concentrated portfolios, and they watch each egg very closely.

It should be no mystery that no great work of art, recipe, or music was ever created by a group. Similarly, I am not aware of any great investment track record that has been created by a committee. Any manager who is truly trying to anticipate future economic trends is bound to take positions that are wildly at variance with what is popular in the market, and this behavior will appear eccentric and ill informed in comparison to the current market favorites.

Thoughtfully zigging when others zag is often the key to success on Wall Street. Blindly going against conventional wisdom isn't any brighter than mindlessly embracing popular opinion, however. In other words, success in growth investing requires an intent focus on the drivers of growth and steadfast objectivity even when this means running against the grain of the consensus. As an example, many growth investors are known as growth mavericks or, in more difficult investment environments, fair-weather outperformers. They rack up disproportionate gains when the economic and market environments are moving higher, but they have a difficult time "rotating" when the weather turns ugly.

There is always a growth market somewhere. At any given time, however, the willingness to adapt to where the growth is now is a discipline that is difficult to stick to.

THINK POINTS

→ Compound interest is the key ingredient to explosive stock performance over time.

→ It's very difficult to find companies that can consistently grow earnings of more than 20%.

→ Cutting losses early on mistakes is critical to avoiding the crushing effects of negative returns.

→ To achieve big investment returns, you have to think independently.

3

High Earnings per Share = High Internal Rate of Return (the Argument)

"I skate to where the puck is going to be, not where it has been."

—WAYNE GRETZKY

IT WOULD BE CONVENIENT IF, to pick tomorrow's winners, you just had to look at past results. Unfortunately, that plan doesn't work because the world is constantly changing.

If you were to look at the leading U.S. industries in 1925, you would find that 23 of the 100 largest capitalization companies were in the railroad industry. Ten were automobile companies, and four were in metals and mining. None of the 100 largest companies were in information technology, health care, or financial services.

Fast forward the clock to 2005. Only one metals and mining com-

THE PAST ISN'T A PROLOGUE TO THE FUTURE		
Number of Companies in the Top 100		
INDUSTRY	1925	2005
Railroads	23	0
Metals and mining	4	1
Autos and parts	10	0

NUMBER OF COMPANIES IN THE TOP 100		
INDUSTRY	1925	2005
Information technology	0	20
Financial services	0	23
Health care/pharmaceuticals	0	17

Source: FactSet, Michael Milken.

pany was among the largest 100 companies, and no companies were in automobiles or railroads. Conversely, 20 information technology companies were among the 100 largest, as were 23 financial services companies and 17 health-care companies.

While we know that we won't find the winners of tomorrow by reviewing the winners of the past, it's instructive to analyze the top-performing companies to learn what to look for when identifying the stars of tomorrow.

→ **TOP-PERFORMING STOCKS, 1995–2005**

To identify the all-stars in the stock market, I evaluated more than 10,000 companies to find the 25 top-performing stocks from 1995 to 2005 on a total return basis. Who made the list was interesting but not that educational—after all, any knowledgeable follower of the market could have picked these in hindsight. And since we know the past isn't a prologue for the future winners, what's noteworthy isn't who made it, but how they got there.

In order to place my convictions in perspective, I analyzed the top-performing companies' characteristics to highlight where growth companies come from and how they create value for shareholders. Notably, many of these companies exemplify the megatrends that prevailed during the study period—a fact that is far from coincidental.

		MARKET CAP ($ MILLIONS)		STOCK CAGR	EPS GROWTH	P/E	
TICKER	COMPANY NAME	12/31 1995	12/31 2005			12/31 1995	12/31 2005
1 AEOS	American Eagle Outfitters	59	3,456	49%	62%	29.0x	12.2x
2 PENN	Penn National Gaming	56	2,734	41%	24%	11.3x	40.4x
3 CELG	Celgene	117	10,992	40%	226%	222.9x	186.2x
4 XTO	XTO Energy	326	15,964	40%	42%	15.7x	18.2x
5 DELL	Dell	3,220	72,097	39%	32%	13.7x	23.2x
6 JBL	Jabil Circuit	199	7,629	39%	31%	17.4x	30.6x
7 BBY	Best Buy	694	21,527	37%	30%	12.5x	21.6x
8 RMD	ResMed	93	2,733	37%	29%	21.4x	40.9x
9 WFMI	Whole Foods Market	256	10,633	36%	21%	24.1x	77.9x
10 EXPD	Expeditors International of Washington	314	7,346	35%	25%	18.9x	41.5x
11 OSK	Oshkosh Truck	129	3,308	33%	27%	12.7x	20.5x
12 URBN	Urban Outfitters	199	4,213	33%	25%	18.4x	35.1x
13 LM	Legg Mason	423	13,510	33%	23%	16.1x	33.9x

1995–2005 ALL-STARS

TICKER	COMPANY NAME	MARKET CAP		STOCK CAGR	EPS GROWTH	P/E	
		12/31 1995	12/31 2005			12/31 1995	12/31 2005
14 SNDK	SanDisk	330	11,472	33%	32%	34.7x	36.1x
15 QCOM	QUALCOMM	2,785	71,406	32%	43%	76.8x	34.1x
16 PNRA	Panera Bread	82	2,061	32%	48%	58.9x	41.2x
17 GLYT	Genlyte Group	86	1,525	32%	25%	11.0x	18.5x
18 MRX	Medicis Pharmaceutical	60	1,760	32%	27%	18.9x	26.9x
19 EV	Eaton Vance	263	3,559	32%	20%	9.8x	24.1x
20 ELX	Emulex	61	1,671	31%	51%	42.7x	24.0x
21 IMDC	Inamed	67	3,197	31%	15%	8.6x	46.8x
22 BRO	Brown & Brown	216	4,274	31%	22%	14.6x	29.3x
23 AMHC	American Healthyways	76	1,573	30%	20%	22.8x	51.0x
24 BIIB	Biogen Idec	294	15,030	30%	23%	36.1x	116.4x
25 USNA	USANA Health Sciences	71	765	30%	34%	27.3x	20.3x
	Mean	419	11,777	35%	38%	31.8x	42.0x
	Median	199	4,213	33%	27%	18.9x	33.9x

Source: FactSet, ThinkEquity Partners.

In the study, the average top 25 company had an initial market cap of $199 million in 1995, grew earnings 27% annually, and experienced an annual P/E multiple expansion of 6% to yield annual price appreciation of 33% through 2005. At the end of the 10 years, the average market capitalization of those same 25 companies had grown to $4.2 billion!

Study of Top-Performing Stocks, 1995–2005

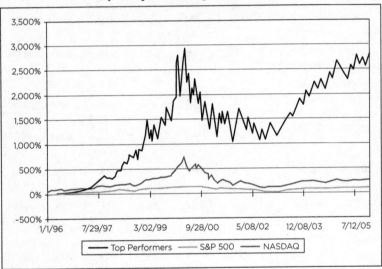

Source: FactSet, ThinkEquity Partners.

As this concise study highlights, profits are fundamental to a growth stock's long-term performance. With a significant portion of the performance being contributed by P/E multiple expansion—despite relatively high multiples at the outset—the market affords a clear premium to companies that are able to consistently capitalize on their market's rapid growth.

This premium of P/E multiple expansion is what differentiates a growth company from a growth stock (i.e., a premium company earns a premium valuation). By comparison, companies that rely upon the broader economy to help them achieve long-term growth will find it far more difficult to achieve a premium valuation in the absence of a strengthening economy, decelerating inflation, and rising consumer and business sentiment.

Just to make sure that this 10-year period wasn't a fluke, we went back to the 10 years between 1985 and 1995 to examine the characteristics of the 25 top-performing stocks during this period.

Lo and behold, the medium market cap for the top-performing companies from 1985 to 1995 was even lower, $134 million. The median P/E was 17.6x and the average earnings growth was 31%. The class of '95 had an average stock price CAGR of 32%.

		\$ MILLIONS)	MARKET CAP			P/E	
TICKER	COMPANY NAME	12/31 1985	12/31 1995	STOCK CAGR	EPS GROWTH	12/31 1985	12/31 1995
1 AMGN	Amgen	147	15,776	49%	88%	14.1x	31.5x
2 HD	Home Depot	313	22,766	44%	39%	22.9x	32.6x
3 AMAT	Applied Materials	134	7,059	41%	40%	14.7x	15.4x
4 STJ	St. Jude Medical	98	3,437	38%	27%	8.8x	25.2x
5 MU	Micron Technology	163	8,202	37%	33%	2.7x	8.5x
6 MDT	Medtronic	657	12,980	35%	22%	12.8x	36.3x
7 PAYX	Paychex	108	2,273	35%	31%	36.6x	50.1x
8 PHS	Pacificare Health Systems	107	2,696	35%	30%	16.7x	23.1x
9 NKE	NIKE	528	9,973	35%	48%	51.9x	20.8x

1985–95 ALL-STARS

TICKER	COMPANY NAME	MARKET CAP ($ MILLIONS)		STOCK CAGR	EPS GROWTH	P/E	
		12/31 1985	12/31 1995			12/31 1985	12/31 1995
10 IGT	International Game Technology	72	1,360	35%	51%	46.2x	14.8x
11 TLAB	Tellabs	156	3,286	34%	31%	22.5x	29.3x
12 DHR	Danaher	80	1,857	32%	31%	16.4x	18.0x
13 ADCT	ADC Telecommunications	120	2,290	32%	20%	15.2x	39.1x
14 BMET	Biomet	112	2,063	31%	35%	31.8x	23.9x
15 FNM	Fannie Mae	1,886	33,818	31%	36%	18.0x	15.9x
16 CBRL	CBRL Group	51	1,039	30%	33%	20.2x	15.5x
17 RHI	Robert Half International	77	1,210	29%	21%	16.0x	30.9x
18 SYK	Stryker	180	2,549	29%	26%	21.7x	29.3x
19 SUP	Superior Industries International	60	766	29%	21%	7.6x	14.9x
20 BRK.A	Berkshire, Hathaway	2,833	38,327	29%	6%	6.5x	48.0x
21 OCR	Omnicare	75	1,178	28%	20%	25.6x	52.3x
22 NOVL	Novell	188	5,295	28%	43%	46.0x	15.8x
23 CD	Cendant	214	6,195	28%	25%	54.6x	69.8x

TICKER	COMPANY NAME	MARKET CAP ($ MILLIONS)		STOCK CAGR	EPS GROWTH	P/E	
		12/31 1985	12/31 1995			12/31 1985	12/31 1995
24 INTC	Intel	3,395	46,592	28%	37%	15.2x	14.2x
25 SFE	Safeguard Scientifics	58	727	28%	16%	17.6x	47.1x
	Mean	473	9,349	33%	32%	22.5x	28.9x
	Median	134	3,286	32%	31%	17.6x	25.2x

Source: FactSet, ThinkEquity Partners.

After considering the profiles of the top-performing companies, it is apparent that long-term stock performance is principally determined by earnings growth, not initial valuation, while the prevailing valuation is the result of historic operating success. The conclusion is that in the future investors seeking to identify the top-performing companies on these lists should not focus on bargain stocks or even "momentum" ideas, but rather identify growth companies that compete in large addressable markets and that possess dynamic long-term growth potential.

In addition, companies that operate in industries propelled by tailwinds will generally outperform the market. A tailwind occurs when a company and/or industry benefits from the trends that are shaping society. For example, companies that provide protection and screening services have received a tailwind from Homeland Security legislation. In contrast, a headwind occurs when negative trends are affecting an industry, such as nonsmoker-rights legislation creating a headwind for the tobacco industry. Those companies that are capable of successfully capitalizing on growing markets, rather than simply relying on the favorable tailwind, will capture larger market shares, be rewarded with premium valuations, and ultimately deliver the greatest shareholder value.

TOP 25 PERFORMERS

AVERAGE	PRICE TO EARNINGS		MARKET CAP ($ MILLIONS)		CAGR		P/E MULTIPLE CONTRIBUTION
	BEGIN	END	BEGIN	END	PRICE	EPS	
10-year study (1995–2005)	31.8x	42.0x	419	11,777	35%	38%	5%
10-year study (1985–95)	22.5x	28.9x	473	9,349	33%	32%	4%

MEDIAN	PRICE TO EARNINGS		MARKET CAP ($ MILLIONS)		CAGR		P/E MULTIPLE CONTRIBUTION
	BEGIN	END	BEGIN	END	PRICE	EPS	
10-year study (1995–2005)	18.9x	33.9x	199	4,213	33%	27%	6%
10-year study (1985–95)	17.6x	25.2x	134	3,286	32%	31%	3%

If we want to identify and invest in the companies that will appear on this list 10 years from now, here are my conclusions: (1) Focus on earnings growth, not the bargain basement. (2) Focus on small-cap stocks. Size forges an anchor to earnings growth!

Source: FactSet, ThinkEquity Partners.

→ PIGS AT THE TROUGH

"Even if you are on the right track, you'll get run over if you just sit there."
—WILL ROGERS

A key principle for successfully investing in emerging growth companies is to be very disciplined about limiting the number of companies you invest in. Knowing intimately what you own allows you to avoid some of the big blowups and stick with companies (or buy more of their stock!) even if they are hitting some bumps in the road.

Professors will tell you how important it is to diversify your portfolio—and if you want mediocre performance, they are correct. The fact of the matter is, to paraphrase Warren Buffett, we think it's better to have fewer eggs in your basket and watch them carefully.

Foster Friess, the highly successful investor who built Brandywine Funds, had a very simple analogy as a framework for how he added and subtracted stocks from his portfolio. He thought of his investments as "pigs at the trough."

I grew up in Minneapolis, which may bias my perspective somewhat, but picture going to the Minnesota State Fair on Labor Day weekend with rides on the Midway, carnival games, and everything one can imagine on a stick (pork chops, pickles, and even fried ice cream). Moving on, you go past the world's largest pumpkin, zucchini, and squash and now find yourself at the livestock exhibit.

After meandering through Rooster House, where it's so loud you can't hear yourself think, you come upon the relative tranquility of the Sow Barn, where you can see 1,300-pound pigs! There, at the trough, is a line filled to capacity with pigs eating things whose names are unprintable. At the end of the trough is a new little pig, but in order to eat, he needs to push aside the weakest pig to make room for himself.

What Foster said was that he was constantly looking at his portfolio "trough" and evaluating which was his weakest "pig" to replace with the up-and-coming one. If all the pigs at the trough were stronger than the new pig he was looking at, the lineup of pigs at the trough would be unchanged.

It's easy in this business to become comfortable with an existing portfolio, but the fact is that things change. Whether it's relative or absolute valuations, fundamentals or a new company that has superior price appreciation potential, we're in a world of limited time and resources, so in order for something to be added, something else needs to be sold.

While small companies in general have proven to be excellent performers, the most attractive opportunities have been, and continue to be, found by focusing on growth.

While the performance statistics for leading growth companies are impressive, being able to identify which companies may top these lists in the next 5 or 10 years is of true value. In my view, these historical performance lists are a good starting point, not in selecting the companies on them today, but in leading us to identify what caused them to top the lists in the past.

→ THREE RULES OF GROWTH INVESTING: EARNINGS, EARNINGS, EARNINGS

Consistent with the results of my top-performer study, the long-term performance of a stock is nearly 100% correlated with a company's earnings. Underlying the 33% average annual price performance of the top 25 companies over the past 10 years was annual earnings growth of 27%. In the five years from 2000 to 2005, annual price appreciation of 50% was supported by earnings growth of 46%, while from 1995 to 2000, 75% annual price appreciation was driven by annual earnings growth of 53%.

What is also borne out in the study is that investors who are early to identify companies with sustainable long-term earnings growth receive a sizable benefit from P/E expansion—the quintessential "double play" of growth investing.

In the 10-year study, P/E contribution added an average of 6% to annual performance. Within that period, the P/E contribution added 20% to the average annual performance in the period from 1995 to 2000, and 10% in the period from 2000 to 2005, or more than twice the long-run average return of the S&P 500!

Notably, the companies identified in the study were not trading at "cheap" initial valuations, with an average starting P/E across all periods of 18.9x. Moreover, in the majority of instances, what likely was initially considered a "lofty" valuation expanded further. Even where valuation did contract from high levels, the sustained growth in earnings ultimately managed to more than offset the negative impact of valuation compression.

This highlights another important facet of the power of growth—great growth companies reduce valuation risk by growing the intrinsic value of their business relative to the potential value that investors have discounted.

→ **THE GROWTH PROCESS**

Investors seeking to identify the top-performing companies need a systematic means to identify growth companies that compete in large, addressable markets or nascent, rapidly growing markets, and that possess dynamic long-term earnings potential.

My research process is structured to accomplish the identification of large, open-ended growth opportunities as well as individual companies that possess the critical elements necessary to capture meaningful market share in these opportunities.

My top-down perspective focuses on megatrends, or the technological, economic, and social forces that develop from a groundswell, move into the mainstream, and disrupt the status quo. We believe that understanding today's megatrends provides us with a road map to where future market opportunities are developing.

My bottom-up analysis is centered on the four Ps—people, product, potential, and predictability—an objective framework to assess a company's potential to realize sustained long-term growth resulting from market megatrends.

→ **EARNINGS DRIVE STOCK PRICE**

"People may bet on the hourly wiggles in the market, but it's the earnings that waggle the wiggles long term."   — PETER LYNCH

At the foundation of my investment philosophy is the principle that over time, share price is nearly 100% correlated with earnings. Accordingly, we want to identify companies that are capable of achieving rapid and sustained earnings growth. This focus is not entirely in a vacuum, irrespective of factors such as current valuation. However, it is my belief that if I am right on the fundamentals that are predictive of rapid, sustained earnings growth, I will better position myself to be on the correct side of the valuation premium.

Rapid earnings growth dictates long-term performance of a company's share price, I believe, which leads us to focus on identifying the most rapidly growing and dynamic markets and, naturally, the companies participating in the growth of those markets or, better yet, driving it. As a corollary to my focus on growth, my search almost inevitably leads me to smaller companies, where even small incremental sales gains have a large impact on a company's overall growth rate.

Smaller companies are typically pure-play investments, with their products and services strategically focused on a particular market's growth. Large, established companies, on the other hand, are typically burdened with more mature businesses, and frequently operate in less related markets than those that smaller companies are focused on. The obvious result is that sales from a fast-growing product or service have a much greater impact on a small company that is squarely focused on a specific market.

It is just as important that a company is able to generate meaningful profits from rapidly rising sales, with a market-defensible position versus competitors. In one respect, small companies have a competitive advantage, with their ability to develop a market niche ahead of others, while their size and focus position them to remain nimble as the market continuously develops. Market focus and agility enable them to adapt more quickly and bring new products and services to market to meet customers' changing demands and preferences, while remaining ahead of larger, less nimble competitors.

In another respect, lack of size can be a competitive liability if a market niche remains underdeveloped or not well defined. This reality leads many small companies to realize subpar profit margins (leaving them inadequately positioned to finance future growth) and, more often than not, to fall behind the industry growth rate (i.e., experience declining market share)—the quintessential "me too" company.

GROWTH STOCKS VERSUS CYCLICAL STOCKS, 1995–2005

GROWTH STOCKS	CAGR		$1 INVESTED	
	EPS	PRICE	1995	2005
Wal-Mart	15%	15%	$1	$4.21
Microsoft	22%	17%	$1	$4.77
Dell	35%	39%	$1	$27.68
Starbucks	29%	28%	$1	$11.43
GROWTH BASKET	25%	25%	$1	$12.02
CYCLICALS	EPS	PRICE	1995	2005
General Motors	NM	−7%	$1	$0.47
JCPenney	−9%	2%	$1	$1.17
PG&E	−2%	3%	$1	$1.31
DuPont	−2%	2%	$1	$1.22
CYCLICAL BASKET	−4%	0%	$1	$1.04

Source: FactSet, ThinkEquity Partners.

Ultimately, to achieve rapid and sustained growth in earnings, a growth company must participate in a dynamic market, such as the information technology, health-care, alternative energy, consumer and business services, specialty retailing, or media and entertainment industries. The most successful of these growth companies are the ones that develop their own market niche and introduce proprietary products and services, with minimal competition, allowing them to achieve sustained, above-average industry profitability and ultimately create tremendous shareholder value.

Using historical examples to underscore my conviction that earnings growth drives stock price, I looked at several classic growth stocks and some more recent growth stocks and compared them to blue-chip cyclical stocks with respect to average annual earnings growth and stock price performance. The takeaway is that $1 invested in the portfolio of growth stocks 10 years ago would have grown to more than $12 today, but $1 invested in well-known cyclicals would have grown to just $1.70.

Why? Because the earnings for the growth stocks had increased at 25% during that 10-year period. On the flip side, the earnings for the four blue-chip but cyclical stocks had increased only 1% during that period.

General Motors had net income of $1 billion in 1984. In 2005, it had net income of −$3.9 billion! It used to be said that as GM goes, so goes the nation. Thankfully, the correct reality is that as growth goes, so goes the United States.

→ HIGH EPS GROWTH + BEATING EXPECTATIONS = MEGAWINNER

We now know that identifying companies that will achieve high earnings growth is the first step to bagging a winner (and over any meaningful period of time, all you need to do).

But to have an explosive stock—one that not only benefits from riding high earnings growth to new stock heights but becomes a megawinner—beating analysts' expectations consistently is a key ingredient to the formula.

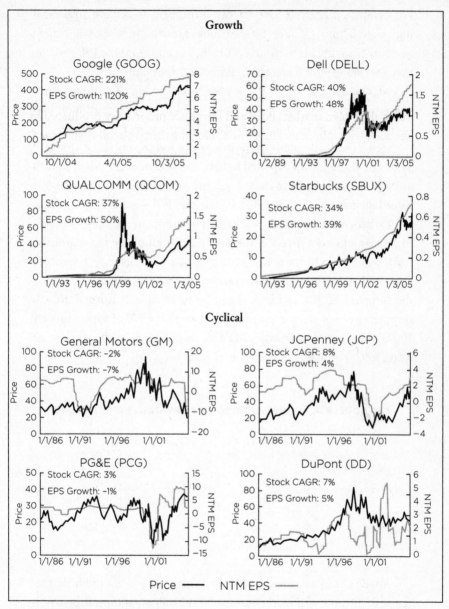

Source: FactSet, ThinkEquity Partners.

Investors love positive surprises, but they hate negative ones. Accordingly, management teams that earn a reputation for "underpromising" and "overdelivering" are often rewarded with high P/E multiples.

For example, if analysts have forecast a company to achieve 20% earnings growth but it achieves 30% earnings growth, the stock will benefit not only from the high earnings growth, but also from the P/E revision that goes along with increased optimism for the company.

Nirvana for a growth stock investor is the combination of high earnings growth and beating expectations—the likely result is the double play of consistently high earnings growth and an expanding P/E multiple.

Here's the quick math of how this works: A company had earnings of $1.00 last year and was expected to have earnings of $1.20 this year, with analysts forecasting a three- to five-year growth rate of 20%. The investors valued the company's shares at 20x (20 times) P/E—or a P/E/G of 100%.

Fast forward the clock one year. The company actually delivered $1.30 earnings, so if investors just kept a 20x multiple on the shares, the stock would be $26 for a 30% return in that year. Instead, if investors began to believe the true growth rate was more likely to be 30%, valuing the company at 30x earnings would be reasonable. A normal-growth company in a normal market should be valued at a P/E of approximately 100% of its expected growth rate. This would result in the stock price being $39.00 or nearly doubling in 12 months.

THE DOUBLE PLAY: HIGH EPS GROWTH + BEATING EXPECTATIONS

	SHARE PRICE	CY EPS	ESTIMATED GROWTH	P/E	ACTUAL EPS	ADJUSTED P/E	PRICE	GROWTH
Scenario 1	$20	$1.00	20%	20x	$1.30	20x	$26	30%
Scenario 2	$20	$1.00	20%	20x	$1.30	30x	$39	95%

Apollo Group is a great case study. When Apollo went public in December 1994, it had a market value of $112 million and promised Wall Street 25% EPS growth. In actuality, Apollo Group achieved 42% EPS growth and met or exceeded Wall Street expectations for 45 quarters in a row. Not coincidentally, Apollo's share price compounded at 59% for that 10-year period.

Apollo Group (APOL)

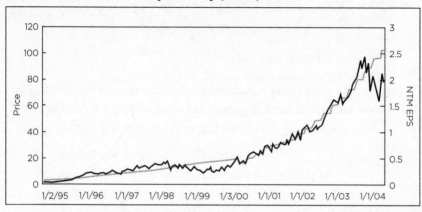

	Date	Actual	Estimates	Date	Actual	Estimates
*Apollo went public in	Dec. '05	0.73	0.70	Dec. '00	0.14	0.09
Dec. '04 with $112 million	Oct. '05	0.65	0.65	Oct. '00	0.12	0.12
market cap and promised	Jun. '05	0.77	0.74	Jun. '00	0.12	0.11
Wall Street 25% long-	Mar. '05	0.47	0.46	Mar. '00	0.07	0.07
term EPS growth.	Dec. '04	0.58	0.56	Dec. '99	0.10	0.09
	Oct. '04	0.52	0.48	Oct. '99	0.09	0.09
*It actually delivered 42%	Jun. '04	0.56	0.51	Jun. '99	0.11	0.11
EPS growth from 1995	Mar. '04	0.35	0.32	Mar. '99	0.06	0.06
to 2005.	Dec. '03	0.44	0.39	Dec. '98	0.08	0.08
	Oct. '03	0.37	0.34	Oct. '98	0.07	0.07
*It had 45 consecutive	Jun. '03	0.39	0.35	Jun. '98	0.09	0.08
quarters of meeting or	Mar. '03	0.24	0.20	Mar. '98	0.04	0.04
beating Wall Street	Dec. '02	0.30	0.23	Dec. '97	0.06	0.06
estimates.	Oct. '02	0.26	0.22	Oct. '97	0.05	0.05
	Jun. '02	0.27	0.24	Jun. '97	0.07	0.06
*Not surprisingly, its	Mar. '02	0.15	0.12	Mar. '97	0.03	0.02
stock CAGR is 48%.	Dec. '01	0.18	0.17	Dec. '96	0.04	0.04
	Oct. '01	0.17	0.16	Oct. '96	0.04	0.03
*$1 invested in Apollo at	Jun. '01	0.19	0.15	Jun. '96	0.04	0.04
IPO is worth $83 today!	Mar. '01	0.09	0.06	Mar. '96	0.01	0.01

Source: Company filings, FactSet, ThinkEquity Partners.

The objective is to find management teams that will underpromise and overdeliver in companies with high and sustainable earnings growth. This is where the biggest winners will be found. Apollo Group is the epitome of this objective.

━━━━━━━━━━━━━━➤ STAR GAZER

JACK LAPORTE
portfolio manager for the New Horizons Fund at
T. Rowe Price

*Jack has been managing the $6.3 billion New Horizons Fund
since 1987. The New Horizons Fund is one of the largest and
most respected small-cap funds in the world. In his reign, Laporte has delivered an 11.8% yearly return, which is 1.6 points
better than the S&P 500 and 5.5 points better than the Russell
2000 Growth Index. When I sat down with Jack, I asked him
about some common mistakes that growth investors make. (To
read my full interview with Jack Laporte, visit www.findingthe
nextstarbucks.com.)*

Often growth investors are not willing to pay what they should
for a truly unique, outstanding growth company. If you have a
high degree of confidence that a company can grow their earnings at 20% a year for an extended period of time, you should
be willing to pay a very high P/E on current earnings. Sometimes I fall into the trap of saying, "Ah, this is a great company
with a great management, but it's too expensive." Well, if it really
is a great company with great management, you should want
to look through the current price (which might seem a little
bit expensive based on current earnings) and realize that if
you're buying it on the basis of earnings out two or three years,
it's actually very cheap.

THINK POINTS

→ Diversification increases the risk of mediocre performance.

→ Following conventional wisdom is another sure way to miss the big winners.

→ Don't drive on the highway looking through the rearview mirror.

→ The stars of tomorrow generally are microcap in size, have a relatively high P/E, and have high earnings growth over a sustained period.

→ High EPS growth and beating Wall Street expectations is the formula for megawinners.

4

Formula for Identifying and Evaluating the Stars of Tomorrow (the Process)

"Here's something to think about: How come you never
see a headline like 'Psychic Wins Lottery'?"

—JAY LENO

ONE OF THE MOST BIZARRE REALITIES of Wall Street is the generally random process security analysts use to evaluate investment opportunities. I was an analyst at Lehman Brothers when it had the number-one-ranked research department on Wall Street. I was director of global growth research at Merrill Lynch when it was ranked number one. I was director of growth research and strategy at Montgomery Securities when that firm did better research than the other two top-ranked firms. And at all three places, the instructions were essentially the same: "Here's a laptop. This is your industry. Go write research and recommend companies."

Was there a Merrill Lynch way? A Lehman Brothers way? Or was there a process to identify, analyze, and recommend stocks? Absolutely not. Basically the "process" for doing security analysis was to hire bright, ambitious people and tell them to do their thing. Sometimes it works. And often it doesn't. It's not a mystery that research analysts are held in such low regard. The way Merrill Lynch and Lehman Brothers have established themselves as world-class firms has nothing to do with their approach to identifying the stars of tomorrow.

But it's not their fault because they haven't been given a process. If Starbucks hired kids off the street and told them, "Go make a latte," very few people would have ever heard of Starbucks.

One of the characteristics of great companies is that they are *systematic and strategic* in how they operate their business. Similarly, if you want to be a great investor, you need to be systematic and strategic in how you analyze companies.

We have created a "recipe book" on how to identify and invest in the fastest-growing companies in the world. It starts with our Think 10 Commandments and then proceeds to our megatrend analysis, our evaluation of a company's four Ps, and a disciplined valuation approach. How is this integrated in my process to identify the stars of tomorrow today?

→ THE THINKEQUITY PROCESS FOR IDENTIFYING AND INVESTING IN THE STARS OF TOMORROW

The ThinkEquity Partners' 10 Commandments are embedded in ThinkEquity's investment process. It's through these simple principles that investors will create the foundation to enhance their investment returns. Obviously, an investor's objective is to make money, but without a method, there is madness!

First, *be right on the fundamentals.* Earnings growth drives stock price. There is essentially a 100% correlation between how a company does and how its stock performs over time. Focus on the fastest-growing companies.

Second, *be proactive, not reactive.* Looking ahead and anticipating where the world is heading is how we catch winners early on. Try to predict what will be in tomorrow's newspapers, as opposed to reacting to what is in today's.

Third, *be rigorous, but don't have rigor mortis.* Looking at the balance sheet to make sure a company has enough cash to support your "blink" decision is important, but it is possible to overanalyze opportunities. The best investments are often easy and intuitive.

Fourth, *when wrong, admit it.* The best investors and analysts are wrong a lot. The worst thing to do is rationalize a mistake. Be intellectually honest. Make decisions based on current facts, not what you had thought to begin with.

Fifth is *the cockroach theory.* You seldom find just one cockroach in a kitchen. Likewise, if you find a problem at a growth company, there are always more behind it. It's rarely a one-quarter issue—the first loss is the best loss.

Sixth, *investment ideas are about information and insight.* Information is valuable if it is proprietary. Insight is valuable if we know what that information means.

Seventh, *the four Ps (people, product, potential, and predictability) are key for any successful growth company.* The first P, people, is the most important.

Eighth, *use five independent sources for each stock you invest in.* If possible, have a regular dialogue with the company management, but remember they will always see the glass as half full.

Ninth, *find three main reasons for a stock to move up or down.* In addition, identify near-term catalysts for price movements. Maintaining a thesis for why you own a stock is key.

Tenth, and finally, *be passionate about investing, but dispassionate about the investment.* The stock doesn't have feelings or know you own it.

The 10 Commandments create a consistent framework to cement my philosophy and are integrated in all that we do. We then start with a top-down view of each growth sector to determine how megatrends and industry drivers are influencing the potential of an industry. From that top-down approach, we create investment themes, which are where we focus our research and resources.

Next, we strive to know and list all the companies within the investment themes we've identified. From big to small, public to private, fast growing to slow growing, we will rank the companies based on the four Ps. We may not have a model on every company, but we will have an opinion on who the best and worst companies are, based on the four P framework.

After we rate the companies within our investment themes, we have a disciplined valuation approach based on earnings growth and price to earnings to determine near-term attractiveness. The reality is that at any given time, there are great companies selling at bad valuations that create near-term risk, as well as bad companies selling at compelling valuations that create near-term opportunities. A disciplined valuation approach focused on future earnings gives us a framework to make informed decisions and manage risk.

The other part of our research process is to have one eye on the short term and one eye on the long term. There is no question that the greatest benefit will be derived from being right in the long term, but we need to be alive to enjoy the success.

Think Recipe for Finding Megawinners

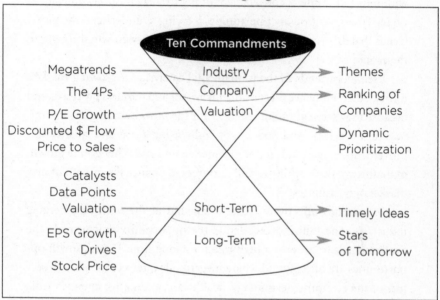

The eye focused on the short term needs to understand catalysts, data points, and valuation. Understanding what will move a stock in the next two minutes, two hours, two days, two weeks, and so on, is highly relevant. The eye focused on the long term assesses earnings growth. As I'll say again and again, earnings growth is what drives stock prices and is nearly 100% correlated with long-term performance.

→ MEGATRENDS—THE DRIVERS OF LONG-TERM GROWTH

"My interest is in the future because I am going to spend the rest of my
life there."   —C. F. KETTERING

The largest market-growth opportunities are those created on the fron-
tiers of the economy, where change at the edge leads to wide-scale change
within the economy. A core element of my strategy in successfully identifying emerging growth opportunities is trying to understand the megatrends that drive change, productivity, and ultimately growth throughout
the economy.

I see megatrends as the fundamental catalysts for growing markets
through their influence on consumer behavior and business processes, and
because they serve as building blocks for the introduction of new products and services. Additionally, by influencing price and quality improvements, megatrends unlock latent demand and reinvigorate growth
in mature markets, while freeing resources to finance the growth of new
market opportunities.

Megatrends effectively create a tailwind at the back of emerging
industries. The tailwinds accelerate the opportunity and provide the
fundamentals to grow at a high rate for a long time. Great growth opportunities are often found where megatrends intersect the growth sectors of the economy: technology, health care, alternative energy, media
and education, and business and consumer services.

Some of the current megatrends affecting consumers, businesses,
and entire economies for that matter are knowledge economy, globalization, the Internet, demographics, convergence, consolidation, brands,
and outsourcing.

In the long run I believe these dynamic forces will drive sales and
profits of entire industries, some directly and others indirectly, while
companies focused on becoming industry leaders will capture the largest
share of these rapidly growing markets and ultimately create tremendous shareholder value.

Megatrends Create Tailwinds

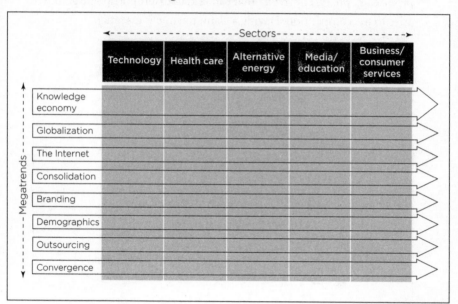

→ THE FOUR Ps

"The only time I really ever lost money was when I broke my own rules."
— JESSE LIVERMORE

Identifying the catalysts behind rapid market growth is an important element of successful growth investing, though finding companies that are able to translate these opportunities into bottom-line results remains my ultimate objective. Companies that are best positioned to accomplish this feat are those that have the most dynamic earnings prospects and that incorporate the four Ps into their business.

I believe the critical components of success for a growth company are the *people* and its growth culture. With young growth companies, this is particularly important, given that a young company won't likely have a measurable track record, but the management and key personnel of the company will.

Next, I look for companies that are leaders in their market, with a proprietary *product* or *service* that can lead to disproportionate gain relative to the competition. Having a claim to fame is essential.

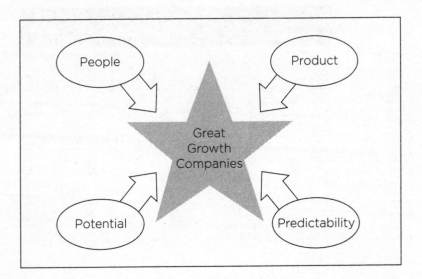

With respect to *potential,* I look for large addressable markets or nascent growth opportunities with open-ended growth, where small, rapidly growing businesses have the opportunity to become big companies. Megatrends play a critical role in assessing how large a market can become and how quickly.

Finally, I assess the visibility of a company's growth—its *predictability.* Does the company have recurring revenue or a formula that produces predictable returns? The best growth companies have high predictability and gain operating leverage as they continue to achieve economies of scale.

Ultimately, I hope to identify companies capable of capitalizing on nascent market growth, rather than relying upon a favorable market tailwind. Those are the companies that will capture larger market shares and be rewarded with premium valuations.

Investors who are early to identify the potent combination of a dynamic market with open-ended growth, and companies executing their business plan to achieve a disproportionate share of the market, will ultimately receive the benefits of the growth premium.

Finding companies with characteristics such as these is as difficult as spotting rare and swiftly moving elephants. The good news is that when we find one, we should know it!

THINK POINTS

→ Great businesses and great investors are systematic and strategic in how they operate.

→ The Think 10 Commandments are an overarching framework to help investors.

→ The recipe for finding and investing in tomorrow's megawinners is to evaluate the megatrends in each growth industry to determine investment themes.

→ Within each industry/theme we rank each company by the four P formula.

→ Use several valuation methods such as P/E to growth and price to sales to determine appropriate value and timeliness.

→ From the top-down process I determine short-term risk and opportunities by analyzing catalysts, data points, and valuation.

→ Last, but most important, look to invest in the company you believe will have the highest earnings growth for the longest period of time.

5

Megatrends

"I don't set trends. I just find out what they are and exploit them."
— DICK CLARK, *AMERICAN BANDSTAND*

IN ESSENCE, MEGATRENDS ARE POWERFUL technological, economic, and social forces that develop from a groundswell (early adoption), move into the mainstream (mass market), and disrupt the status quo (mature market), driving change, productivity, and ultimately growth opportunities for companies, industries, and entire economies.

Megatrends play a key role in how social, economic, technological, and political changes take hold, and as we look backward through history, their effects are easily seen. In real time, however, megatrends tend to go underappreciated. The nature of megatrends is that they are relatively slow to develop, driven by bottom-up, "local" events that slowly gain in critical mass until they come to define large-scale and pervasive change.

In his 1982 book *Megatrends,* John Naisbitt identified several trends that were in various stages of restructuring an industrial economy that was regionally concentrated and national in focus, with corporate America best characterized by industrial giants and extensive management hierarchies. Technological improvements were often feared, particularly by workers and unions. Politically, power remained concentrated, polarized by business, labor, and social issues, and focused on short-term solutions.

In the midst of this restructuring, which the consensus had yet to appreciate and fewer still wanted to embrace, Naisbitt anticipated what most feared: the continued decline of manufacturing and the rise of the information economy.

The trends he identified more than 20 years ago have steadily progressed, with many information technology companies as recognizable and mature today as industrial bellwethers were then. Aside from identifying the trends themselves, one of Naisbitt's key insights was that the most powerful of the trends occurred independently, across geographies and throughout communities, only later becoming a large collective trend.

What Naisbitt was able cull from these seemingly disparate trends were common factors, or megatrends, that were in effect catalyzing the restructuring of the past, present, and probable future.

Megatrends continue to play just as important a role today as they have over the past 10, 20, and 50 years. What is changing are the smaller but related trends resulting from today's more visible megatrends. For example, while globalization is clearly not a new trend, in combination with greater geopolitical openness, economic development, and more robust information and communications technologies, the pace of globalization, trade, and outsourcing has rapidly accelerated.

Likewise, with the explosion in the number of products and services to address a growing number of global markets, the value of brands is growing exponentially, as companies find it a necessity to differentiate their products and defend their markets with the value embedded within their brands.

Information technologies have been around long enough for IT companies to now be mature, although the application of IT continues to rapidly broaden beyond traditional business investments and consumer electronics, spurring growth in new areas of biotechnology and nanotechnology as well as consumer and business services.

Identifying new trends is always difficult. As the venture capital community notes, by the time something becomes a trend, it is too late for many investors to reap benefits. That said, only by continuing to look for the forces that shape the realms of businesses and consumers can we hope to understand and capitalize on emerging growth markets in today's global economy.

Within these megatrends are themes that become increasingly pervasive through economies, though they generally remain unrecognized until they are firmly considered the status quo. Below we augment the themes first posited by Naisbitt, which represent recurring themes across the economic and social megatrends currently at work.

EVOLUTION OF MEGATREND THEMES		
1960–80	1980–2000	2000–20
Industrial society	Information society	Knowledge economy
Forced technology	High tech/high touch	Internet/invisible computing
National economy	World economy	Globalization/economic clusters
Short-term	Long-term	Convergence
Centralization	Decentralization	Outsourcing
Institutional help	Self-help	Demographics
Hierarchies	Networking	Consolidation
Either/or	Multiple options	Brands
Representative democracy	Participatory democracy	Feedback democracy

Source: ThinkEquity Partners, John Naisbitt, *Megatrends.*

As I mentioned earlier, I have identified eight megatrends that I feel are the key drivers for waves of opportunity. The knowledge economy, demographics, globalization, the Internet, and outsourcing will drive market growth and competition, while convergence, consolidation, and brands will be the key enablers of what become successful products, technologies, companies, and industries.

Those companies best able to recognize and harness the growth opportunities made available by these megatrends will be those that first capitalize on, then extend their lead from, the competition; recognize the rewards of being an early mover; and leverage productivity improvements for the benefit of their customers and their own growth potential.

In the coming years, these megatrends, as well as many new ones, will continue to create the largest market opportunities, providing the fundamental catalysts to growing markets through their influence on consumer behavior and business processes, serving as the building blocks for the introduction of new products and services, as well as creating growth opportunities within more mature markets.

My view of current and future trends is that they likely will be extensions of past megatrends, though the pace of change will be more accelerated, rapidly capitalizing on cumulative advancements in technology, demographic shifts, changing consumer preferences, and improved business efficiencies. The time it takes to innovate and commercialize to meet current and latent demand will continue to collapse toward real time.

In my mission to find the stars of tomorrow, I rely heavily on understanding the megatrends that are creating significant market growth opportunities. In the years ahead, I anticipate that the dynamic changes that have taken place during the past bull market will serve as stepping stones for future growth opportunities.

→ MEGATREND 1: THE KNOWLEDGE ECONOMY

"If investments in factories were the most important investments in the Industrial Age, the most important investments in an Information Age are surely investments in the human brain."

—LAWRENCE SUMMERS,
FORMER PRESIDENT OF HARVARD UNIVERSITY

Mind Over Matter: Human Capital in the Knowledge Economy

Throughout history, whether in preindustrial or industrial times, great nations developed based on their access to physical resources or their ability to surmount physical barriers. England and Spain crossed the oceans, Germany turned coal and iron into steel, and the United States exploited a wealth of agricultural and industrial resources to become the world's breadbasket and industrial superpower.

The advent of the personal computer, the Internet, and the electronic delivery of information has transformed the world from a manufacturing, physically based economy to an electronic, knowledge-based economy. Whereas the resources of the physically based economy were coal, oil, and steel, the resources of the new knowledge-based economy are brainpower and the ability to acquire, deliver, and process information effectively.

THE 10 FASTEST-GROWING OCCUPATIONS IN THE UNITED STATES, 2004–14

OCCUPATION	EMPLOYMENT ('000s)		CHANGE		MOST SIGNIFICANT SOURCE OF POSTSECONDARY EDUCATION OR TRAINING
	2004	2014 (EST.)	NUMBER	PERCENTAGE	
Home health aides	624	974	350	56%	Short-term on-the-job training
Network systems and data communications analysts	231	357	126	55%	Bachelor's degree program
Medical assistants	387	589	202	52%	Moderate on-the-job training
Physician assistants	62	93	31	50%	Bachelor's degree program
Computer software engineers, applications	460	682	222	48%	Bachelor's degree program

OCCUPATION	EMPLOYMENT ('000s)		CHANGE		MOST SIGNIFICANT SOURCE OF POSTSECONDARY EDUCATION OR TRAINING
	2004	2014 (EST.)	NUMBER	PERCENTAGE	
Physical therapy assistants	59	85	26	44%	Associate's degree program
Dental hygienists	158	226	68	43%	Associate's degree program
Computer software engineers, systems software	340	486	146	43%	Bachelor's degree program
Dental assistants	267	382	115	43%	Moderate on-the-job training
Personal and home care aides	701	998	297	42%	Short-term on-the-job training

Source: U.S. Census Bureau.

With some of the greatest developments in new technologies arriving late in the 20th century, widespread optimism surrounding the 21st century has led futurists to predict a period of rapid growth of the magnitude of the Industrial Revolution, if not greater, with the advent of the knowledge-based economy. In this economy, knowledge workers form the cornerstones of successful businesses, emerging industries, and economic growth. In this new environment, however, the labor force is presented with an unprecedented challenge as it must continuously upgrade its skills to keep pace with innovation as companies increase their R&D expenditures. Of the 10 fastest-growing occupations over the next 10 years, 6 require postsecondary education and all are knowledge-based jobs. Even more telling, the number of patents issued in the United States per year nearly doubled over the past 10 years, and the pace is accelerating.

Today's economy is a knowledge economy based on brainpower, ideas, and entrepreneurship. Technology is the driver of today's growth economy, and human capital is its fuel. The knowledge economy is people-centric, having evolved from being manufacturing-intensive to being labor-extensive. Fundamental to success in the new economy is how companies obtain, train, and retain knowledge workers.

Patents Granted in the United States

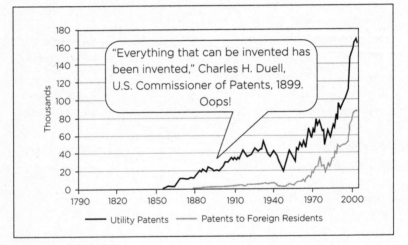

Source: U.S. Patent Office.

Ubiquitous and untethered PCs and high-speed bandwidth will facilitate access to knowledge anytime, anywhere. The Internet democratizes knowledge, increases access to it, lowers its cost, and ultimately improves its quality. I believe that combining the richness of an offline experience (such as a one-on-one conversation with a professor) and the reach that only the Internet provides creates a network effect that allows scalable knowledge enterprises to be born. Moreover, I see significant potential advantages that offline operators can achieve by leveraging their experience and brand online. For example, Target has combined its position as the merchandiser of affordable forward fashions with its white-hot brand and has created an online powerhouse.

The information revolution that began with the birth of the PC has evolved into the knowledge revolution. E-commerce is to the knowledge revolution what the railroads were to the Industrial Revolution. I think enterprises building "knowledge tracks," or infrastructure, into the corporate market are poised to enjoy explosive growth.

In the knowledge economy, education is the fuel that powers new enterprises. Integrating quality educational content with testing/assessment and certification programs is the new education paradigm for the 21st century. Assessment is the currency with which all skills are valued. The four engines of the new economy—computers, telecommunications, health care, and instrumentation—employ approximately 50 knowledge workers per 100 employees and are growing. Employment in these technology-intensive industries is rising three to six times as fast as economy-wide job growth.

The Internet is all about disproportionate gains to the leaders of a category. By focusing on knowledge enterprises that contain the four Ps and other key differentiating factors, it is generally possible to distinguish the Yahoo!s from the yahoos and gain outsized investment returns from outsized opportunities.

In today's world, knowledge is making the difference not only in how well an individual does, but also in how well a company does and, for that matter, in how well a country does. The future possibilities of the knowledge economy look both exciting and, at the same time, daunting. Education as a proxy for knowledge shows that the pay gap between somebody who has a high school education and a person with a college education has more then doubled in the past 20 years—strong evidence of the realities of the knowledge marketplace we are in.

In today's knowledge-based global marketplace, human capital has replaced physical capital as the source of competitive advantage. A key result of the confluence of technology and the Internet economy is the need for better and smarter workers. The reality of a 5% unemployment rate in the United States, the "free agent" mindset of the most talented workers, and the fact that only 24% of the U.S. adult population has a college degree is making this task more difficult than ever before.

E-commerce forces even traditional businesses to operate at Internet speed, with time-to-competency now a major factor in determining the competitiveness of all companies.

Fast forward to 2011. Unfortunately, the supply of students coming

NEW VIEW OF HUMAN CAPITAL AND LEARNING IN THE KNOWLEDGE-BASED ECONOMY	
INDUSTRIAL ECONOMY	KNOWLEDGE ECONOMY
Wages	Ownership/options
Four-year degree	Forty-year degree
Learning as cost center	Learning as number-one source of competitive advantage
Help wanted	Talent needed
Learner mobility	Content mobility
Distance education	Distributed learning
Résumé	Competence
Employee	Talent
Physical capital	Human capital
One size fits all	Tailored programs
Geographic institutions	Brand-name universities and celebrity professors
Just-in-case	Just-in-time

Source: Michael Moe, Merrill Lynch.

out of America's schools doesn't promise much relief. In a recent international comparison, U.S. twelfth-graders finished dead last and next to last in the key new-economy subjects of math and science, respectively.

Hence, the fundamental and massive problem of global competitiveness and obtaining knowledge workers reaches all the way down to the K–12 level. As the human capital demand funnel is triggered, global corporations need to more effectively recruit knowledge workers, provide lifelong learning for their employees, and create supply for the future by improving the K–12 education system. The Internet acts as a major enabler linking corporations to people, providing management systems, anytime/anywhere learning, and a catalyst to help revolutionize a failing primary education system.

The truly revolutionary impact of the Internet is just beginning to be felt. Historically, geographic distance mattered. It mattered to people seeking goods and services. It mattered for teachers and their students. With the Internet came the death of distance and the rapid reshaping of the world into one marketplace.

At no previous time has human capital been so important. This means that finding, developing, and retaining knowledge workers will be mission-critical functions—and high-growth sectors—in the new economy. Accordingly, I look at the continuum of human capital solutions holistically—a knowledge web—and believe the most important companies will have an appreciation for and/or involvement in a comprehensive solution. I believe that those companies that can link different elements of the human capital value chain—stretching from recruiting to assessment to training and, finally, retention—while leveraging the Internet's capabilities to deliver a total solution will be the big winners.

People Power at the Center of the Knowledge Economy:
The Human Capital Value Chain

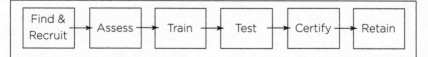

Source: Michael Moe, Merrill Lynch.

Democratizing Knowledge

The Internet creates one economy and one market. As large as the online higher education market (consisting of colleges and universities) is in the United States, the global opportunity is significantly greater. Unlike in the United States, where postsecondary education is relatively available, access to world-class postsecondary institutions in many parts of the world is limited. Currently, there are about 84 million students enrolled in higher education worldwide. Global demand for higher education is forecasted to reach 160 million by 2025. If online learning captures even half of this growth, there will be 40 million students for online education.

Widening Pay Gap as Knowledge Workers Are Rewarded

A company's earning power rises due to its return on human capital. Companies, in turn, must reward employees with "productivity wages" or risk losing them to competitors. When this happens, the earning power of knowledge employees rises in the job market. Those without the necessary education, however, do not reap similar benefits. Accordingly, we have seen the income gap between those with a bachelor's or higher degree and those with just a high school education widen significantly, and I expect this trend to continue as long as the marketplace rewards knowledge-intensive companies.

Moreover, the computer has replaced many "left-brain," task-oriented jobs as it performs these functions faster, cheaper, and better than humans. For example, now more often than not, phone companies use voice recognition technology provided by companies such as Tellme Networks to provide the number you seek. A significant challenge and opportunity for corporations lies in creating knowledge workers from today's existing labor pool.

Human Capital Drives Market Valuations of Knowledge Companies

Growth companies today are dependent on human capital. Those companies that have created growth by leveraging their "off-balance-sheet" human capital assets have, in turn, seen their share prices rewarded with higher valuations. It is illustrative to compare valuations of the largest 10 companies in the industrial economy with those of the largest 10 companies in the knowledge economy.

LARGEST COMPANIES BY MARKET VALUE, 1980, 2005	
1980	**PRICE-TO-BOOK**
IBM	2.4x
AT&T	0.7x
Exxon	1.4x
Schlumberger	6.9x
Mobil	1.3x
Chevron	1.5x
Atlantic Richfield	2.1x
General Electric	1.7x
General Motors	0.8x
Royal Dutch Petroleum	0.8x
Median price-to-book	1.5x

2005	PRICE-TO-BOOK
General Electric	3.3x
Exxon Mobil	3.2x
Microsoft	5.8x
Citigroup	2.2x
Wal-Mart Stores	4.0x
Bank of America	1.8x
Johnson & Johnson	4.9x
American International Group	2.0x
Procter & Gamble	13.3x
Pfizer	2.6x
Median price-to-book	3.3x

Source: FactSet, ThinkEquity Partners.

Most telling, as I mentioned earlier, the wage gap between someone with a high school education versus a college education increased from 50% in 1980 to 111% in 2005. This fact shows that corporate focus has shifted to human capital from financial and physical capital. Given the intangible nature of human capital, it simply cannot be "line-itemized" on a balance sheet as tangible assets are. I believe rising price-to-book ratios reflect, in large part, the fact that the productive assets driving growth are increasingly off-balance-sheet assets.

As the rise of the knowledge economy accelerates and knowledge employment within industries experiences exceptional growth, human capital liquidity (knowledge workers efficiently seeking and being sought for knowledge jobs) will become an increasingly important factor for employers. We expect that this will continue to push up the wage gap between the highly educated and the less educated. In addition to competitive compensation, I anticipate that growing human capital liquidity will also encourage companies to provide other benefits such as child care and specialized education and training—benefits that increase worker loyalty, encouraging them to apply their creativity and brainpower to growing these companies.

Growth Jobs Are Knowledge and Service Jobs

"The killer app for the next decade is talent acquisition and retention."
— JOHN DOERR

To understand the future, it's critical to understand the past. In the 1780s, when the United States was formed, we had an agrarian economy in which 90% of all jobs were related to farming. By 1850, 49% of all jobs were in farming as the Industrial Revolution began to have its impact. By 1900, only 39% of jobs were in farming, just 3% of the adult population in the United States had a college degree, and only 15% had a high school degree. Today, less than 2% of U.S. labor force is in farming, 24% of the population has a college degree, and 85% has a high school degree.

During the Industrial Revolution, the labor force was equipped with the skills to enter into manufacturing-sector employment, and the assembly line merely required the theory of work organization to be put into practice. Workers were required to do no more than perform specific tasks and later operate specialized machinery that performed the actual work. Nonetheless, the changes that this innovation brought were enormous. By 1950, 40% of the U.S. workforce was employed in the manufacturing sector, and this increased productivity 50-fold. Workers accrued the majority of the benefits—half in the form of sharply reduced working hours, and the other half in a 25-fold increase in real wages.

The rise of knowledge workers (who succeeded industrial workers) began 50 years ago with roots in the GI Bill, the "Management Revolution," and the rise of the service sector. Since 1950, employment in the

U.S. Economic Development

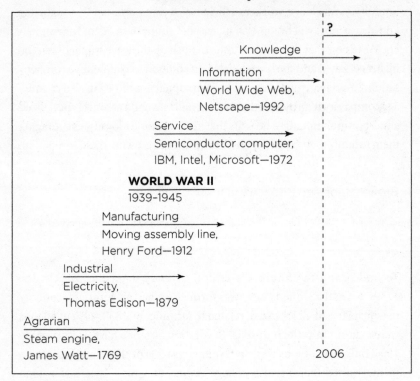

Source: ThinkEquity Partners.

manufacturing sector has fallen from nearly 40% of total employment to less than 10% currently, while service sector employment has risen from less than 14% to more than 76%—essentially flip-flopping from where it had been in 1950. During this period, demand for an educated workforce grew. Increased competition from abroad (particularly from emerging economic regions) has resulted in continued substitution in the U.S. manufacturing sector away from workers and toward technology, increasing the productivity of the remaining workers. Domestically, the service sector has attracted the more highly skilled workers away from the manufacturing sector. Low-skilled factory jobs have been absorbed by less-developed countries.

Just as gains in manufacturing productivity, greater access to higher education, and an affluent middle class fueled the transition from a manufacturing to a service-based economy, the extensive adoption of information technology is now creating the need for a highly skilled knowledge-based economy. While service sector job growth has been increasing overall, the more technically intensive industries have experienced the most rapid growth. Knowledge jobs such as IT, health, and business services, on the other hand, are growing three to six times as fast as jobs economy-wide.

Understanding how a company fits into the knowledge economy and what it's doing to obtain, train, and retain the smartest people in the marketplace is critical for investing in future stars.

STAR GAZER

MICHAEL MILKEN
financier of innovation and entrepreneurs

Michael Milken is arguably the most influential financier of the 20th century, having almost single-handedly created the market for high-yield bonds in the 1970s and 1980s. Milken "democratized" access to capital for innovative entrepreneurs who literally created new industries. Milken founded a number of companies related to education and is currently a principal— along with Lowell Milken and Steve Green—in Knowledge Universe Education, the world's largest operator of early childhood education centers. In 2003, Milken started Washington, D.C.-based FasterCures, which seeks greater efficiency in researching all serious diseases. In a 2004 cover story, Fortune magazine called him "the man who changed medicine." He also founded the Milken Family Foundation in 1982 to support medical research and education. I had a chance to sit down with Michael Milken, and here are some highlights from our talk.

Michael Moe: *Mike, you've been an innovator for nearly 40 years in finance, education, health care, and wellness. How do you decide where you're going to focus your energy for opportunities?*

Michael Milken: I try at least one, two times a year just to sit down and think about what might happen in particular areas. So, at the end of 2005, I literally took two days when I didn't take any phone calls. My wife, Lori, and I went away and just read and thought. From 1970 to '78, I'd had this enormous luxury of a 2½-hour commute in each direction, or 5 hours a day when no one actually spoke to me, so I could reflect and think. Now I don't have that opportunity as often, so I try to just block everything out and decide what really are the issues of society to deal with. I've been a strong believer that the best opportunities come where I can identify the challenges and the needs of society. It's a trite line, "doing good is good business," but it's true.

As I think about the decisions I've made over time, it was really after the Watts riot that I decided that I needed to work in the field of finance and that access to capital was a civil right. It took a long time and it wasn't an easy process to try to innovate to get people to understand that the individual that you're financing is the key in that decision making. You're going to finance the future; not finance the past.

Today when I sit down and think about things, I'm concerned that health care is the largest part of the U.S. economy and potentially the largest part of all economies worldwide. How to significantly reduce that cost is one of the defining issues in society. Recall the case of polio. People had estimated the solution to polio was going to cost $100 billion, and we got it down to $100 million—with a vaccine.

Michael Moe: *What are the most important areas today?*

Michael Milken: Two elements in the health-care area have been driving me in the last 12 or 13 years. One, how do we accelerate science? We decided to form FasterCures under the Milken Institute. Two, how do we make things happen faster? It's no longer the technology that's the inhibiting factor. It is the infrastructure. It's the processes. We concluded that we're using 19th- and 20th-century ways of approaching medical problems and not using 21st-century data-collection technology that's available to us.

We're really focused in this effort on accelerating the cures for life-threatening diseases by changing how the processes work, or changing legislation or dealing with things like HIPAA requirements or reporting requirements, so we can get more out of the data. We can move faster in medical research because of the dramatic reduction in telecommunication costs and storage costs and dramatic increase in the speed of computing capabilities. If you can figure out how to do that, there are large economic benefits for business, and tremendous benefits to society in increasing the value and the quality of life. I would say it's not only a passion. It's something I think will make a great contribution.

Michael Moe: *How do you go about analyzing all this?*

Michael Milken: The basic concept that permeates my thinking is that human capital—the skills, education, and experience of individuals—is the primary asset on our planet. Depending on whose estimates you use, it makes up 75 to 95% of the assets.

There are two things that empower the increase in the value of that asset. One is medical, increasing the quality and length of life. And two is education that increases the productivity of that life. Both of these were enhanced by the financial revolution that allowed capital to flow to individuals with ability, which I believe has occurred in the United States and is slowly occurring throughout the world. With that as my basic premise, trying to figure out how to change the perception of medical research, or collection of medical data, or dissemination of medical data obviously would serve that effort to increase the quality and length of life.

As for education, I would say I'm using finance as a benchmark of what can be done. In the 1970s, my firm was probably the first to computerize our trading records and data, which gave everyone access to information so they could make better decisions. Today, probably 30% of the most valuable companies in the world are in the financial service industry. I believe this industry, more than any other, has used technology to analyze and substantially reduce costs.

The elimination of paper and the ability to increase the velocity of money is an enormous benefit of deploying technology. The first day I worked on Wall Street, my first assignment was to eliminate the movement of the stock certificates and the bond certificates, which was potentially going to bankrupt the Wall Street firms in the late 1960s. The sheer fact that you wouldn't be paid until you had a physical delivery of a certificate from Missoula, Montana, was essentially bringing the financial system to a halt. Today there is a central depository, you have electronic transfers, and it's no different from our going to the bank and withdrawing money or depositing money. The whole method of finance has changed.

Michael Moe: *How does this apply to health care?*

Michael Milken: When we're looking at medical today, we're thinking the same way. If we can eliminate paperwork, research will move faster. Medical is motivated to deploy technology more than education is. We think about education the same way. We want to make it available to everyone worldwide. I think it all stems from the premise that the most productive thing one can do is enhance the quality and length of an individual's life and then give that individual all the tools he needs to be the most productive he can be. And that takes the form of education. That's why I've moved from finance to health care and education.

Michael Moe: *You helped to create huge industries and companies, such as MCI in telecommunications and Turner Broadcasting in cable, from the very early days. What did you look for in a company that you were going to get involved with, and how important were the people to that?*

Michael Milken: When I think about financing or investing in a company, I first step back and focus on the industry. What is the industry? Where is it going? What's its role? Who are the competitors? What effect is technology going to have on that industry? Take the cellular industry, for example. Growing up in the '50s and the '60s as a *Star Trek* fan, I'd see Scotty being told by Captain Kirk to "beam" him up, so it just seemed to me that there could be a wireless device with the basic technology so that people could speak to each other and could travel through the air. Why would anyone ever want to have a phone hooked into a wall if you could do it wirelessly? There's the concept that your communication device is where you are, not that you go to a communication device to communicate. I was watching an old James Bond movie with my daughter, and when Bond finally had some information, he was rushing around trying to find a phone booth to make a call from, as I recall. She thought it was the craziest thing she ever saw. Why is he driving around? Why doesn't he just take out his cell phone?

If you have an idea of who is going to succeed and can identify the visionary thinkers, such as Craig McCaw or Ted Turner, you look for a product that you think will be well accepted and individuals who can accelerate the technology and the concept of that technology—individuals who can manage a large ramp-up particularly, such as Bill McGowan. I would say it's no different than with Steve Wynn. He limped into my office; I think he had a broken leg at the time. He was in his midthirties, I was in my early thirties, and I saw his passion, his ideas, his creativity. The concept was an adult Disneyland, creating structures, environments that adults would love to spend time in, whether it was due to the beauty of a hotel or restaurant, the entertainment, or the sheer structure of the building. And what I saw was an industry in gaming that was more of a sports rink for individuals where they thought they could actually win.

Financially backing a person such as Steve Wynn, who had the passion and ability to create structures all wrapped into one, was a tremendous opportunity for me and a very well-wrapped way of creating the development of an industry that was so misunderstood by public investors at the time.

Michael Moe: *It all goes back to the people, right?*

Michael Milken: Whether it is Steve Jobs with Apple or Bill McGowan with MCI, it's an individual name. I met Bill McGowan in the early 1970s and my own firm would not allow me to finance him. They were very concerned about what AT&T was saying. The chairman of the board of the firm was on the board of

Continental Telephone and they didn't want us to "finance competitors."

In the late 1970s, I gave a presentation telling them they were right, I had looked at the various assets and stepped back, and when I thought about it, it really wasn't a fair competition. They thought I was going to give up on financing MCI, but I said, "No, the 1.3 million people who work for AT&T are not enough to offset Bill McGowan and his senior management team of 11 people; they might need five million people to do that."

I think of these opportunities to marry capital, new forms of securities, with people of talent, whether this individual is John Malone of TCI or Bill McGowan of MCI or Steve Wynn at what became the Mirage, today part of MGM/Mirage, or Kirk Kerkorian or Bob Toll or Bruce Karatz. These industries have grown, and the companies have been successful because (1) they ran great businesses and had great vision in these industries, and (2) financial technology was adapted to further accelerate the growth of these industries. They, as individuals, understood how to use that financial technology.

Michael Moe: *Mike, is there anything more you want to say about the opportunities you see in health care and education?*

Michael Milken: Let's compare education to the media industry, where, let's say, Steven Spielberg spent $1 million a minute for special effects. It changed what one expected on the movie screen. Our view on education is that the teacher is essential in that classroom. However, we've never invested in a digital product where you capture the best teachers, with the best techniques and the best learning, and put it online. In the case of

K12 Inc., the teacher stands up in front of the classroom today and is teaching science in the elementary schools in Philadelphia using the same curriculum that is online that students in virtual charter schools or home schools might be using, but here you have a teacher interacting with that child. You've completed the home–school connection.

I envision that, in the next decade or two, some percentage of every class that every child takes, beginning in first grade and increasing as they get older, will be online, whether they're taking that class at home, the Boys' and Girls' clubs, the school's computer lab, or a local library redefined as to what a library is. And therefore you can invest tens of millions of dollars in curriculum because you are going to advertise it to millions of children around the world. You can bring the best curriculum, the best teaching methods, and empower that teacher in the classroom, or that parent who's helping the child at home, or some other care provider or tutor with the best, and you get immediate feedback as to how that child is doing and how children all over the world are doing, and you can adapt the deployment of late-20th-century, early-21st-century technology so it allows you to have a dynamic textbook that is changing every day based on your results, on how people learn, and on what's going on in the world. We all recognize that any textbook is obsolete on the day it is printed because it is based on things that occurred at that point in time, so by the time it gets to the student in the classroom—whether it's an example used in mathematics or whether it's history that's being taught, or science—it's all dated. By using technology, you'll be able to be more in tune, to know how a person learns best, to present the material in the best way that they learn, to deploy technology.

The paradigm is changing with technology. The key issue is that teachers need to be comfortable with technology. It's been a problem in the past, but it will get better in the future.

Michael Moe: *Where is medicine going?*

Michael Milken: The IBM chip for Sony Playstation Games can do two trillion calculations per second. Use this for individuals and their diseases. Use the power of technology to diagnose and solve problems, calculate all the data and go through all the permutations. Then medicine will evolve and go from productive, to predictive, to preventive. A full 60% of all health-related problems involve lifestyle—whether you smoke, exercise, eat fruits, etc. It makes sense to launch companies that promote healthier living. Wellness will be adopted by society to lower costs and improve the quality of life over the next decade or two.

→ MEGATREND 2: GLOBALIZATION

"It has been said that arguing against globalization is like arguing against the laws of gravity."

—KOFI ANNAN, SECRETARY GENERAL, UNITED NATIONS

The megatrend of globalization has been impacting business since Christopher Columbus set off to find a shorter route to India and ended up in the Bahamas. Technology has been the major accelerator of this trend, with the telephone, the airplane, and the Internet playing major roles in making the world smaller and flatter.

Tom Friedman, the *New York Times* columnist and globalization spokesperson, brilliantly lays out his view on the future impact of globalization in *The World Is Flat.* Through cheap technology, abundant

The Global Top 20

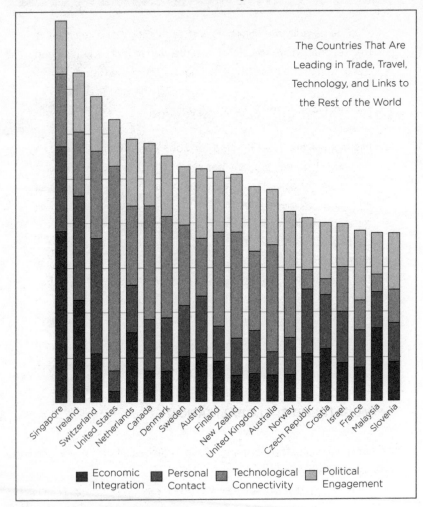

The Countries That Are Leading in Trade, Travel, Technology, and Links to the Rest of the World

Economic Integration Personal Contact Technological Connectivity Political Engagement

Source: AT Kearney Global Top 20, 2005.

bandwidth, and the continuation of the globalization megatrend, Bangalore has effectively become a suburb of Boston.

The 10 "flatteners" that Friedman cites as the major influences for globalization are:

1. *11/9.* On November 9, 1989, the Berlin Wall came down. Perhaps the greatest legacy of Ronald Reagan's presidency

came when he stood outside the Berlin Wall and shouted, "Tear down this wall, Mr. Gorbachev." And, of course, as he did, communism collapsed, and free enterprise and markets became the economic metrics for the world.

2. *Netscape.* It went public on August 9, 1995. And with that, the world became your oyster with the click of a mouse.

3. *Development of workflow software.* This decreased the effect of manufacturing delays. With it, time and geography become irrelevant.

4. *Apache server.* The result was the acceleration of Web site design.

5. *Y2K outsourcing.* This showed the world (through necessity) how India could be used for reliable outsourcing.

6. *Offshoring.* China became the hub for multinational manufacturing and assembly work.

7. *Supply chain.* Wal-Mart is the poster child for dynamically optimizing the process for bringing products to the consumer.

8. *Insourcing.* This is in-house job sharing. UPS leads the way here.

9. *Web search engines.* It is frightening what Google finds at lightning speeds.

10. *Steroids.* Technology such as Voice over Internet Protocol (VoIP) and mobile phones integrate us faster, cheaper, and all the time.

For decades, investors such as Sir John Templeton have shown the importance of thinking globally for investment opportunities. Looking to the future, being a global investor will be a redundant term—*to be an investor you will have to think globally.* As the U.S. economy continues to mature, looking to emerging markets for growth opportunities will be an important part of the growth investor's playbook.

WORLD EXCHANGES		
COUNTRY/REGION	MARKET VALUE	PERCENTAGE OF WORLD MARKET VALUE
Mexico	$267 billion	1%
India	$475 billion	1%
Middle East and Africa	$546 billion	1%
Eastern Europe	$593 billion	2%
Hong Kong	$687 billion	2%
China	$772 billion	2%
Australia	$972 billion	2%
Canada	$1 trillion	3%
United Kingdom	$3 trillion	8%
Japan	$5 trillion	13%
Asia	$8 trillion	21%
Western Europe	$11 trillion	28%
United States	$16 trillion	41%
North America	$17 trillion	44%
World	$39 trillion	100%

Source: FactSet.

But what globalization really illustrates from my perspective of identifying the stars of tomorrow is how it helps or hurts a business opportunity. You can't say it doesn't matter because globalization affects essentially everything.

Medicine provides an example of a traditonally localized business that is affected by globalization. Whereas historically if you were injured or sick, you basically had access only to the physician in your community, now X-rays can be e-mailed to the other side of the globe to be examined by an expert there. Sourcing product from the most competitive vendor is another global exercise. Companies outsource noncore functions routinely, making it impossible to compete without embracing the realities of globalization.

Pure plays on globalization are seen in the travel industry, which directly benefits from the increased integration of the planet. In many ways, it's easier to get from San Francisco to Shanghai than from San Francisco to Des Moines. Businesspeople I know don't think twice about going on a two-day trip to Singapore from San Francisco. They *do* think twice about a two-day trip to Birmingham, Alabama. To get to Birmingham, you're likely to have to change planes twice, and by the time you're back home, it feels as if you've been through a war, sometimes without measurable benefit. On the other hand, going to Shanghai requires only one direct flight, and you're able to get a ton of work done undisturbed. Payback from the trip is usually huge (and could only have been gotten by going). In 2003, the world's airlines carried 1.7 billion passengers—equivalent to 25% of the world's population—and 500 million people traveled on international flights.

Despite airlines having been a notoriously horrible industry with the cumulative loss by all U.S. airlines reaching approximately $25 billion since Orville and Wilbur Wright took wings, globalization and the demographic of aging populations retiring and having more time to travel make it impossible not to be bullish on the travel industry.

As English is the global business language, another pure play on globalization is English-language training. China, always looking ahead, has made English classes mandatory starting in the second grade. Berlitz is a company with the theme of English-language training. Pearson and Thomson are two terrific global media companies that have sizable English-language businesses.

Identification technology such as biometrics is an obvious benefactor of a global world. While for now a driver's license is generally sufficient identification in the United States, and a passport is acceptable abroad, in a global world where people are traveling in multiple countries frequently and commerce is conducted without geographic boundaries, physical and virtual security will be enhanced by more infallible identification.

AIRLINES I LIKE

AIRLINE	NET SALES	MARKET VALUE	ESTIMATED LTG
GOL Intelligent Airlines	$7.1 billion	$5.6 billion	36%
JetBlue Airways Corp.	$1.1 billion	$2.5 billion	22%
Southwest Airlines	$1.5 billion	$13.1 billion	19%
Ryanair	$1.9 billion	$8.7 billion	14%
Singapore Airlines	$7.8 billion	$10.4 billion	10%
EOS	Private company		
Virgin Atlantic	Private company		

Industries That Benefit from Globalization

Medicine
Airlines
Language programs
Identification technology
Security companies
Education

Financial services
Consumer brands
Entertainment

Capital and customers are scouring the globe 24 hours a day, 7 days a week for the best return on investment for products and services. Globalization accentuates the need for a company to have a claim to fame and accelerates the exposure of mediocre business models. Company and product branding (a megatrend I will discuss later in this chapter) becomes increasingly relevant with globalization, which is great for great businesses but fatal for ordinary ones.

→ **"BIRDS OF A FEATHER FLOCK TOGETHER"**

In today's global economy, where access to capital, technology, information, labor markets, and commodities is increasingly available worldwide, the concept of geographic "clusters" may seem a paradox. However, globalization has had the greatest impact in stepping up the pace of global competition, rendering productivity—not access to low-wage workers and inputs—the key to a company's success.

LOCAL GLOBALIZATION	
METROPOLITAN REGION OR STATE	INDUSTRY CLUSTERS
Silicon Valley	Infomation and communications technology Biotechnology Venture capital
Los Angeles	Media and entertainment Defense and aerospace Shipping

METROPOLITAN REGION OR STATE	INDUSTRY CLUSTERS
Seattle	Software Aircraft equipment and design Shipbuilding
Las Vegas	Leisure industries and casinos Regional airlines
Dallas	Real estate development
Omaha	Telemarketing Hotel reservations Credit card processing
Colorado	Computer integrated systems Computer programming Engineering services
Nashville	Hospital management Entertainment
Phoenix	Aerospace Optics Analytics instruments
Minneapolis	Publishing and printing Medical devices Transportation and logistics
Detroit	Auto equipment and parts
Boston	Asset management Biotechnology Software and communications equipment Venture capital

METROPOLITAN REGION OR STATE	INDUSTRY CLUSTERS
New York	Financial services Advertising Publishing Multimedia
Pennsylvania/ New Jersey	Pharmaceuticals
North Carolina	Furniture Synthetic fibers IT research and development
Southern Florida	Health technology Tourism

Source: Institute for Strategy & Competitiveness, Cluster Mapping Project, Harvard Business School.

Clusters (geographic pockets of companies tied together by a common industry, though not necessarily companies within the same industry) enable firms within the cluster to be more specialized, benefiting the growth and competitiveness of the entire cluster. While clusters may be defined by the principal industry, such as information technology and venture capital in Silicon Valley, media and entertainment in Hollywood, asset management in Boston, or even wine in Napa Valley, the breadth of the companies within the cluster will not conform to the standard industry classification.

In effect, while clusters may appear to be comprised of only loosely connected industries, the reality is that clusters are highly specialized in their particular trade or service as it applies to the cluster's principal industry, such as in legal and financial services, manufacturing, marketing, transportation, construction, and educational institutions.

The three principal means in which competitiveness is affected are through (1) increasing the productivity of companies within the cluster by promoting specialization, (2) spurring the pace of industry innovation across the network cluster, and (3) promoting the growth of new companies as a result of the cluster's competitiveness, productivity, and, ultimately, success.

As clusters reach critical mass, benefits become more widespread, allowing individual companies to reap scale economies as a result of the cluster's size, while maintaining the nimbleness and flexibility of a smaller firm. Furthermore, much as outsourcing allows more mature firms to shed noncore aspects of their business as their operations grow, cluster economies enable growing firms to focus on the growth of their strategic assets while relying on specialized firms to manage the growth of nonstrategic operations—the negative side effect of growth and success.

What the growth of industry clusters is increasingly highlighting in today's global marketplace is that competitive advantage is more and more being driven by "local globalization"—the specialization of industry linkages, business relationships, local knowledge, and labor markets—which drives productivity growth in the immediate relationships between companies as opposed to just the productivity within a company.

As we are hunting for the stars of tomorrow within defined sectors, scouring the region that is home to the industry cluster can be very fruitful. For example, in trying to find the next big thing in medical devices, one would be wise to troll in the Minneapolis market, home of Medtronic, St. Jude, and Guidant.

Globalization will continue to expand new growth markets for products and services, though even more important, the global marketplace will serve as a means to "economize" through a combination of labor market cost advantages, production efficiencies, and access to global markets as well as coordinating postproduction, sales, and services. The advantage of going and thinking globally will free up valuable resources for growth opportunities.

It is not inconceivable that in the near future, the majority of companies will engage in R&D locally, with product components manufactured in China, then assembled in South America or Eastern Europe, and then redistributed as finished products back into the global marketplace, where local product positioning, sales, and advertising are tailored for the local-global marketplace.

In the aftermarket, customer service will be handled in India, with product issues sent back up through the supply chain. Fixes will be handled

Rising Importance of Global Trade to the U.S. Economy

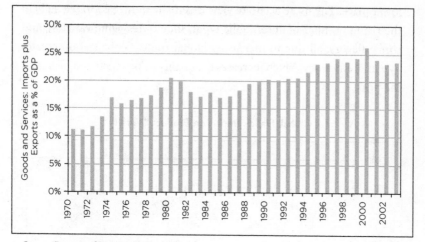

Source: Bureau of Economic Analysis.

by global product engineers and identified enhancements will be incorporated into the continual R&D process back at the original R&D center.

I see globalization as opening up not only new end markets to businesses, but also new markets for essentially every business function that was once performed in-house. The result will be greater capture of global cost advantage and the bringing of market forces to business functions that were once protected inside of organizations.

It is widely appreciated that rising global trade between developed and developing countries has important benefits such as holding down inflation in mature economies and promoting rapid growth in developing economies. What often goes underappreciated is the increase in variety—growth in the types of essentially the same product.

Most think of expanding global trade as a substitution of production and consumption of a domestic product for a foreign product—decline in one and growth of another. The reality is that rising global competition increases variety, giving consumers as well as businesses more choices. In fact, rising competition couldn't occur without an increase in variety.

The traditional view of trade overlooks this and focuses on the potential loss to overseas companies that export "the same" product at a lower price. The more accurate view is actually quite easy to see daily in the rising number of automobile types, shoe styles, wine varietals, and coffee flavors, all due to increasing global trade. Globalization creates dynamic efficiency, which increases the quality of products and decreases the price.

Global Trade's Impact on Product "Variety"

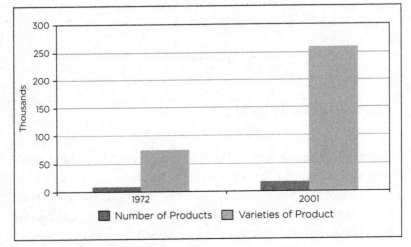

Source: Federal Reserve Bank of New York.

In a recent study of the impact of variety emanating from global trade, it was estimated that the dollar benefit to U.S. consumers amounts to about 3% of GDP, or roughly $300 billion. In the same study, it was found that the number of varieties of products had risen from approximately 75,000 (7,700 products) in 1972 to nearly 260,000 (16,390 products) in 2001—a near doubling in the number of varieties per product.

This increase in variety has implications for not only consumers' standard of living, but the entirety of the retailing industry, where growth thrives from being able to increase product assortment to better match consumers' ever-evolving preferences.

Moreover, with increasing global trade and rising variety, the dynamics of brand equity shift further toward servicing consumers' evolving preferences, with the most adept retailers being those that view their value proposition from the standpoint of being first and foremost a purchaser for their customers, obtaining the most sought-after products at the best possible price, and providing customers with the largest assortments. These companies recognize global markets and global sourcing as a competitive imperative for growth, because their first focus is purchasing for customers.

Contribution to Rising U.S. Import Product Variety, 1990–2001

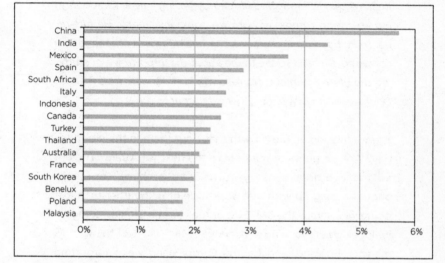

Source: Federal Reserve Bank of New York.

STAR GAZER

RICHARD DRIEHAUS
chairman of Driehaus Capital Management and
architect of the investment philosophy

Driehaus Capital Management, established in 1982, manages $3.7 billion for institutions and high-net-worth individuals. Richard's track record of success has firmly entrenched him among the top echelon of U.S. equity managers. In particular, Richard has distinguished himself by having a nose for identifying emerging trends and growth companies early. He has repeatedly been ranked among the top U.S. equity managers in the world. Richard spoke to me about the importance of studying the global markets. (To read my full interview with Richard Driehaus, visit www.findingthenextstarbucks.com.)

Are we missing all the growth that's out there in the world today? Are we going to miss out in the next 100 years? The answer is, in a great sense, yes. That's the problem. I'm talking about keeping up with real worldwide growth rather than just doing well versus the S&P 500 or the Morgan Stanley composite index. We're looking at America (which is 5% of the world's market), England, and Central Europe—and we're forgetting about 80% of the world population. In other words, we're investing where the billion people are wealthy and not where five billion people are increasing their resources and their positions.

China—The Wild West in the Far East

"If GE's strategy of investing in China is wrong, it represents a loss of a billion dollars; if it is right, it is the future of this company for the next century." —JACK WELCH

It's become almost a cliché that China is the next big thing. Ambitious young people from around the globe are flocking to Shanghai and Beijing much as they did to San Francisco in the California Gold Rush of 1849 or the Internet frenzy of the 1990s.

I hate being in the camp of conventional wisdom, but I'm a believer. In fact, I think China and the Internet are the two major forces that will shape the world for the next 50 years.

Why am I so bullish? There are at least 1.3 billion reasons—the sheer size of China and its demographics are staggering.

China has created an economic miracle. If you have the chance to fly into Shenzhen, you will be amazed by the thousands of skyscrapers, commercial and residential, under the giant wings of the jumbo jet. Shenzhen, a small, impoverished town in Southeast China with merely 20,000 in population in 1978, has transformed into the fourth-largest city in China today. It has more than 10 million residents and created 342 billion Yuan (or $42 billion), or 2.5% of the nation's GDP in 2004. As an experimental field for capitalism, Shenzhen was handpicked as China's first Special Economic Zone, which marked the beginning of the impressive economic growth in the Middle Kingdom.

In just 27 years, China's GDP grew from 362 billion Yuan (or $44 billion) to 13.7 trillion Yuan (or $1.7 trillion), representing a compound annual growth rate of 15.6% (or 9.7% in real terms). This is even before the country's GDP revision in December 2005—China believes its GDP is at least 10% more than reported mostly due to past underestimates of its service sector output. China is now the seventh-largest economy in the world and the second-largest if measured in purchasing power, behind only the United States. Individuals are getting wealthier too as per capita GDP, over the same period of time, increased from 379 Yuan (or $47) to 10,502 Yuan (or $1,295). Annual GDP growth is expected to be 8% until 2020.

China has 100 cities with one million people or more. The United States has 9!

China is already the number-one market in the world for mobile phones (373 million users), the number-one steelmaker, the number-one coal producer, the number-one investment recipient in developing countries with $500 billion plus, and the number-two market in the world for PCs. In addition, China is expected to be the number-one market in the world for automobiles by 2010.

GDP Distribution in China and the United States, 2004

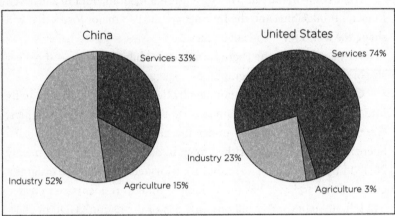

Source: World Development Indicator, World Bank.

Real GDP is $1,700 per capita versus $41,800 in the United States. An estimated 150 million peasants will move to the city in the next decade, spurring rapidly growing consumer demand. Already, the Chinese have squirreled away $1.7 trillion into money market funds. The Chinese save 47% of their incomes.

Right now, there are more than 50 Chinese stocks traded in the United States and approximately 1,400 listed in the two Chinese exchanges in Shanghai and Shenzhen. It's expected that there will be more than 10,000 Chinese IPOs in the next 20 years.

In order to grow to the next level, which is called "a harmonious society" by the Chinese government, I believe that China has to make significant progress in social security, health care, and education reforms, and strengthen its ailing financial system over the next few years. When and only when the ordinary Chinese see the existence of a safety net do I believe they will be willing to reduce their savings and increase spending. Only in this case could the massive domestic demand be unleashed, driving sustainable economic growth.

Currently Asia (minus Japan) has 9.5% of the world's GDP, 10% of the world's equity capital market, and 60% of its population (nearly four billion people). Contrast this with the United States, which has 30% of the world's GDP, 46% of the equity market, and 5% of the world's population. With the world's highest growth rates, Asian capital markets should at least equal their share of world GDP.

REGION	PERCENTAGE OF GLOBAL GDP	EQUITY CAPITAL MARKET	POPULATION
United States	30%	41%	300 million (5%)
Asia (except Japan)	9.5%	10%	4 billion (60%)

Source: CIA World Factbook, FactSet, ThinkEquity Partners.

Key trends include the growing middle class, urbanization, and growth in inter-Asian trade. These will all result in greater demand for products and services such as television sets, computers, automobiles, and travel.

Looking forward, China is dedicated to quadrupling its 2000 GDP ($1.1 trillion) by 2020, implying an annual growth rate of 8% or more. At this rate, and assuming a 3% annual growth rate for the United States, China will become the largest economy in the world in 50 years (or in just 12 years if GDP is measured in purchasing power)! China, standing where the United States was in the late 1880s and Japan in the early 1950s, has the potential to become one of the greatest growth stories in the decades to come.

Accelerating Urbanization Process in China

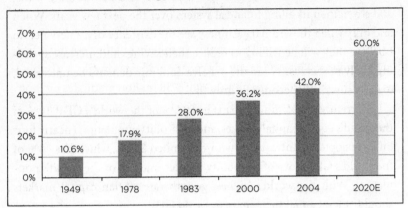

Source: National Council Center for Economic Development and Research.

The direct result of accelerating urbanization is that it will release up to 300 million low-cost laborers into the market. This is equivalent to the entire population of the United States, and triple the U.S. labor force. Cheap labor, working with sufficient capital, creates a formula for good returns. For this reason, I believe the manufacturing sector in China will maintain its advantages and momentum for several decades to come.

My investment thesis for Chinese companies specifically is that companies will experience rapid earnings growth, price/earnings multiple expansion, and currency reevaluation. The analogy I use to view China in terms of an investment opportunity is post–World War II Japan with 1990s U.S. technology.

A senior official in Beijing once told me, "China is like an old locomotive running at 100 miles per hour. It is a challenge for us to fix the problems in the system while keeping it moving at a high speed; however, stopping it to do the work is not an option." This might be the best description of the situation in China, and it matches my view—a country consists of both dangers and opportunities. To identify promising opportunities and avoid potential pitfalls is not easy, but it is my research goal. As I discussed in chapter 2, compounding earnings growth at a high rate for a long time is a beautiful thing, but it can be all for naught with a down 50, 60, or 70% investment.

Creating enough jobs is still a paramount task for the Chinese government in the years to come. According to a report from the Commission for Development and Growth, the country's central planning body, the labor supply in 2006 will be roughly 25 million but the demand is for only 11 million. The job market for college graduates in China continues to be tough. In 2005, roughly 30% of 3.38 million graduates did not find the jobs they wanted. In 2006, the number of graduates will be 4.13 million. If the historical pattern holds, more than one million college graduates will not be able to find jobs after graduation in July.

Whether it's looking at investing in Chinese companies or analyzing what a company's China strategy is, there is no more important a megatrend than China.

Population Versus Market Value

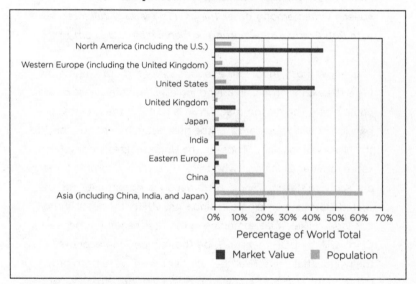

Source: CIA World Factbook, FactSet, ThinkEquity Partners.

STAR GAZER

BOB GRADY
managing partner at Carlyle Venture Partners

Carlyle is one of the largest and most influential private equity firms in the world, with more than $20 billion in assets under management. Bob Grady serves as managing partner for Carlyle's U.S. venture operation, Carlyle Venture Partners. In addition, Mr. Grady coordinates Carlyle's global venture capital group, which has more than $1.7 billion under management in five funds. Mr. Grady has an incredibly rich history both in finance and in politics, having served as President Bush Senior's speech writer, among other things. (To read my full interview with Bob Grady, visit www.findingthenextstarbucks.com.)

The single most important economic event in our lifetime, by far, is the explosion in China. Nothing else has come close or will come close. The reason that is true is that it is the greatest expansion in living standards for the greatest number of people in the history of mankind. Those in the United States who want to sabre rattle at China and who think that this is a terrible threat are sadly mistaken. This is a tremendous opportunity for the United States to participate in global growth for the next century. It is indeed likely that sometime in the next handful of decades China will, by GDP measures, be the number-one economy in the world. That's fine. We'll be number two. If we're both growing at high rates and enjoying productivity growth and rising standards of living, that's a wonderful thing for the United States. It's not the worst thing that another economy is growing even faster than ours. We stand to be a principal beneficiary, and we should not lose sight of that.

India—Be Our Guest

"If you want to know what India feels like, take out a champagne bottle and shake it for a half hour and then take the cork off. You don't want to get in the way of that cork." —THOMAS FRIEDMAN

As much as it's tempting to put China and India in the same megatrend bucket, they have as many differences as similarities. But one thing is for sure: the impact China and India will have on global business and the opportunities that are being created are mind-blowing.

First, the common denominators between the two countries are core to my growth opportunity thesis.

Like China, India has a lot of people—one billion of them, in fact. India is expected to surpass China in population by 2030.

As in China, the urbanization of India and a rapidly growing middle class will fuel consumerism. In fact, according to McKinsey & Company, India's market for consumer goods will be a $400 billion market by 2010, making it the fifth largest in the world.

China and India are both producing huge numbers of engineering graduates—about three times the number at U.S. universities, according to some studies. In a global marketplace and knowledge-based economy, this is a huge advantage for both countries.

While China has a communist government, its religion is capitalism, and its language is money. India is the largest democracy in the world with the second-largest English-speaking population. The caste system still permeates Indian government, business, and society, creating a dysfunction that contradicts the principles of democracy and meritocracy.

In China, while decisions are centrally planned, change can occur with mind-blazing speed. In India, the bureaucracy is so embedded that change can be mind-numbingly slow. A modern infrastructure to support growth is woefully behind the need for it. In the racing high tech center of Bangalore, leaders are increasingly militant about the need to upgrade India to the 21st century.

While China is a hotbed for manufacturing and growing consumerism, India's claim to fame is services. IT outsourcing and business process offshoring are, combined, a $300 billion industry growing at 25%.

That said, creative industries are booming. In 2002, India was the top film producer in the world, making 1,200 films. The United States produced 543—less than half the number produced in India.

In India, a recent college engineering graduate working for a company like Google in Bangalore can expect to earn a salary of about $18,000, or $14,000 after taxes. This is enough for a two-bedroom flat, a maid/cook, and a small car. As a point of comparison, a similarly qualified student in Silicon Valley can expect to earn about four times that much, but can barely get by.

In India, a haircut costs about 30 cents, as does a maid for a day. In Silicon Valley, a haircut costs $15 and a maid costs $75. Not surprisingly, this situation creates incentives for more and more Indian graduates to stay home, rather than traveling abroad to work.

The combination of a four-to-one labor arbitrage (cost difference between similarly qualified workers) and abundant supply of educated people will continue to rocket India into the services center of the world.

Microsoft, Intel, and Cisco have committed to investing nearly $5 billion for research and development over the next five years. Legal services, accounting services, customer service, financial analysis, and software programming will continue to migrate to India.

In looking for and evaluating the stars of tomorrow, trolling the Indian waters for opportunities will be crucial, and understanding domestic companies' Indian strategies will be too.

TALE OF THE TAPE

CHARACTERISTIC	CHINA	INDIA	UNITED STATES
Population	1.3 billion	1.1 billion	296 million
Real GDP	$2.2 trillion	$720 billion	$13 trillion
GDP (purchasing power parity)	$8 trillion	$4 trillion	$13 trillion

CHARACTERISTIC	CHINA	INDIA	UNITED STATES
GDP growth	9%	7%	4%
Real GDP per capita	$1,700	$772	$41,800
GDP per capita (purchasing power parity)	$6,200	$3,300	$41,800
Engineering graduates	644,106*	215,000	222,335
Foreign investment	$60 billion	$6 billion	$106 billion
Size of capital market	$772 billion	$475 billion	$16 trillion
Government	communist	democracy	democracy
Internet users	111 million	51 million	226 million
Cell phone users	269 million	26 million	150 million
TVs per 100 households	46	34	100
Cars per 1,000 people	7	6	600
VC investors	Warburg Pincus, Carlyle, Doll Capital, Redpoint	Draper, Norwest Battery, Mobius, Matrix Partners, Mayfield, Bessemer Venture Partners, Trident, Worldview Technology	everyone
Key public companies	Sina, Baidu, 51 Jobs	Wipro, Cognizant	Microsoft, Exxon, Google

*May include equivalents of auto mechanic.

STAR GAZER

PROMOD HAQUE
managing partner at Norwest Venture Partners

Promod Haque joined Norwest Venture Partners in 1990. He has been ranked as a top dealmaker on the annual Forbes Midas List for the past five years, and in 2004, Forbes named him the number-one venture capitalist, based on performance over the past decade. Promod focuses on investments in semiconductors and components, systems, and software and services, and is one of the most active investors in India. (To read my full interview with Promod Haque, visit www.findingthenext starbucks.com.)

I think there are different opportunities emerging in India. You've got a fairly significant middle-class population that in recent years has acquired a noteworthy amount of purchasing power, fueled by the idea revolution that's taken place in India. Broadband penetration is really starting to take off—it's where China was five years ago. The same is true with wireless penetration. Wireless and mobile penetration are increasing significantly to the tune of about 40 million subscribers a year, and currently are at the level where China was about four years ago. You look at a lot of those drivers and vectors and come to the conclusion that the consumer Internet market is poised for tremendous growth in India.

→ **MEGATREND 3:**
THE INTERNET—INVISIBLE COMPUTING

"The historical records show that humans have never, ever opted for
slower."   —STEPHEN KERN

History has a way of repeating itself.

When a game-changing technology hits the scene, people overesti-
mate how quickly it will overtake the old technology, but underestimate
the long-term potential.

The movie goes like this:

Scene 1: Revolutionary discovery is made public and gets everybody
excited. *BusinessWeek, Fortune,* and *Newsweek* all write about it the same
week.

Scene 2: Thousands of new companies get created in the industry in
a nanosecond. Students are dropping out of school so they don't miss
the "gold rush." Cocktail conversations among the rich and famous are
dominated by this new technology. Zillions of dollars in capital are invested in hundreds of companies—many with half-baked business
plans, but with all the right buzzwords.

Scene 3: The mania is in full swing. *BusinessWeek, Fortune, Newsweek,* and *Ladies' Home Journal* have cover stories on the new age's
poster boy, calling him or her the new Edison or J. P. Morgan. The market value of the 20 new public companies is greater than the GDP of
Great Britain. Companies that are in radically different businesses are
tossing their old business plans to reinvent themselves for the new era.
Cab drivers in New York City are retiring from the winnings they have
made on tips from newly wealthy customers, and shoe shine people give
new-era stock advice with the authority of Jim Cramer.

Scene 4: The music stops. At first, few people notice it because they
are too busy partying and having a good time. A few of the more pru-
dent participants start looking for a place to sit down.

Then the police come and tell everyone to go home. Some do, but
many go looking for another house to go to where the music will go on and

the party will continue. Everything's shut down. Those without a chair are now frantic for some shelter. Too many partiers, not enough seats.

Scene 5: The same people who were lauded as visionaries and heroes are being roasted as frauds and scam artists. Many go bankrupt. Some go to jail. Nobody is ever the same.

All the old codgers laugh at the misfortune of the new-era folks and are smug, knowing the world is going back to the way it was and is supposed to be.

Scene 6: After the nuclear winter, spring starts to emerge with a few flowers popping up. Nobody really knows what to make of it, but it's kind of nice to have some of these guys still around. Remembering how bad their hangover was, most people stay away with not even a sniff.

Scene 7: Flowers are now everywhere. The ones that were first obvious in the spring seem to be growing out of control (i.e., Audrey II in *Little Shop of Horrors*). Others are growing in places nobody had seen them before or could imagine.

This sounds just like the script from the *Internet Story*—mixed metaphors and all, right? Maybe it does, but the Internet isn't the only industry whose story this tells. It's the story of railroads, automobiles, the computer, the telephone, and more.

In 1823, America had 15 miles of railroad tracks. By 1890, there were 166,703 miles of railroad track, but only two years later, $2 billion of capital was destroyed by excess capacity and overdevelopment. Today the railroad industry is a $100-billion-plus industry with 173,000 miles of track.

Between 1904 and 1908, more than 240 automobile companies were created. By 1923, there were 108 automobile companies, with 10 responsible for 90% of business. In another characteristic crash, within the next three years, 65 automakers dissolved, leaving only 43 U.S. firms, and no manufacturers entered the U.S. automobile market afterward. Today there are 3 U.S. automobile makers with $630 billion of revenue.

The world population adopted the Internet more quickly than any other new technology in the history of the world. It took commercial aircraft 54 years before 25% of the population had used it. It took electricity 46 years. VCRs took 32 years. Cell phones took 16 years. Only 7 years after the commercialization of the Internet, 25% of the world's population had used it.

Number of Years to Attain 25% Market Penetration

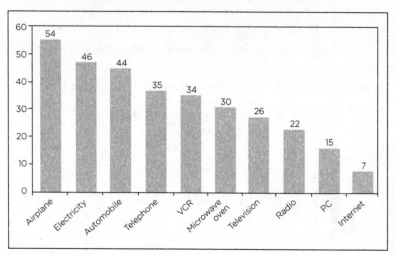

Source: Michael Milken, Andrew Rosenberg.

Given the rapid adoption of this new technology with seemingly open-ended potential, billions of dollars were invested in start-up Internet companies and hundreds of billions of market value were attributed to fledgling public Internet enterprises.

When the bubble popped, it wasn't pretty: $8 trillion of capital was destroyed—more than the GDP of Great Britain, France, and Germany combined. But now, with the sun coming up in the East again, the full impact of the Internet is beginning to be felt.

I don't view the Internet as an industry, but as a megatrend that impacts all industries. While there are pure Internet businesses, the Internet as an agent for change impacts everything from government to automobile manufacturers to music companies. For example, iTunes provides digital music content downloaded onto your iPod and made possible by the Internet. Certainly, Google is one of the most powerful and important companies in the world and at the epicenter of the Internet megatrend. But as we look for the most important emerging growth companies of the future, it is necessary to analyze how the Internet will create opportunity and also change business models.

Think about the United States Postal Service. With the success of the

WORLD INTERNET USAGE AND POPULATION STATISTICS

REGION	POPULATION (2006 EST.)	PERCENTAGE OF WORLD POPULATION	INTERNET USAGE	PERCENTAGE OF POPULATION USING INTERNET	PERCENTAGE OF WORLD USAGE	USAGE GROWTH 2000–05
Africa	915 million	14%	23 million	2%	2%	404%
Asia	3.7 billion	56%	364 million	10%	36%	219%
Europe	807 million	12%	290 million	36%	28%	176%
Middle East	190 million	3%	18 million	10%	2%	454%
North America	331 million	5%	226 million	68%	22%	109%
Latin America/Caribbean	554 million	9%	79 million	14%	8%	337%
Oceania/Australia	34 million	1%	18 million	52%	2%	132%
World total	6.5 billion	100%	1 billion	16%	100%	182%

Source: Miniwatts Marketing Group, www.internetworldstats.com.

Internet, e-mail has made "snail mail" less relevant, but it has also been a boon to traditional mail services by increasing the number of high-cost, high-margin packages commissioned via e-commerce.

The Internet can potentially turn the very traditional education system on its ear by providing online education. The Internet can democratize education by increasing access, lowering the cost, and improving the quality. Supply induces demand.

INTERNET SPOKES
Communication—VoIP, instant messaging, e-mail, blogs
Services—travel, on-demand, open-source
Entertainment—games, movies, podcasts, music
Purchasing—e-commerce, exchanges, business-to-business
Learning—postsecondary, research, market surveys

Skype, with its 241 million free Internet downloads that enable people all over the world to talk for free over their Internet connections, shows what the Internet can do to the traditional communications industry. In the software industry, the Internet has made huge waves of on-demand software and open-source software possible. Even in retail, through the Internet, mass customization is possible, allowing customers to pick and choose features in real time and receive the product at their doorstep in only a day or two.

Today there are more than 800 million Internet users across the globe with approximately 25% of those in the United States. E-commerce is a $6.8 billion industry growing at 9%.

Ubiquitous computing and abundant bandwidth will further accelerate Internet adoption, usage, and applications. Whether it's in communications, services, entertainment, purchasing, or learning, the Internet is going to be at the heart of the action.

I-BUSINESS MODELS TO MONETIZE THE WEB	
MODEL	DESCRIPTION
Access	Companies that sell or provide dial-up and/or dedicated network connections or other network management services. Business models can be based on monthly fees, or can be provided for free under a contractual agreement. Free access may include free PCs for classrooms as well as connectivity and is typically covered through advertising.
Content	Companies that provide what you see when you go online. This includes both "portals," which organize and provide access to content created by other companies, and "destinations," which create specialized content (K–12 field trips, university courses, etc.). The typical business model is based on advertising, sponsorship, subscription fees, and e-commerce.
Commerce	Companies that sell merchandise or facilitate the matching of buyers and sellers. The typical business model resembles that of a catalog retailer or auctioneer, although as the industry develops, it will likely begin to encompass advertising as well. Commerce companies operate in business-to-consumer (B2C) and business-to-business (B2B) arenas. In e-learning, commerce is seen as an important means of covering the costs of free content and monetizing traffic, particularly in K–12, where advertising can be a sensitive issue.
Software	Companies that sell software that facilitates inter- or intra-enterprise communication and commerce. The typical business model is composed of software license fees, software maintenance fees, consulting services, and, increasingly, software hosting and operation services. Learning information systems and training management systems are two evolving software forms.
Services	Companies that provide a wide variety of services necessary in the online ecosystem, including hosting, application rental, transaction processing, information databasing, consulting, design, and implementation. The typical business model is based on "per-click" transaction fees, time-and-materials fees, or subscription fees.

Source: Michael Moe, Merrill Lynch.

In order to invest successfully, we need to ask ourselves how the Internet can impact an industry or accelerate the opportunities within it. Further, to properly evaluate a company's business opportunities, I use the framework on page 114, which provides a lens for evaluation. By analyzing an Internet business through the lens of one or more of these five business models (access, content, commerce, software, and services) on the Internet, I can better analyze a company's prospects.

The Technology Revolution

Technology has transformed our society and economy, having a profound impact on U.S. corporations. This impact is explicit in the increased investment in technology over the past three decades. In 1970, approximately 5% of corporate capital expenditures were for computer and data processing equipment aimed at improving the productivity of human capital. By 2004, nearly 52% of capital expenditures by corporations were high tech related. IT has become the new property, plant, and equipment.

Composition of Business Equipment Investment

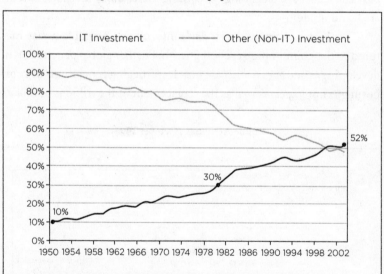

Source: Bureau of Economic Analysis.

Internet Opportunities—Game Changers

Broadband
Mobile

Search

Personalization

User-generated content (RSS, blogs, audio, etc.)

Music and video

Payments

Interactive entertainment

VoIP

Pay per call

Ubiquitous connectivity

Market research

Open-source everything

Private exchange

Unlike the highly visible ramp of business investment in IT equipment and software, and the explosion in consumer electronics over the past 20 years, I see technology becoming increasingly invisible, untethered, and ubiquitous.

This is not to imply that today's information technology has matured to the point of pure cyclical growth. Further global penetration of developing economies, which are now leapfrogging generations of computing technologies, as well as the replacement of the trillions of dollars

Online Activities (October 2003)

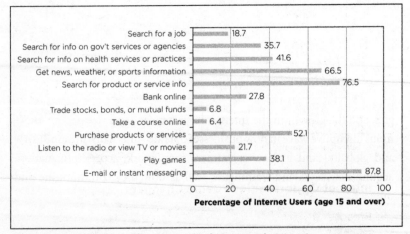

Activity	Percentage
Search for a job	18.7
Search for info on gov't services or agencies	35.7
Search for info on health services or practices	41.6
Get news, weather, or sports information	66.5
Search for product or service info	76.5
Bank online	27.8
Trade stocks, bonds, or mutual funds	6.8
Take a course online	6.4
Purchase products or services	52.1
Listen to the radio or view TV or movies	21.7
Play games	38.1
E-mail or instant messaging	87.8

Percentage of Internet Users (age 15 and over)

Source: National Telecommunications and Information Administration.

Major Computing Cycles

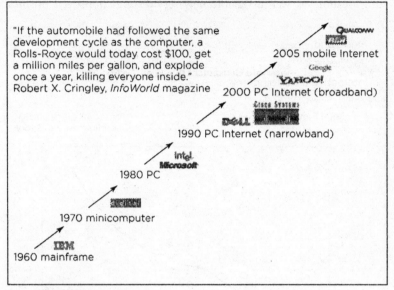

"If the automobile had followed the same development cycle as the computer, a Rolls-Royce would today cost $100, get a million miles per gallon, and explode once a year, killing everyone inside."
Robert X. Cringley, *InfoWorld* magazine

2005 mobile Internet

2000 PC Internet (broadband)

1990 PC Internet (narrowband)

1980 PC

1970 minicomputer

1960 mainframe

Source: ThinkEquity Partners.

of existing IT capital stock, will continue to drive secular IT-industry growth that will be 1.5 to 2 times greater than that of the broader economy. However, these more mature markets will increasingly become shaped and reliant upon how today's emerging technologies alter the needs of businesses and the preferences of consumers.

The past explosion in IT investment and consumption was driven by the principle of "faster, better, cheaper," which induced rapid cycles to innovate, develop, and bring "faster" technology to market. This resulted in rapid quality improvements, a sharp reduction in prices, and ultimately mass-market penetration across the business and consumer sectors.

The convergence of telecommunications and information technologies, and the growth in the Internet in particular, have released an enormous disruptive wave in how businesses operate (internally, intraindustry, and globally) and in how consumers shop, work, access information, acquire new skills and training, as well as how they communicate and interact.

Looking ahead, early stages of ubiquitous technologies are already rapidly emerging, ranging from telematics and biometrics to digital sensors and smart tags that will digitally mark virtually every product and location, as well as enable new services and improved business processes.

Business and Consumer Outlays on Technology

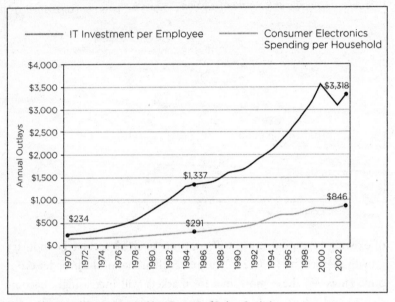

Source: Bureau of Economic Analysis, Bureau of Labor Statistics.

Within the highly visible consumer electronics market, networking technologies that were once the domain of businesses are now driving the growth in the "networked home," while the declining cost of wireless devices is redefining the mobile nuclear family and driving the computer-to-user ratio from 1-to-1 to many-to-1, as the important statistic shifts from adoption per household to usage per individual. In other words, technology adoption continues to explode, albeit in more subtle and more valuable ways than simply upgrading to the latest family computer or buying the latest version of software. It is now driving the growth in interconnectedness with multiple "computers" per user, increased accessibility to high-value networks of information, and online communities that are now rapidly proliferating.

By asking how the Internet impacts the business opportunities for an emerging star, or how it influences a more traditional industry, you will be in a better position to catch the largest waves of opportunity.

→ STAR GAZER

JOE McNAY
chairman and chief investment officer of Essex Investment Management Company

Essex Investment Management Company has $4.4 billion under management. Joe McNay is a portfolio manager who also oversees Essex's investment strategies. He managed the now famous 54/50 portfolio, the Yale class of '54's intended gift to their university for their 50th class reunion, which over 21 years (from their 25th reunion in 1979 to 2000) increased from $75,000 to $90 million, for a CAGR of 40%. When I sat down with Joe, I asked him about key lessons that he has learned as a growth investor and how he stays informed about new opportunities. (To read my full interview with Joe McNay, visit www.findingthenextstarbucks.com.)

I learn more from my mistakes than I do by being right. The real wake-up call is when something doesn't work rather than when it does. First of all, it brings you back to reality. When things go correctly, you think, "Oh, I'm so smart! I never do anything wrong," or "I always do it right." But, when you make a mistake, you know you were wrong. It's painful. And you look at it, you analyze it, and you say, "What was my mistake? Why did I make it? What happened?"

A lot of it comes from getting exposed to what is going on and recognizing when things are occurring that appear to have real substance and can really be something important. You spot change by awareness, by reading, by having a background in what is going on, and you see the kinds of things that occur. That is where the growth really comes from. Right now I read the New York Times, the Wall Street Journal, and IBD [Investor's Business Daily]. IBD has become one of the most important suppliers of information, but a lot of it comes from observing public things and observing people and what they do, what they like, and what they will do.

Some of the great successes I've had, I was in earlier than anybody else. I was in the medical area, I was in the waste management area, I picked up the cellular area before anybody, I picked up international telephones, but above all I picked up the Internet. One of my early very successful investments in the Internet was a local company in the Boston area called CMGI. I saw it for what it was and for $4 a share we accumulated and became the second-largest owner in it in the United States with Fidelity being first. Of course, they were 1,000 times bigger than we, so it was more important to us. I bought it as a public venture capital firm in the Internet, and as the Internet developed, the bubble developed, and the stock ultimately went from $4 to $160.

→ MEGATREND 4: DEMOGRAPHICS: SEEING IT COMING FROM A MILE AWAY

"Weather forecast for tonight: dark."   —GEORGE CARLIN

Generally, I don't pay any attention to the weather reports because I find them often wrong, and some general observation can basically prepare me for the day ahead. If it's raining outside, I'll grab an umbrella. If it's 40 degrees, I'll wear a coat. But a long time ago I quit planning my activities based on the weather forecast for the week ahead. I don't flip a coin to make decisions, and I don't listen to a meteorologist.

But, if I want to schedule a ski vacation in Colorado, I'll plan it for March. If I want to go waterskiing in Minnesota, I'll do it in July, and if I want to watch the cherry blossoms in Washington, D.C., I'll arrange my trip for April.

While day-to-day weather is random, the seasons are predictable. It's cold and snowy in the winter, warmer and wet in the spring, hot and drier in the summer, cooler in the fall. The days are longer in the summer, shorter in the winter. I know these things and I can plan around them.

Similarly, understanding demographics gives investors a very predictable window to the future.

An aging population is going to require more health care, travel more, and be looking for ways to enhance their retirements. Premium wines, beers, and coffees benefit. So do financial services.

As women become a larger percentage of executives in business, nanny services and corporate child care become more in demand, and takeout food and premade dinners are trends, as are tutoring, maid, and gardening services.

In the I-Generation, most kids can't remember when the Internet wasn't always on. To them, the cell phone is like the automobile was to our parents—a way to exercise their independence and exhibit self-expression. Ring tones, text messaging, games, and movies are what the I-Generation expects in one smart device.

The Hispanic population is the fastest-growing ethnic group in the United States. Currently 14% of the U.S. population is Hispanic; it is expected to be 20% by 2020. With this growth comes great opportunities for targeted marketers, focused media, and smart retailers.

Immigration will continue to increase rapidly, though it will likely slow from some parts of the developing world as growth and liberalization in developing countries improve opportunities at home. In the United States, minority populations will continue to rapidly move into the mainstream. The Latino population's growth in numbers and purchasing power will make it the first minority group to meaningfully redefine the retail, media, and financial services industries in the United States.

U.S. Hispanic Population

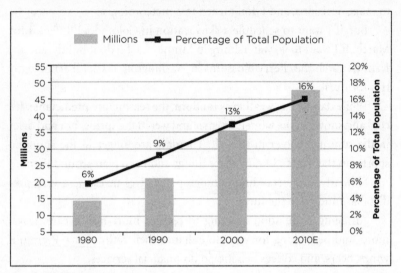

Source: U.S. Census Bureau.

The combination of an aging population and the events of 9/11 have provided a catalyst for a religious revival. In 1994, a Gallup Poll asked Americans whether they felt the need to experience spiritual growth, and 20% said yes. By 1999, 78% said yes, and this was before 9/11! Rick Warren has sold 25 million copies of *The Purpose Driven Life,* and *The Passion of the Christ* is one of the most successful movies of all time, grossing more than $600 million (to the great surprise of "the experts"). With up to 80 million evangelicals, $7 billion of Christian music and $2.24 billion of Christian books were sold in 2004, according to *Billboard.* Christian music, books, and other media are obvious winners; family restaurants such as Potbelly's, family entertainment such as Six Flags, and virtuous apparel retailers (the anti–Abercrombie & Fitch) win big too.

Demographic trends over the next 20 years will prove incredibly dynamic. The oldest of the baby boomer generation will begin to leave the workforce and enter retirement around 2008, but 90% of Generation Y (the echo boomers) will have entered the labor market by that time, and thanks to the size of Gen Y, the effects of the vanishing workforce will nearly be offset. Of course, replacing seasoned employees with new entrants will present new challenges for companies.

Generational Labor Force Composition

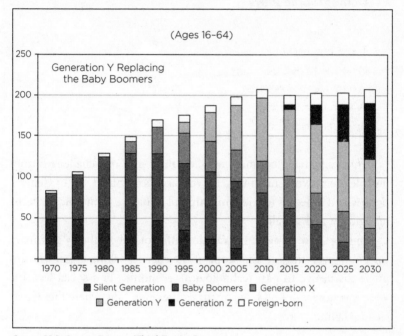

Source: U.S. Census Bureau, ThinkEquity Partners.

Generation Y will be the first generation to grow up with information technology—leap-frogging Generation X's mere comfort with technology—as a result of the Sony Walkman, Atari, Apple 2E, Commodore 64, and VCR. Beyond using technology, Generation Y's experiences will extend to understanding how information technology works, and can work, when applied to things so far untried by prior generations.

Across numerous industries, baby boomers and the younger generations will create polarizing forces: Boomers frequenting stores to shop (and spending more time shopping), Generations X and Y bypassing them almost completely; travel industries seeing sharp growth in leisure demand, while business travel wanes; financial services restructuring to cater to retirees, while commercial, merchant, and "venture banks" build out new capabilities to meet the explosion in new business ventures and restructuring of more mature industries.

Demographic Plays

Health care
Travel and leisure
Minority marketing
Womencentric services
Wealth management
Spiritual products

Politically, baby boomers will face their first real challenges from outside their own demographic, as the larger combined size of Generations X and Y begins to wield meaningful influence economically, technologically, and socially.

In short, emerging demographic shifts not only will play a primary role, but, given the size and scope of the changes taking place, will also prove disruptive to past technological, economic, and social legacies. Wise investors will find huge opportunities emerging where these legacies are falling away.

STAR GAZER

ED MATHIAS
managing director at The Carlyle Group

Ed has one of the richest backgrounds among investors in emerging growth companies and is regarded as an expert student of the market. Ed has been a general partner at The Carlyle Group since 1993. He has experienced finance at all levels, including as senior portfolio manager of New Horizons Fund and as a member of the board of directors at T. Rowe Price as well as from his involvement with the formation of New Enterprise Associates. I spoke with Ed about his advice for growth investors. (To read my full interview with Ed Mathias, visit www.findingthenextstarbucks.com.)

I think people who want to be growth investors have to be willing to venture out on their own, do their own research, and make their own decisions. They're not going to have as much information as the hedge funds or the money managers with huge research staffs, but they may have a dose of common sense, which could help a lot. The people who really succeed, as in any field, are those who have a passion and spend a lot of time, and I think you can do that as an individual, but it's not easy. I would say the two key factors are to understand your own situation and also have control over your emotions— understand how you make decisions, look at your record over time, and sort of adapt your strategy to that.

→ **MEGATREND 5: CONVERGENCE— SEEING THE WHOLE FIELD**

"Convergence is when your site finally loads just as your laptop's batteries die."
—STUART CHIRLS, EDITOR, *THE JOURNAL OF COMMERCE ONLINE*

Ten years ago, Bill Clinton was elected to his second term as president, Nicholas Cage won an Oscar for best actor in *Leaving Las Vegas*, O. J. Simpson was on trial for murder, Timothy McVeigh was on trial for the Oklahoma City bombing, and Atlanta hosted the 100th anniversary of the Olympic Games.

Do these events seem as though they happened just yesterday? My point is that 1996 wasn't that long ago. Yet, while most businesspeople were using a cell phone and many professionals were using a pager, nobody could imagine one device that could act as a phone, messaging service, e-mail system, camera, calendar organizer, computer, alarm clock, and entertainment center.

Research in Motion (RIMM), maker of the highly addictive Black-Berry smart phone, had by January 2006 built a $12 billion market cap company by being able to integrate all these seemingly distinct functions onto one device the size of your palm.

In the game of football, great quarterbacks do two things that separate them from average quarterbacks. First, they see the whole field and don't get trapped by focusing narrowly on one receiver or zone. This makes it possible to take advantage of opportunities wherever they may present themselves and makes competing against them magnitudes harder. Second, great quarterbacks are able to see two or three moves ahead. As with a great chess master, being able to play out scenarios to optimize outcomes is the key to success.

Similarly, to be able to identify the stars of tomorrow, investors need to see the whole field and be able to look at least two or three moves ahead in terms of where the industry is heading and converging.

Convergence is the coming together of two or more distinct entities or phenomena. This is a megatrend that is increasingly prevalent in an IT world where cell phones take pictures and televisions surf the Web. Much of the emerging area of nanotechnology is around the converging fields of computer storage, semiconductors, biotechnology, manufacturing, and energy. In health care, convergence will affect targeted drug delivery, gene therapy, and a variety of future applications for medical technology.

POTENTIAL CONVERGENCE OPPORTUNITIES AND TIMING	
OPPORTUNITY	LIKELY TIMING OF TAKE-OFF
Implantable drug pumps	Next 2 to 5 years
Targeted drug delivery	Now

OPPORTUNITY	LIKELY TIMING OF TAKE-OFF
Closed-loop diabetes management systems	Next 2 to 5 years
Noninvasive in vivo diagnostics	Next 2 to 5 years
Remote monitoring and therapy management	Next 2 to 5 years
Targeted cell/gene therapy delivery	Next 5 to 10 years
Image-guided surgery	Now to the next 2 years
Noninvasive therapies/intervention (e.g., radiotherapy, cryotherapy, heat therapy)	Now to the next 5 years

Source: Windhover Information, Inc., and Bain & Company.

The real point of convergence is that solutions can be created in the spaces between traditional disciplines. Convergence is really about appreciating solutions without needing to reveal or understand what had to come together to reach that solution. Studying the underlying software code for salesforce.com is unnecessary; appreciating the business proposition and return on investment (ROI) for its customers is the key issue.

Figuring out how TiVo works hurts my brain and makes me question my existence, but understanding how it alters the dynamics of the television experience and economics is the investor's puzzle.

Analyzing how convergence will impact specific company opportunities requires investors to redraw the lines of how industries are defined. Wall Street—which likes to think of the world in nice, convenient brackets with a rearview mirror as its navigating device—rarely sees what is ahead.

By looking over the horizon and crossing the boundaries, by thinking "what if" as opposed to mastering the obvious, we can find the big winners.

Convergence Landscape

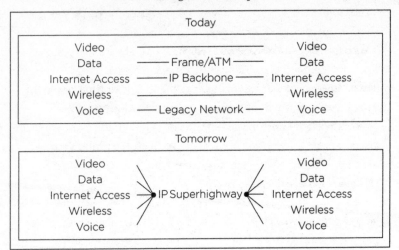

Source: Acquicor, ThinkEquity Partners.

Convergence fuels the search for efficiency, and collaboration between experts in different fields is the catalyst driving convergence. Convergence in telecommunications is effectively the foundation of the knowledge economy. Convergence increases information flow between businesses and consumers, and it drives out inefficiency and creates exponential growth in a network's value.

Widespread adoption of the Internet by businesses and consumers initiated the convergence of voice and data networks, though this remains in its infancy. The past growth of the Internet was driven by access, then by access at faster speeds, and ultimately by access to the Internet from every device. However, the Internet largely remains a destination, with its value derived from being able to reach information.

Today, value is increasingly being derived from communication. The next stage of development will be driven by the ability to communicate and collaborate, with the near-term infrastructure focus being VoIP and longer-term focus being XoIP (Anything over Internet Protocol), enabling voice, interactive data, video, and applications over a common IP-based network.

Beyond user-to-user and business-to-business communications, sensors and smart tags will allow businesses to wring greater inefficiencies out of their operations—specifically their supply chains—and increase responsiveness to end-market demand and changing customer preferences.

Digitally "tagged" products, such as Wal-Mart has requested of its suppliers, will allow businesses to better manage product and inventory flows, taking unnecessary float out of the supply chain and effectively moving closer to matching customer demand in real time, while minimizing the commitment of resources to unneeded inventory.

Smart tags, or small-scale chips linked to local databases, will be increasingly tied together through Web services, bringing peer-to-peer computing to small-scale technologies that transmit information when and where it is needed—or on the fly. This further enables information to shift to the edge of a business's network, where supply-chain logistics, distribution, and customer responsiveness occur.

The result is that critical information will be accessible anywhere, anytime, and will be capable of leveraging the converged network. Of course, this trend will create a new bottleneck in the form of securing network information flows. In order for companies to fully leverage the information embedded in their business and their relationships with suppliers and customers, security technologies will have to mature to

Convergence Is Dramatically Changing the World

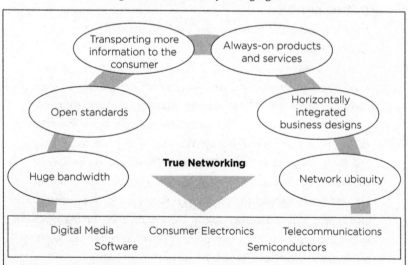

Source: Acquicor, ThinkEquity Partners.

enable a higher level of comfort for companies to open their networks. With this final bottleneck broken, however, business users, consumers, and suppliers will expect or demand that information be available to them anywhere, anytime, and as a matter of necessity.

The convergence of communications is the emerging key to the "electrification" of the network, bringing computing power into the real world, closer to where business decision making, job functions, and consumer and social interactions take place. The initial applications of the converged network and technologies such as VoIP and tags will deliver value through replacing today's technologies, but will ultimately help to define how business is conducted tomorrow. Again, underlying the drive toward convergence is the goal of wider collaboration and the increased recognition that linked knowledge is of far greater value than disconnected knowledge. Investors should be looking for smart and integrated technology that solves problems and delivers return on investment that is made possible only through convergence.

STAR GAZER

DAVID SPRENG
founder and managing general partner of
Crescendo Ventures

David's global venture capital investment firm Crescendo Ventures has more than $1 billion under management and offices in Palo Alto, Minneapolis, and London. He is a core team member of the World Economic Forum Working Group on "Nurturing the Early Stage Investment Climate in China" and a member of the board of the National Venture Capital Association (NVCA). He has been named to the Forbes Midas list of top venture capitalists. I asked David about the importance of management. (To read my full interview with David Spreng, visit www.findingthenextstarbucks.com.)

Great management is great leadership. Leaders instill a great-culture. They have clear vision, and they get their people feeling like they are doing something important and meaningful. I have built a network, and I strive to stay in touch with that network. I look to find one great person—a magnet—and then build around him or her. I spend time with people in multiple environments to really understand what makes them tick. Great leaders know where they are going. They are intellectually honest and are bold, but not delusional. It is critical that they work well with and through others. Also, they are respectful, passionate, and smart. They communicate well and are especially good at listening. It is also important that they enjoy what they are doing.

→ **MEGATREND 6: CONSOLIDATION—
MAIN STREET VERSUS WALL STREET**

"History doesn't repeat itself, but it rhymes."   —MARK TWAIN

The story goes like this: Boy gets out of high school, maybe a state university, and goes to work at the first job he can get. He realizes quickly he is pretty good at business and hates working for somebody else, so he starts a business by getting a second mortgage on his house, borrowing from his in-laws, maxing out his credit cards, and/or raiding his children's college fund.

He works around the clock—six, often seven, days a week. His wife takes care of the house, but also helps out at work, doing whatever needs attention. After surviving a number of near-death experiences, the business is going pretty well. He's not taking any big salary, but he can pay all the bills and is expanding the business. Excess profits are plowed back into growth.

Despite the fact that he went to public schools, he sends his three children to private schools. He joins the country club but rarely uses it. However, his kids love it and are good golfers and tennis players.

Business clicks right along. The company becomes prominent on Main Street, and he's also been able to expand to other cities within the region. Numerous local and regional awards attest to the company's achievements.

He sends his kids off to elite colleges. He tells anybody who will listen about his children's success. During summers, he offers his children opportunities to apprentice in different parts of the business, but they always travel to Europe instead.

The company has become a money machine, but he has trouble retaining the top talent. Most people at the company assume (because the CEO has said so) that he expects his children to take over the company from him when he retires. Given these circumstances, it's impossible to keep a strong number two at the company.

The kids finish college and grad school. After bumming around for a few years, they convince their dad that it would be better for the business if they got some experience at another company or in another industry before they come back.

To begin their careers, the kids move to New York City, Chicago, San Francisco, and London, where, remarkably, a lot of their friends from school are living.

Dad still works six days a week, but he finds he actually is starting to enjoy going on vacation and playing golf. His kids have been promising him for 10 years that "next year" they are going to move back to join the family business.

New technology is coming into the industry. Dad doesn't really understand how it works, but fears if they don't use it, he could get left in the dust. ABC, a company he has known for years through the industry association (he's a former president), just went public at a huge multiple. Now with a public stock, they are buying up everybody.

Having seen ABC's IPO, some of his longtime customers start asking questions. A few even start to do some business with ABC on its e-commerce site (something his company doesn't even have yet). All sorts of issues start arising, such as China, India, and outsourcing. Things were a lot simpler when all he had to do was make the customer happy and keep his costs low.

ABC is getting more and more of his business. They are charging 20% less, which he thinks is insane. When he talks to his lost customers, though, they say a combination of factors attracted them to ABC— doing business with them is cheaper, faster, and better. He looks at ABC's public financial statements and can't believe his eyes. Despite charging less, they have higher margins!

His health is starting to concern him. His doctor has told him he needs to slow down—at the time his business needs him to speed up! He calls his children to see if they are ready to come back. They each tell him no, adding that it wouldn't be fair to *their* kids, but they do thank him for setting up his grandchildren's trust funds and paying for their private schools—it really helps.

Reluctantly, he calls the CEO of ABC and says they should have that dinner. They talk, they dance, they merge.

ABC's stock goes up as the acquisition is accretive. He leaves after six months as he disagrees with decisions being made at the top. Sealing his frustration was a phone call with the CEO, in which the response to his complaints was "Last time I checked, we bought you."

Sound like a unique story? It isn't. This happens every day on Wall Street.

Consolidation occurs when a business grows through buying other businesses in its industry. In a classic fragmented mom-and-pop industry, the consolidator typically gets advantages of scale that give it ongoing competitive advantage. Couple that with cheap currency provided by Wall Street and you get the makings of a consolidation story—Main Street versus Wall Street.

One of the key abilities investors need to form is to be keen observers of society, business, and politics. By being able to see the whole field, an investor can anticipate a future opportunity before it becomes obvious. Being able to see where consolidation of products and/or services may emerge is critical to investing in the stars of tomorrow and avoiding being run over by a truck.

The obvious consolidation opportunity is like the general situation described at the beginning of this chapter. The classic recipe for a consolidator is where there is a wildly fragmented industry that is dominated by mom-and-pop businesses.

As an industry starts to consolidate, the consolidator benefits from scale and service advantages that make it increasingly difficult to compete against. Where a public company buys a private company, there is also often the boost of public-market versus private-market arbitrage.

For example, a leading public-company consolidator may have a P/E of 25x but be able to buy a private company at a P/E of 12x. Shareholders benefit not only from the strategic synergy in the combination, but also from the arbitrage in valuation. The arbitrage in the public and private multiples results in the merger being accretive to earnings, which will likely result in an even higher stock price. The "currency" often used for a consolidation strategy is the consolidator's stock.

An interesting irony in a consolidation investment thesis is that the higher the valuation of the consolidator, the more attractive its stock theoretically should be for an investor. The reason is that its rich stock "currency" will be able to buy more earnings for less and therefore be that much more accretive. It's tough to get your brain around that concept, but once you do, it's pretty powerful.

Consolidators

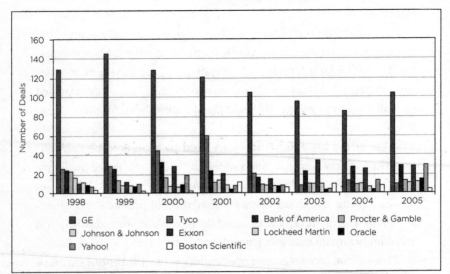

Source: FactSet, ThinkEquity Partners.

While consolidation is a megatrend and can be a very attractive component of an investment thesis, there are a lot of pitfalls. The biggest warning flags for consolidations are mergers based solely on public/private arbitrage or those that lack strategic logic.

A second issue to understand is integration. Consolidation always makes sense on paper, but from cultural issues to systems and communication, the biggest failures occur where an acquisition wasn't integrated well.

Another issue to understand is the broader global concern impacting an industry. Often you see consolidation in maturing industries where merging parties might be sensing their own vulnerabilities. Just like people on a date often don't bring up all their faults and insecurities, merging companies have incentive to show themselves in the most positive light.

Looking in a very narrow silo, it may have seemed really smart for the facsimile industry to consolidate, but then came the Internet, which made such mergers completely unattractive from a growth standpoint because the industry was going to move away from facsimile altogether.

Consolidation Rules

1. Have a good strategic rationale.
2. Have a solid integration plan.
3. See the broad picture.
4. Use conservative accounting.
5. Verify that it is accretive to earnings.

Beyond the classic roll-up of an industry, where many small companies roll into one large one, some of the most interesting opportunities can be found when companies buy companies that develop services or technologies that give the consolidator an unfair advantage in its industry.

When eBay bought the start-up online payment processor PayPal for $1.5 billion, everyone thought eBay was nuts. It turns out that was a brilliant move because it created a competitive moat around eBay that seems almost insurmountable. More recently, eBay bought VoIP-provider Skype for $2.6 billion, and the critics are out in full force again. We shall see.

Similarly, Internet leaders Google and Yahoo! have been actively acquiring businesses and technology to enhance their competitive positions.

In biotechnology, there are hundreds of publicly traded products—consolidation will occur to leverage distribution networks and marketing cost. Companies with a single blockbuster product will be better able to market that product if they partner with a larger company complete with an established customer base and marketing arm.

The consolidation wave in software is in full swing, which will result in an industry that looks a lot like the medical device industry—a barbell—with one end being the Goliaths and the other end the innovative emerging companies.

Consolidation Plays

Medical devices
Software
Biotechnology
Consulting
Insurance
Education software
Asset management
Oil services
Financial services
Internet

STAR GAZER

DUNCAN BYATT
co-founder and president of London-based
Eagle & Dominion

Duncan Byatt began his investing career in Edinburgh, Scotland, in 1984 as a graduate trainee at Ivory & Sime, where he gained experience with U.S. and European investments. He went on to work as a corporate finance analyst in London, started a fund management operation for a major Japanese insurance company, and spent time in both Japan and the Pacific Rim. From 1991 to 1998, he ran the U.S. Emerging Growth Funds for Gartmore Investment Management in the UK, which were among the largest and most successful funds of their type in London and were AAA-rated by Fund Research. I asked Duncan what he looks for in a company that he is thinking of investing in. (To read my full interview with Duncan Byatt, visit www.findingthenextstarbucks.com.)

Typically, to assess people, we sit down and spend quite a lot of time talking with the management team. Very often, we'll go and visit the company on the ground as well and meet with the guys who are actually running the operation. You immediately get a sense of it. Is it buzzing? Is it very busy? Do the people look as though they're really enjoying what they're doing? Or is it kind of quiet? Are people looking a little glum like they really wish they were somewhere else? You pretty rapidly get a sense of whether the business is ticking positively or not.

Typically, companies that we invest in fall into two camps: consolidators and innovators. We're looking, ideally, for a company that I call a 20-20-20 company. A 20-20-20 company is

20% revenue growth, 20% profits growth, and, over time, the ability to get a 20% return on equity. So within the 20% revenue growth, the consolidator normally is a slightly larger, slightly more mature business in a more mature industry—very often a fragmented industry. And they may be growing 7 or 8% internally, but they can probably double that through acquisition. That's a very large part of their growth.

→ MEGATREND 7: BRANDS— THE GIFT THAT KEEPS ON GIVING

"A brand for a company is like a reputation for a person. You earn reputation by trying to do hard things well."   —JEFF BEZOS

Raymond Babbitt was right—Kmart sucks. Fourteen years after Dustin Hoffman's autistic savant character muttered those lines in 1988's Oscar-winning *Rain Man,* Kmart filed for bankruptcy.

If Raymond had said, "Wal-Mart sucks," or "Target sucks," the line would have fallen like a lead balloon. It resonated with audiences in a perverse way because most people hated shopping at Kmart. The Kmart brand meant low-quality products, nonexistent service, and a horribly bad shopping experience. Kmart sucks!

Starbucks started with a promise of delivering exceptional-quality coffee and friendly service. The brand equity the company created through its performance against expectations allowed Starbucks to expand its offering to everything from alternative drinks to music. Because Starbucks has established this connection with its patrons, it has been able to expand the relationship. In fact, investors anxiously await the introduction of Starbucks' next product or service because they expect the customer to like it.

Apple has always been a cult brand, but has now been able to expand into the masses. Macintoshes, iPods, Video, iTunes, Shuffle, iSight—

everything Apple makes, we want. It's a badge of coolness to have your Apple Notebook out on the plane. The Apple stores, which didn't exist five years ago, do more than $2 billion in revenue, or more than $20 million per store. For comparison, the gigantic Best Buy superstores do around $30 million per store! Not bad for a new boutique.

We have become a culture where one arm extends to hold a Starbucks cup, and our ears reveal neon-white iPod earphones.

Intel Inside is a brilliant brand. It gives consumers confidence in the technology and gives Intel a higher margin. Is AMD's chip as good as Intel's or better? Perhaps, but Intel has the brand.

Ralph Lauren's Polo is another incredible brand. For two or three times what a consumer would pay for a comparable product, he or she can get the pony as an outsourced endorsement of good taste and fine lifestyle.

Google is the brand for Internet searches. While there are numerous other search engines and sites, when you need to know, you go to Google. It stands for being powerful, accurate, efficient, and simple.

Most of Dell's components and services are provided by somebody else, but because Dell's products have the Dell name attached, consumers have confidence in buying.

Harvard, Stanford, and Princeton are educational brands. It is presumed that people who graduate from these schools are smart because of it. Goldman Sachs is *the* brand in investment banking. You could probably find equally smart people at other places and have your transactions done more cheaply, but if you are going to sell your business or take it public, you want the Goldman stamp of approval.

On the flip side, ill-will brands like Kmart seldom overcome the negative stigma associated with them.

A brand is a promise between the company and the consumer about what to expect from the relationship. It takes years to build brand goodwill, but once it's achieved, it gives the company permission to introduce other products and services consistent with that promise.

General Motors has a huge upside battle ahead of it. Radio Shack is a bad brand. In a global marketplace and Internet economy, having a powerful brand is more important than ever before because a brand provides the shortcut that time-pressed consumers and executives need to make decisions. Brands provide assurances. Brands provide comfort and confidence. Successful businesses of the future need their brands to create a relationship with the customer and sustain integrity behind the promise.

The volume of global advertising continues its steady increase, consistent with nominal GDP growth, but an increasing share of advertising continues to move online. Within the global context, advertising growth in developing economies continues to outpace global growth, as consumers in developing economies move up the purchasing power curve and companies move aggressively to maximize the lifetime value of their brands with emerging market consumers.

I see many factors combining to create a more dynamic environment for establishing, promoting, and protecting brand equity: increasing competition from low-cost foreign markets, growing purchasing power in developing global markets, dynamically changing distribution channels, growth in Internet retailing, changing demographic needs (aging baby boomers, rising spending power of Gen Y, and multiple ethnic markets), niche-market segmentation, and an explosion in the number of competitive products.

In more mature economies, consumers are confronted with an escalating number of advertisements each day across a growing number of mediums for a growing number of available products and services.

Media, marketing, and advertising companies are now coping with their clients' extensions into new global markets, a proliferation of mediums, and emerging technologies, which in some cases augment traditional advertising channels, while in many other cases, they displace them.

At the core of branding are the developing challenges for businesses in terms of how to promote their brands, how consumers perceive advertising, and how brands influence purchasing decisions.

For businesses, the multimedium aspect brings new challenges of balancing the potential for more targeted advertising with some risk of brand dilution. The Internet in particular epitomizes this opportunity and challenge, as it enables niche-customer advertising, though also results in a larger number of varying messages. For mass-market products, this is arguably less of a problem. But for products where differentiation plays a critical competitive component, this is a potential risk—being all things to all people results in product "premiums" being commoditized.

Fortunately, along with new advertising channels have come improved methods for matching advertising content with target markets, ranging from analytical techniques being applied to market identification and segmentation, to increasingly rapid feedback on customer responses to both tangible and intangible brand attributes.

From the consumer perspective, the number of touch points (places a consumer encounters advertisements for products and information about products) continues to grow rapidly. By all appearances, these touch points extend outside of the traditional means where companies

HOTTEST BRANDS

TOP 10 GLOBAL BRANDS		TOP 10 HOTTEST BRANDS
1. Coca-Cola		1. Google
2. Microsoft		2. Apple
3. IBM		3. Starbucks
4. GE	vs.	4. IKEA
5. Intel		5. BlackBerry
6. Nokia		6. Motorola
7. Disney		7. eBay

TOP 10 GLOBAL BRANDS		TOP 10 HOTTEST BRANDS
8. McDonald's		8. Red Bull
9. Toyota	vs.	9. Manchester United
10. Marlboro		10. Virgin Mobile

Source: BusinessWeek, Interbrand.   *Source: ThinkEquity Partners.*

have a direct influence on product positioning and their brands through means such as product experience.

During the Internet's short history of online retailing, it has had two clear impacts aside from driving online sales: (1) providing a means for consumers to conduct their own research on products and (2) increasing the accessibility of peer recommendations through such simple methods as online product reviews. With peer recommendation second only in importance to the touch-and-feel experience available through store visits, online customer reviews have become a powerful trend in retailing (online and offline) as well as a significant factor affecting brand value.

A dynamic emerging facet of creating and sustaining brand value is interactive peer assessment. Through online social networks, consumers are now able to ask peers which product is best, gaining information through grassroots recommendations. This in turn enables the consumers to discover a product's value through what peers determine its quality and value to be, rather than by what the quality and value are advertised to be. As these communities grow in relevance, peer evaluation is likely to be an increasingly important factor behind brand equity and therefore an important component for companies and advertisers to understand, lest they risk losing credibility with real-world customer experience.

This said, what continues to trump all other aspects in determining brand value is a desirable shopping experience, consistent delivery of an

Preferred Shopping Information Resource

Consumers reporting which was the most useful information source in making a major household purchase

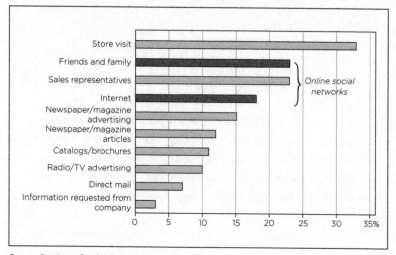

Source: Institute for the Future, Household Survey.

array of products and services that match consumer preferences, and a reputation for quality. Companies that recognize the challenges of low-cost sourcing, increasing numbers of distribution channels, and shifting preferences (demographic, cultural, etc.) as opportunities to improve quality, access, assortment, and price points, are those that will best serve their customers and ultimately benefit from the development and sustained value of their "brand."

Companies that ignore the importance of the brand megatrend will be swept away in an onslaught of information, as will the investors who do the same. A strong and visible brand is a key ingredient in the formula for strong products.

STAR GAZER

DAN LEVITAN
co-founder of Maveron

Dan Levitan co-founded Maveron, a venture capital firm, in 1998 with Starbucks chief executive Howard Schultz. They hit the jackpot with their early investments in eBay and drugstore.com. Dan was previously a managing director at Schroders, where he headed consumer investment banking. I asked Dan for his advice to investors. (To read my full interview with Dan Levitan, visit www.findingthenextstarbucks.com.)

The way to be successful in investing in tomorrow's stars is having some combination of curiosity, looking at a lot of things, being incredibly open-minded and, last, giving yourself a glass of cold water and applying a healthy set of discipline in terms of understanding where the weaknesses are that could prevent the execution of an otherwise good idea. If you blend that curiosity, passion, and discipline and spend the time to really look at a company from not just your own perspective, not just management's perspective, but from the customer's perspective and the marketplace's perspective, I think you have an interesting opportunity to find some things that can be really big.

→ MEGATREND 8: OUTSOURCING

"Don't focus on how to spend less money. Focus on how to make more money."
— LYNDON FORMAN

After Lou Dobbs aborted Space.com to return to his earth-based chair on CNN's *Moneyline,* he took on the crusade against offshore outsourcing. His 2004 book *Exporting America* advocates balanced trade over globalization.

Dobbs created an "Exporting America" list that calls about every company I can think of traitors to America: 3M, Accenture, Albertson's, AMD, Agilent, American Express, Apple, AT&T, AOL, Applied Materials—and that's just through the As!

The reality is that in an ever-increasing global marketplace and in a world where time and distance have collapsed due to the Internet, the outsourcing toothpaste isn't going to be squeezed back into the tube. While outsourcing isn't a new trend, it is a megatrend that is with us to stay.

Reasons Companies Outsource

Save money and cost
Focus on core business
Improve service
Gain access to experts
Flexibility

To compete and to win, leading companies need to determine what their core competencies are and outsource basically everything else. The origins of outsourcing were in saving a buck, but today it's about comparative advantage and optimizing time and resources.

IT technology is the most prevalent area for jobs to be outsourced, with 28% of all outsourced jobs in the IT areas, and the global IT service market being an estimated $1.2 trillion in 2006. Global investment banks are expected to invest $356 billion in India for outsourcing projects. Human resources and sales and marketing are the other areas most commonly outsourced.

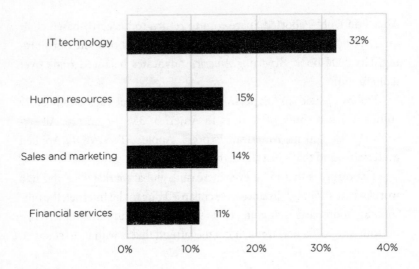

PERCENTAGE OF INDUSTRY OUTSOURCED

Source: CIO magazine.

Leading growth companies of the future will be aggressive outsourcers to produce the highest-quality, lowest-cost products. Think of the movie studio model of assembling the right actors, producers, writers, marketers, and distributors to make a particular movie who then go their separate ways after it's completed. This model may be adopted in many other industries.

Not only will leading growth companies be companies that outsource, but outsourcing companies will continue to be leading growth companies. BPOs (business process outsourcers) will continue to thrive. Payroll, benefits, customer service, human resources, and procurement are a few areas that will continue to benefit from the outsourcing megatrend.

Sectors That Will Benefit from Outsourcing

Payroll

Benefits

Customer service
Tax compliance
Human resources
Procurement
Research
Internet services
Voice network management

Outsourcing will continue to evolve beyond simply shedding non-core activities to outside companies and shifting production to low-cost labor markets such as India, China, and the Philippines. Outsourcing will continue to extend into higher areas of a company's value chain, including those once considered core competencies. This trend is already rapidly emerging, with an increased number of functions being outsourced from within companies' executive and R&D domains—both traditionally considered the ultimate of core competencies.

One of the commonly overlooked side effects of successful companies is the growth of noncore activities and infrastructure investment, such as customer service, IT infrastructure, and "back-office" functions generally, each of which limits a firm's flexibility to maintain a focus on their actual business. With information and telecommunications technologies enabling specialized firms to cost-effectively target these activities inside of companies, growth opportunities are opening up in an increasing number of outsourceable markets.

Cumulatively, the trend toward outsourcing is raising business profitability, enabling companies to extract greater profit from each dollar of sales as well as to increase the return on invested capital. This is evident not only in rising profit margins throughout the business sector, but also in the record net corporate cash flows achieved even since the last economic downturn—currently up nearly $400 billion since the first quarter of 2001. This has important consequences for how companies fund future growth, making them less reliant on external financing and better aligning internal capital sources with investment opportunities.

As implied, outsourcing continues to evolve from being a cost-conscious consideration to being a strategic value proposition, enhancing companies' total return on investment (ROI) and competitiveness.

Outsourcing contributes to profits going up

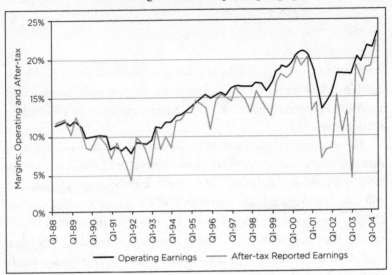

Source: ThinkEquity Partners.

Outsourcing contributes to cash increasing

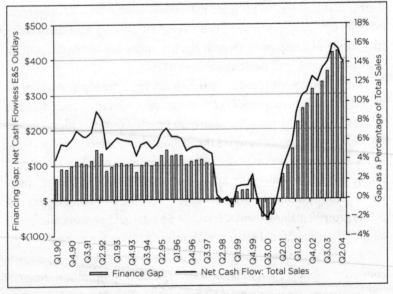

Source: ThinkEquity Partners.

Firms are increasingly embracing outsourcing, leveraging cost-savings opportunities (contract manufacturing, customer support) helping to enlarge profit potential in their addressable markets, as well as utilizing highly specialized services (intellectual property rights management, contract R&D) to recognize the benefits of increased business flexibility. Combined, this leaves them to concentrate on new opportunities and future products, and it positions them to better capitalize on their innate strategic strengths.

The general rule of thumb is that the more knowledge-intensive a business or industry becomes, whether due to technological, production, or global marketplace complexities, the greater the number of functions that will need to be outsourced to others to sustain competitive advantage.

The ability of a company to innovate and meet customers' changing needs is progressively more dependent upon how effectively it manages organizational change around its most strategic assets. With production becoming increasingly services-dominated and services becoming more technical, companies that embrace outsourcing at every opportunity will create sustainable competitive advantage in their marketplace by remaining focused on their core competencies.

GLOBAL LEADERS IN OUTSOURCING			
REGION	MARKET SIZE	TOP-RANKED COUNTRIES	UP-AND-COMERS
Central and Eastern Europe	$3.3 billion	Czech Republic, Bulgaria, Slovakia, Poland, Hungary	Romania, Russia, Ukraine, Belarus
China and Southeast Asia	$3.1 billion	China, Malaysia, Philippines, Singapore, Thailand	Indonesia, Vietnam, Sri Lanka

REGION	MARKET SIZE	TOP-RANKED COUNTRIES	UP-AND-COMERS
Latin America and the Caribbean	$2.9 billion	Chile, Brazil, Mexico, Costa Rica, Argentina	Jamaica, Panama, Nicaragua, Colombia
Middle East and Africa	$425 million	Egypt, Jordan, United Arab Emirates, Ghana, Tunisia	South Africa, Israel, Turkey, Morocco

Source: BusinessWeek, from A. T. Kearney Global Services Location Index, 2005.

→ STAR GAZER

CLIFF GREENBERG
portfolio manager of the Baron Small Cap Fund

Since 1997, Cliff has been the portfolio manager of the $2.8 billion Baron Small Cap Fund, where he invests in classic growth companies, fallen angels, and special situations. His performance is impressive when compared to his peers: Baron Small Cap has outperformed 90% of the funds in the small-cap growth universe over the past five years. (To read my full interview with Cliff Greenberg, visit www.findingthenextstarbucks.com.)

I'm not looking for great companies; I'm looking for great investments. I'm looking for the opportunity to make big returns as a shareholder. The best way to do that is to find unique compa-

nies with big opportunities that have defensible niches and have
entrepreneurial managements and cultures that can take a little
idea, a little company, and turn it into a big company. Its shareholders can really prosper along the way. And that's what I do
for a living: try to invest in small companies that I believe are
special and different enough and run by really good people and
can grow much larger than they are when I purchase them, and
make myself and my investors a lot of money.

→ **POSTSCRIPT**

I expect the dynamic developments that took place over the past 15 years
to continue to thrive and to serve as the cornerstones of future growth
opportunities.

Accumulated advancements in information technology (IT) and organizations restructuring around IT, as well as exponential growth in
knowledge networks (internal, business-to-business, and business-to-
consumer) are catalyzing the growth of knowledgecentric industries.
Dynamic and simultaneous demographic shifts (baby boomers, the
echo boom, and abroad, the aging of Japan and Europe) and growing international market opportunities are increasingly globalizing labor markets, changing human capital requirements, and blurring the distinction
between foreign and domestic.

The emerging knowledge economy remains in its infancy, with the
so-called information economy from which it is to grow still relatively
mired in data overload. Only recently has the information economy
truly flourished, with information being extracted from the mountains
of data within organizations, the tastes of multiple demographics, and
the latent regional and global markets, as well as from the entrenched
business-to-business processes.

As companies increasingly capitalize on the reams of data now being turned into useful and accessible information, their accumulated in-tellectual capital and knowledge assets are enabling growth in more strategic and profitable directions. Until this point in the modern corpo-rate economy, success has brought with it the side effects of growth—internal operations (IT equipment and software included) and services infrastructure that are peripheral to a company's business.

With increasing information, history, and analytics to benchmark and assess the strategic value of retaining or outsourcing these assets and functions, companies are recognizing improved profitability and higher returns on investment by being able to invest in what they know—the products and services of their business—while minimizing or avoiding altogether growth in noncore operations. Technology will help large companies to have continued growth.

A consequence of outsourcing is the emerging development of eco-nomic and industry clusters, where companies provide services specifi-cally catered to an industry's needs. This enables the principal industry players to grow unencumbered by the side-effect demands of their pri-mary business. Ultimately, this enables a company's growth to internally finance the primary business and not the services that grow with their success, while unlocking new market growth opportunities from within established service sector industries.

With the increasingly successful integration of IT and reorganiza-tion around it, emerging technologies are being developed that press forward with information and communications technology being em-bedded into virtually everything ordinary, and enabling extraordinary tools as well. In other words, the application of IT to areas outside of IT and into everyday products and business processes is enabling enor-mous efficiency gains in established markets, driving the digitization of products and services in one form or another, while creating new mar-ket opportunities to manage business processes and end-market cus-tomer relationships differently, meaning better than before.

Small-scale technology, such as digital tags, is poised to replace ex-isting technologies while driving growth in new and existing markets. Tags can perform the same function as bar codes and do it far better by embedding *information* at the edge of a business's network, rather than storing a piece of *data* within a single company's network. Retailing, as an example, brings automated accounting and real-time inventory management nearer to reality and minimizes costly supply-chain float.

RFID tags represent an enabling technology that extends what companies have been learning to do with earlier technologies—better track and manage inventory, cut costs, and streamline supply. Moreover, processes and information that result from the implementation of RFID will drive demand for Web services, wireless devices, and wireless enterprise software, as well as reinvigorate growth in more mature markets such as enterprise resource planning (ERP) and supply-chain management applications.

Globalization will continue to expand new growth markets for current and future products and services, though, even more important, the global marketplace will serve as a means to "economize" through a combination of labor market cost advantages, production efficiencies, and increased varieties of products available to global consumers.

It is widely appreciated that rising global trade between developed and developing countries has important benefits such as holding down inflation in mature economies and promoting rapid growth in developing economies. What is underappreciated is the growth in product variety. Most think of expanding global trade as having a substitution effect on a country's production and consumption (i.e., replacing a domestic industry or product through foreign competition). The reality is that rising global competition increases variety, giving consumers as well as businesses more choices. In fact, rising competition couldn't occur without an increase in variety.

While increasing variety due to rising global trade will improve global consumer welfare, it will also introduce new challenges, ranging from supply-chain logistics to brand equity. Consumers will have to sift through more choices before making purchases. In turn, retailers will need to establish stronger brands in order to compete in an ever-increasing market.

These are just a few brief perspectives on what is currently under way that will increasingly be recognized as an opportunity or enabler of a significant opportunity in the years ahead.

THINK POINTS

→ Megatrends are the long-term forces that create tailwinds for growth industries.

→ Megatrends will be a common denominator among most of the important growth companies of tomorrow.

→ Megatrends that will create tailwinds are the knowledge economy, globalization, the Internet, demographics, convergence, consolidation, brands, and outsourcing.

→ While China and India are part of the globalization megatrend, both are so important that they need to be evaluated on their own.

6

The Four Ps

"Here's to the crazy ones. The misfits. The rebels. The troublemakers. The round pegs in the square holes—the ones who see things differently. They're not fond of rules and they have no respect for the status quo. You can praise them, disagree with them, quote them, disbelieve them, glorify them or vilify them. About the only thing that you can't do is ignore them. Because they change things."

—APPLE COMPUTER AD, 1997

INVESTMENT PROFESSIONALS often try to make investing sound complicated, but I've found that the better investors make complicated ideas seem simple. Warren Buffett, whose annual Berkshire Hathaway reports are a must-read for any investor, explains investing so that it's understandable. Peter Lynch has talked about being able to explain an investment so a sixth grader could understand.

With simplicity as the objective, I use the four Ps (people, product, potential, and predictability) as the key elements I'm looking for when identifying and investing in the stars of tomorrow.

After looking for industries driven by key megatrends and finding opportunities within these industries that have potential for a high and sustainable earnings growth rate, I use the four Ps to differentiate the stars of tomorrow from the ordinary companies. Finding stars that exhibit the four Ps isn't simple, but in my view, it's the key to long-term investment success.

→ PEOPLE—FOLLOW THE LEADERS

"Take our 20 best people away, and I can tell you that Microsoft would become an unimportant company."   —BILL GATES

I believe that more than 50% of the secret to success in investing in tomorrow's big market winners is evaluating the people running a company. There is no shortage of interesting ideas, but it's always the people that make the difference. In business, sports, or life, winners will find a way to win, and my goal is to find that winning team and stick with it.

Often it's the vision and passion of an entrepreneur that ignite the business opportunity. Sam Walton of Wal-Mart had a vision of bringing value and convenience to rural America. Bill Gates had a dream of making computers easier to use. Howard Schultz's vision was to bring the experience of the Italian coffee bar to America, and Irwin Jacobs's was untethered communication everywhere.

In sports, it's easy to see the effect of an individual. My friend Michael Milken—who funded a number of important nascent businesses that became large, such as MCI and Turner Broadcasting—uses the example of Michael Jordan and his impact on the Chicago Bulls when he joined as a rookie in 1984. At the time, Chicago had the worst record in the NBA. That's why they had the opportunity to draft Michael Jordan. Not coincidentally, the Bulls also had the worst attendance in the NBA in the year prior to Air Jordan joining the team. The basic economics for the Bulls show they had an average attendance of 261,000 per year with an average ticket price of $15—giving Bulls, Inc., approximately $3.9 million in gate revenue for the year.

Five years later, the Bulls were sold out, with a total attendance for the year of 737,000 at an average ticket price of $30. Bulls, Inc., ticket revenue was $23 million, a difference of nearly $20 million! This doesn't even factor in the multiplier effect of fair-weather fans that a winning team has. Clearly, one person made a huge difference.

Cute sports story, but how does it apply to the business world?

When Bill Campbell joined Intuit as CEO in 1994, its revenues were $200 million. In 2000, when he became chairman, it had $2 billion. Sim-

People Make the Difference

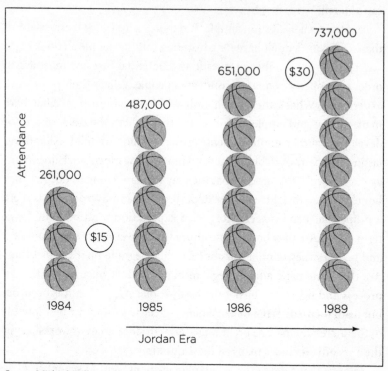

Source: Michael Milken.

ilarly, when Mickey Drexler joined the GAP, GAP's revenues were less than $1 billion. In 2002, when he retired, it had nearly $14 billion. When Bill McGuire joined UnitedHealth Group in 1989, it had revenues of just over $400 million. Now it has $44 billion. Finally, when Jack Welch became CEO of General Electric in 1981, it had revenues of $26 billion. When he left in 2001, it had revenues of $126 billion—that's a $100 billion increase! This makes it obvious that key players can have a dramatic impact, even within mediocre teams.

The goal, however, is to find a great leader at the head of a great team. After all, I've never heard an investor say, "They were bullish on the long-term outlook for a company despite the mediocre management team" (although Warren Buffett has remarked, "When a management team with a reputation for brilliance meets a business with a reputation for poor economics, it's often the business's reputation that remains intact").

Obviously, nobody ever wants to invest in average people, but how can you tell?

Unfortunately, it's not simple. It requires a lot of leg work. Many of these companies don't have long histories, but the people all do.

There are a number of questions a potential investor must ask in order to properly evaluate a company's people. What's their prior work experience? What's their reputation within the industry? What have management and employee turnover been? What's the track record for developing and promoting talent? Is there passion to build a significant lasting company or to build it up and flip it? How much stock does management own? Do they do what they say they are going to do? Are they honest and forthright? Do they underpromise and overdeliver? Is there a proper balance between short-term expectations and building long-term value? Are they building a culture where everybody shares a vision and believes they're on a mission? Do they degrade their competition? Are they systematic and strategic in building their business? Is there a process and history of hiring the best people? Are they not egocentric, but team focused? Is the management concerned about the best interest of the shareholders? The preliminary growth stock analysis worksheet in the appendix includes many of these questions.

Notice that I didn't list where management went to school as a key criterion. Often Wall Street is enamored with Ivy League degrees or the equivalent (full disclosure—this author went to the University of Minnesota, which isn't often confused with Harvard). While academic background can be relevant—and certainly Yale, Princeton, and Stanford have their fair share of business success stories—it's definitely not a prerequisite. Sam Walton went to the University of Missouri; Howard Schultz, Northern Michigan; Warren Buffett, the University of Nebraska; Don Fisher, University of California; and some of the most notable, such as Bill Gates, Larry Ellison, and Michael Dell, didn't even finish college.

Ultimately, it's a lot of little things that will add up to one big thing when we analyze whether management is world-class. Often, this is indeterminable at first, but over time (could be a few quarters; could be years) evaluating how management executes against its promises and opportunities is the key to finding the megawinners.

DROPOUTS TO BILLIONAIRES

DROPOUT	EDUCATION	COMPANY	NET WORTH
Bill Gates	Left Harvard	Microsoft	$51 billion
Paul Allen	Left Washington State University	Microsoft	$23 billion
Michael Dell	Left University of Texas	Dell	$18 billion
Larry Ellison	Left University of Illinois	Oracle	$17 billion
Steve Jobs	Left Reed College	Apple and Pixar	$3 billion
Alan Gerry	Dropped out of high school	Cablevision	$1 billion

Source: Forbes 400 Richest, ThinkEquity Partners.

➤ STAR GAZER

TIM DRAPER
founder and managing director of Draper
Fisher Jurvetson

Tim Draper was an original venture capital investor in Parametric Technology, Tumbleweed Communications, Overture.com, Digidesign, Preview Travel, Four11, Combinet, and Redgate. His suggestion to use "viral marketing" in Web-based e-mail to geometrically spread an Internet product to its market was instrumental to the successes of Hotmail and Yahoo!Mail and has been adopted as a standard marketing technique by hundreds of businesses. He was also an early investor in Skype. I sat down with Tim and asked him what he looks for in companies. (To read my full interview with Tim Draper, visit www. findingthenextstarbucks.com.)

For me, it is all about the people. Are they leaders? Do they have a mission in life to do what they are proposing to do? Will they continue to pursue this vision against all odds, with no money, when life gets them down? And is their vision clear? Does it eventually become profitable?

How do I assess great people? I test them. I see what makes them tick. I ask the tough questions even if they might be embarrassing. There is no 400-pound gorilla left in the room when I am finished. I look for the passion, for the vision. I ask them why they do what they do. If it is about the money, that is usually not enough. We saw that en masse with the crash of 2001. The people who did it for the money generally gave up. The ones that were in it for the vision are mostly still around.

→ PRODUCT—WHAT'S THE CLAIM TO FAME?

"Innovation distinguishes between a leader and a follower."
— STEVE JOBS

In searching for great growth companies, I am looking to invest in companies that are leaders in what they do. Attractive companies need something that makes them special or great—they need a claim to fame. Starbucks is the preeminent provider of gourmet coffee. Callaway is the leading innovator in designing and manufacturing premier golf clubs.

"Me too" companies—businesses that participate in the leader's industry, but due to market share, growth, and/or quality are imitators rather
than innovators—are of zero interest to me. In the business world, it is
ultimately the survival of the fittest—I want to be involved with the
companies that not only survive, but thrive, during their corporate evolution. Ultimately, companies that aren't leaders fall into oblivion.

Companies that dominate a niche and help shape its future are leaders. Companies that may be smaller than the gorilla but have better
products, better and more sustainable margins, and/or higher and more
visible growth can become leaders. Watch out for them.

The best of all situations is a "one-of-a-kind" company that has no real
competition. eBay is a one-of-a-kind company. Apple Computer is a one-
of-a-kind company with its iPod. Harris & Harris, a holding company of
early-stage nanotechnology companies, is a one-of-a-kind business.

In evaluating a company's leadership position within an industry,
there are many things to analyze. What is the company's market share? Is
it increasing or decreasing?

For a company to be a leader, it needs to be expanding its market
share profitably. Generally, this means that a company should be gaining
share among its competitors without decreasing margins. Great growth
companies have pricing elasticity and control over their margins. Starbucks has been raising what it charges for a cup of coffee for fifteen years
amid increased competition, but hasn't missed a beat. Coffee prices have
fluctuated greatly, but Starbucks' margins have steadily increased.

There are exceptions to this—I call it the Wal-Mart doctrine. Wal-
Mart became the largest retailer in the world by charging its customers
less so it would make more. For years, Wal-Mart made less in gross margins but actually did make it up in volume so that operating margin remained stable while market share soared.

Here's the quick math on how this strategy works. Wal-Mart had
been shaving margins for almost a decade so that by the end of the
1990s, Wal-Mart's gross margin was 23 to 24% versus Kmart, its main
competitor, at 29 to 30%. By this time, Wal-Mart's sales per square foot
were almost $400, more than double Kmart's $178.

Wal-Mart made almost twice as much in gross profit for the same
theoretical square foot of retail space, while at the same time delivering

superior value and selection to its customers. Coupled with the superior efficiencies that Wal-Mart derived from its high productivity, Wal-Mart produced vastly more profit per square foot (and more profit per dollar of investment) than did its key competitor.

HOW WAL-MART OVERWHELMED KMART

	WAL-MART	KMART
Sales per square foot of gross store space	$395	$177
Gross margin rule	24–25%	29–30%
Gross profit/square foot	$97	$52
Operating expense rate	17.5%	26.0%
Operating expense/square foot	$69	$46
Operating margin rate	7.1%	3.5%
Operating profit/square foot	$28	$6

Source: ThinkEquity Partners.

Dell thought out of the box by selling computers directly to consumers and building them to order. Apollo Group built the largest private university in the United States because it treated working adults like customers—a radical idea to most colleges and universities. Thinking differently is a key quality of most big winners.

Costco is another brilliant business where the Wal-Mart doctrine applies, but Costco has gone one step better. Costco's goal is basically to sell as much merchandise as can be optimized by pricing its product very aggressively (at less than half of Wal-Mart's discount store gross margin) and being so efficient (partly because of the volume) that the company earns only slightly better than a 1% pretax margin on sales of merchandise. Don't get Costco confused with one of those Internet-era business models like dog.com where the more they sold, the more money they lost. For Costco, earning 1% on merchandise sales is more than enough.

In some ways, Costco's business model works more like an insurance company than a traditional retailer. An insurance company's objective is to break even on the policy itself but make its profit on the "float"—the use of that money until it has to be paid out. For an insurance company, you pay your $1,000 in auto premiums in January, and the insurance company expects that by December, on average, it will pay out $1,000 on claims and claims expenses. The insurance company makes its profit by having the use of your money and investing it during the year. If it makes an 8% return, its profit is $80.

One of Costco's objectives is to get the float on the money you give them today to purchase jumbo Corn Flakes, with Costco paying the vendor about 30 days later, by which time Costco has had the use of the cash proceeds from the sale of the vendor's inventory. Selling gas at only the slimmest of profit margins makes sense if the total investment required to sell gasoline can turn, as it does for Costco, more than 300 times per year (almost every day). "Turn" is the number of times a company's inventory is sold during the year. With investment turning like that, it's possible to see a triple-digit ROI with hardly any profit margins at all. It also makes sense if the business model creates *free* cash today that doesn't need to be used for new capital expenditures.

The profit margin on the merchandise sale may not appear very attractive, but the return on investment is. It's even more attractive overall: Costco members also pay a fee to support their addiction to Costco's low prices.

The American Express Traveler's Check was a classic float business. Travelers would deposit money with Amex before going on a trip, and Amex would have use of that cash to invest until it was redeemed (often much later, and sometimes not at all). Amex's cost of capital was negative.

The fact is, while it's exceptionally difficult to find truly world-class management teams, it's just as difficult to find companies that have a truly great or unique product. The only way to find them is to do a lot of digging. You have to kiss a lot of frogs before you are going to find a prince.

With companies that provide a service, three metrics tell the story of whether I have found a star or not:

1. Revenue per employee
2. Recurring revenue from existing customers
3. Nonforced employee turnover

Revenue per person is a critical metric for comparing a company to others in its industry because it shows productivity and value ascribed to the provided service. The higher revenue per person is vis-à-vis competitors, the better the indication of quality of people and noncommodity service. Also, having the highest revenue per person suggests that the company can pay its people more, which will help in keeping them.

Goldman Sachs has the most envied brand in investment banking, and, not coincidentally, its revenue per person is the highest in the industry. Lehman Brothers has leapfrogged others in its stature, with a corresponding rise in revenue per employee.

REVENUE PER EMPLOYEE AT TOP INVESTMENT FIRMS	
Goldman Sachs Group	$1,934,939
Lehman Brothers Holdings	$1,373,358
Morgan Stanley	$968,715
Bear Stearns Companies	$944,077
Merrill Lynch	$860,546

Source: FactSet.

Recurring revenue is an important metric as it is a leading indicator of how customers perceive the value of the service and whether it's viewed as fungible or not. It depends on the business, but companies that have 90% or greater recurring revenues are terrific. A company with a high proportion of its revenue as recurring almost always sells at higher multiples to its growth rate. A red flag for a service business is when its recurring revenue is decreasing or it's losing a disproportionate number of customers.

For companies in general, but in particular for service companies, having low nonforced turnover is a good thing. On the one hand, great companies do ask people who aren't performing or are killing a culture to leave. At McKinsey, you could be a partner for 20 years, but if you aren't carrying your weight, they will politely make you an alumnus. On the other hand, having a big percentage of service employees or knowledge workers walk across the street because they perceive a better opportunity there is a big problem. Generally speaking, a professional services firm should have less than 15% nonforced turnover. The better the company, the lower the nonforced turnover.

Product Checklist

1. What's the company's claim to fame?
2. What is its market share? Is it growing or decreasing?
3. Is it the fastest-growing company in the industry?
4. Is pricing stable or increasing?
5. Are margins stable or increasing?
6. How do margins compare to the three leading competitors in the industry?
7. How does the growth rate compare to three leading competitors?
8. Is there brand value?
9. What's the revenue per employee? How does it compare to three leading competitors?
10. When they lose a sale, why did they lose it, and to whom?
11. What is the quality of the sales force?
12. Is it the product-quality leader?
13. What percentage of revenues do they invest in R&D?

Another leading indicator of the quality of the product is the quality of the sales force. Salespeople are generally a very fluid group. They migrate to where they will have the best product to sell and make the most money. Seeing experienced salespeople leave a blue-chip company for a relatively new company may be a sign that something is going on.

Well before it became obvious to everybody that Google was a special company, top salespeople from the Valley were flocking there in droves. Foxhollow, which has been a rocket ship in the medical device area since going public in 2004, was attracting leading medical device salespeople before anybody in the mainstream had heard of the company.

With technology companies, tracking where the top engineers are heading provides a window to who has the leading-edge product. In the 1980s, the electrical engineers were all heading to Seattle to work for Microsoft. Now they are going to Google and Apple.

Analyzing the percentage of revenue committed to R&D is also important in understanding a company's commitment to quality and innovation. The rule of thumb for a technology company is that it spend at least 7% of revenue on R&D.

LARGE-CAP LEADERS IN R&D SPENDING

COMPANY	MARKET VALUE (MILLIONS)	SPENDING ON R&D AS PERCENTAGE OF REVENUES
Celgene Corp.	$11,993	36%
Genentech Inc.	$92,228	23%
Broadcom Corp.	$24,055	23%
Analog Devices Inc.	$14,552	21%
Eli Lilly & Co.	$65,413	21%
Freescale Semiconductor Inc.	$10,711	20%
Siebel Systems Inc.	$5,624	20%
Maxim Integrated Products Inc.	$13,854	20%
Advanced Micro Devices Inc.	$16,102	20%
Infineon Technologies AG	$7,132	19%
Altera Corp.	$6,996	19%
Amgen Inc.	$87,283	19%
Adobe Systems Inc.	$24,097	19%
STMicroelectronics N.V.	$16,806	18%
Tellabs Inc.	$5,640	18%

Source: FactSet.

Understanding a company's commitment not only to maintaining its competitive position, but also to enhancing it, is critical. The best companies are leaders in investing in innovation through R&D. Google has its people spend 20% of their time dreaming up new ideas. 3M expects that 25% of its revenue in five years will come from products that currently don't exist. New products are often key to fueling growth.

STAR GAZER

RANDY KOMISAR
partner at Kleiner Perkins Caufield & Byers

Randy Komisar joined Kleiner Perkins Caufield & Byers in 2005 as a partner. For several prior years, Randy partnered with entrepreneurs creating businesses with leading-edge technologies. He was a co-founder of Claris Corporation, served as CEO for LucasArts Entertainment and Crystal Dynamics, and acted as a "virtual CEO" for such companies as WebTV, Mirra, and GlobalGiving. He was a founding director of TiVo, where he is currently chairman of the Nominating and Governance Committee. Randy has also served as CFO of GO Corporation and senior counsel for Apple Computer, following a private practice in technology law. Randy is a consulting professor of entrepreneurship at Stanford University and author of the best-selling book The Monk and the Riddle. (To read my full interview with Randy Komisar, visit www.findingthenextstarbucks.com.)

Probably the most valuable lesson I've learned is the importance of subordinating your ego in order to understand how to most effectively inspire and motivate the people around you, so that you can get the most done. I've learned to take less credit for my successes, and I've learned to suffer less in my failures. The business of entrepreneurship, and the business of start-ups are the business of experimentation. By nature, experimentation will lead to many failures, in terms of not being able to achieve the desired result. But even those failures have success built in them if you can learn from them and if you can take away whatever the wins are that are available to you. So the lessons that I've learned tend to be kind of ethereal and philosophical. But fundamentally, they've made me a lot more humble, and a lot more flexible, and a lot more appreciative of people and the opportunities that I've had to work in.

→ POTENTIAL—HOW BIG COULD THIS BECOME?

"Before you build a better mousetrap, it helps to know if there are any mice out there." —MORTIMER B. ZUCKERMAN, CHAIRMAN AND EDITOR IN CHIEF, *U.S. NEWS & WORLD REPORT*

My framework for finding the stars of tomorrow, companies that have the biggest potential, is to identify *problems* and *pain* in the marketplace. I then look at the growth sectors of the economy—technology, health care, media, education, and business and consumer services—and analyze how megatrends are creating tailwinds of opportunity. Where the growth sectors intersect the megatrends is where I believe the stars of tomorrow will be found. This intersection is the best place to focus research and resources!

To find long-term winners in the stock market, it's essential to invest in companies that have great people and a leading product. In order to have gigantic winners, you also need huge potential.

When I was determining the market potential for Starbucks, I thought about the billion cups of coffee consumed every day, and estimated that about 999 million of them were bad! This made me believe there was a lot of potential. More seriously, I researched the number of

Starbucks stores in San Francisco versus the number of McDonald's units and, based on this calculation, predicted potential for three times as many Starbucks stores.

There are numerous nice little companies that are clipping along, but they will always remain nice little companies because of the size of the market they are in. Moreover, a company could be in a relatively large market today, but the market could be shrinking. The best typewriter companies in the world essentially disappeared after the PC and WordPerfect arrived on the scene. Facsimile machines are in that boat. So are cigarette manufacturers. Traditional travel agencies are going the way of the dinosaurs. Simply put, the home run ball is going to be hit where small companies have the potential to be big companies. The market doesn't have to be big today (or even exist!) to have enormous potential.

The classic investment opportunity is where there is a problem—the bigger the problem, the bigger the opportunity. Where is there pain?

The education market is an obvious place where there are big problems and big opportunities. Online education wasn't a market 10 years ago. Now it's a $6.3 billion market and it's growing.

The biggest potential opportunities are often found where megatrends intersect the growth sectors of the economy—technology, health care, media, education, and business/consumer services. From this I get a growth accelerator that can lead me to the home run opportunities.

Within megatrends there are minitrends that develop. Minitrends might be huge in terms of opportunity but narrow as they relate to impacting all of the growth sectors. An example might be within the megatrend of branding. The minitrend of one-on-one marketing is big, but only to a relatively narrow list of sectors. Open-source is a huge trend in software and media (made possible by the Internet, another megatrend), but it is a minitrend because it's unlikely to have broad enough sector implications.

Minitrends I like include one-stop shopping (consolidation), wellness (demographics), obesity (demographics), spirituality (demographics), woman power (demographics), Internet learning (knowledge economy and Internet), China (globalization), travel (globalization), India (out-

Megatrend	⟶	Minitrend
Brand	⟶	One-stop shopping
Internet	⟶	Open-source
Demographics	⟶	Wellness
Demographics	⟶	Obesity
Demographics	⟶	Woman power
Knowledge economy and Internet	⟶	Internet learning
Globalization	⟶	China
Globalization and outsourcing	⟶	India
Globalization	⟶	Travel
Internet	⟶	Peer-to-peer
Internet	⟶	Digital everything

sourcing and globalization), peer-to-peer (Internet), and digital everything (Internet).

In having a framework for determining where the world is heading guided by megatrends and minitrends, it's equally important to understand where the world is not going. Investing in a buggy whip after Henry Ford created the Model T wasn't going to be fruitful no matter how good a buggy whip it was. *Negatrends* are secular shifts in society, the market, and/or politics that will result in a shrinking market opportunity. Mom-and-pop shops are a negatrend as shown by the disappearance of the corner drugstore or local hardware store. Megatrends that negatively impact mom-and-pop shops are brands, consolidation, and globalization.

Unskilled workers are a negatrend influenced by the knowledge economy, the Internet, and outsourcing. Other negatrends I see are mass marketing (Internet and brands), pay phones (the Internet), closed economies (globalization), and middlemen (Internet and globalization). Regrettably, some negative trends that aren't negatrends—because the market is increasing (not shrinking)—include terrorism, identity theft, and pirating.

As I look to the future, I see that companies that benefit from the four Ps as well as megatrends and minitrends will be the big winners.

Megatrend		Negatrend
Brand	⟶	Mass marketing
Consolidation	⟶	Mom-and-pop shops
Internet	⟶	Pay phones
Globalization	⟶	Closed economies
Internet and globalization	⟶	Middlemen
Knowledge economy, Internet, and outsourcing	⟶	Unskilled workers

Whether oil prices are $60, $100, or $20 a barrel, the fact is that there is a finite supply, which is a problem. At $60 a barrel, that problem starts to become painful to consumers, and opportunities in alternative energy, such as clean fuel and solar power, become attractive. Energy technology is a big part of the solution for the future and an area of opportunity for growing companies and investors.

With an aging population, all sorts of problems become acute. What kind of health care will be provided? Where will the elderly live? How will the elderly have enough money for retirement? What are they going to do with their spare time?

It's critical when evaluating the potential to distinguish between a *fad* and a *trend*. Charles Schwab has said that the first fad he was involved with as an investor was the "bowling bubble" in the spring and summer of 1981. According to analysts at the time, every American was going to go bowling for an average of two hours a week.

180 million people × 2 hours per week = a LOT of bowling!

But this was absurd! Just because you can do the math doesn't mean the math makes sense. Quantifying realistic long-term potential and scrubbing assumptions are necessary in order to understand what the real opportunity is.

VINOD KHOSLA
founder of Khosla Ventures, affiliated partner at
Kleiner Perkins Caufield & Byers

*Vinod Khosla has been universally regarded as one of the top
venture capitalists in the world for the past 20 years. He was
ranked number one on the Forbes Midas list in 2003. He was a
co-founder of Daisy Systems and founding chief executive officer of Sun Microsystems, where he pioneered open systems and
commercial RISC processors. Vinod serves on the boards of
Agami, eASIC, Indian School of Business, Infinera, Kovio, Met-
ricstream, Spatial Photonics, Xsigo, and Zettacore.*

Michael Moe: *Vinod, explain your investment philosophy.*

Vinod Khosla: I sort of think of myself as a private-market investor and, even then, somebody who focuses on technology,
not private equity. I know nothing about public markets. I almost
never trade in public markets just because I feel pretty incom-
petent there.

MM: *Let's start with how you look at opportunities. What are the
things that you factor in when you're trying to find ideas to get
involved with?*

VK: From my perspective, focus is very important. As you
might guess, from an investing point of view, you want to be in
areas where you know more than the others do, which means
you pick areas and then you focus on those. I'm not a portfolio
investor, unfortunately. I'm a focused investor.

In my world you can lose only one times your money, but you can make 50 or 100 times. That says two things. One, you work in areas where you know you have some sort of a comparative advantage in picking growth segments. Large markets forgive a lot of mistakes. In the high-growth segment, they tend to be newer markets. When markets are new, there's a lot about the market that's uncharacterized. To me, it's crucial to realize that you won't understand all of it. But you'll be ahead on the learning curve compared to people coming behind you. I think the investing process is one of making the mistakes and getting smarter about a market before others do, but the market wave is large enough that it's quite forgiving while you're learning.

The other thing I like to see in these markets is short-term advantages and long-term advantages. In the end, the short-term advantages generally end up being technology.

You get some patents. There are technical advantages. Then the business strategy over time becomes trying to parlay a technical advantage into a permanent long-term advantage.

Look at Apple. Basically their advantage with the iPod was a better design and some neat technology, but nothing earth shattering. In the end they will have 50 million or 100 million people with their music library locked into their service. That's a permanent advantage, not a technology advantage. You start with your foot in the door, generally with a technology advantage, and parlay it into something more permanent. It could be a brand; it could be locking in consumers; it could be distribution; it could be any of the traditional things that businesses talk about.

MM: *What else is key for you?*

VK: The other component of this is people. I find most investors say they want great people, but they don't pay enough attention to them. They don't realize what having good people means, especially in growth markets.

It's okay to say you're looking for great people. It's much harder to say you'll take 10% of the company's equity and give it to a great CEO. It's just not a decision too many people in the investment business will make, especially in the later stage of private equity. I'm always arguing about it.

If I find a great person who might be willing to join a company, I'll always look to find an excuse, create a position within the organization so you can fit the person in as opposed to saying, "Oh, we don't need another head of marketing. We already have one." Every time I find somebody good, I will twist around the whole structure to try and fit them in, as opposed to focusing on just what we need—because the people add value independent of title.

MM: *I believe great businesses are systematic and strategic. Do you have a different point of view?*

VK: Process matters in mature industry and process matters in growth markets too. But in growth markets, what's different is instinct and what I call an organized-chaos style of management. You need a great process-oriented manager who has all the right metrics, weekly staff meetings, and corporate goals and evaluation against goals and bonuses—all the usual stuff of managing a company. You also need entrepreneurial instincts. That's much harder for a process-oriented person. That's where I think growth equity becomes a little bit different because entrepreneurial instincts are very, very critical, unlike in your traditional industries, where you pretty much know what works and what doesn't because people have already tried it. In new markets and growth markets, that's not the case.

You need a different style of person who's willing to take more risks. For example, in a management style geared toward growth, you want to reward failure if it's an intelligent risk. You want to reward good judgment even if it doesn't always succeed.

Not only is paying attention to people important, the mix of people is very important. I call that engineering the gene pool of a company to have the wild guys and the process guys and the experienced operating guys and the guys who think the impossible is doable. The constructive tension is really important.

It's not a sergeant style of management where you have a whole army marching in step. It's more like where you'll see a shepherd herding sheep in a general direction, but the sheep within are probably going leftward, rightward, and backward, discovering new pastures of green grass. That's sort of how you manage growth equity: you keep changing the trajectory and start dealing and experimenting at the edges of a herd, while the herd generally is following the direction. It's not the rigid management style where you lock in four- or five-year plans.

MM: *What other observations do you have?*

VK: I find it's much easier to build entrepreneurial companies in markets that don't exist but have the potential to be large, than it is to build them in existing markets that analysts have covered in sort of defined metrics, because the guys with the much higher resources generally ruin it. Let me give you a classic example on both sides. Nobody thought the market for Google was big enough when Google started, right? In fact, the first market they were in was the online advertising market. Their business model centered around advertising was as important as their search technology. People thought it was a geeky start-up, but, in fact, it was about adding advertising value proposition to small companies. Suddenly you could see a $5,000 or $10,000 ad campaign. The guy I buy my sheepskin rugs from could have a $1,000 advertising campaign. And if it paid off, he could invest another $1,000.

So it was a change in business models and it was new. Contrast that to another high-growth market like, say, mobile. If everybody knows the market, then the guys with the biggest resources, the Verizons and Cingulars, are the ones who are going to win. So, this issue is picking markets that haven't yet been figured out. You have to pick your markets a little bit carefully to be much more focused on large markets that are what I call zero-billion-dollar markets instead of zero-million-dollar markets.

MM: *As you look ahead, what areas are the most interesting for you?*

VK: I'm spending a lot of time on energy because my other rule is that every missed problem is a major opportunity. It's just a fact of life. Then there's—off the fringes—technical capability. I like operating on the fringes. When I first mentioned synthetic biology a year and a half ago to people, they looked at me weird. In fact, 90% of biologists won't have heard of it.

But the problem with operating on the fringes is you never know what technology will have a huge economic impact. Energy is an important area. Synthetic biology is on the fringes where technological change can cause a huge economic impact in major areas. Now, that's not to say there aren't opportunities where there's no technological change. I'm just saying that's not for me. I just focus on what I do well. So when people started doing growth retail investing, I stayed out of it. I didn't want to touch it because other people knew a lot more about retail than I did, but in an area like synthetic biology or alternative energy, where nobody knows anything, I can have an advantage.

→ **PREDICTABILITY—HOW VISIBLE IS THE GROWTH?**

"Well done is better than well said."   —BENJAMIN FRANKLIN

One of the biggest challenges for a young, fast-growing company is delivering operating results that are predictable.

Investors reward management teams that underpromise and overdeliver, and they punish companies that habitually miss expectations—often to extremes that seem illogical on the surface. As I mentioned before, Apollo, the top-performing stock from 1994 to 2004, promised Wall Street 25% earnings growth, delivered 42% earnings growth, and its stock had a CAGR of 48%.

Early in my analyst career, I followed Discovery Zone, a rapidly growing provider of indoor entertainment centers for children. The company had a management team led by Don Flynn, a former senior executive of the famously successful Waste Management Corporation.

Discovery Zone was the leader in a new market and its Discovery Zone centers were wildly popular with parents and children as a way to entertain kids on a rainy afternoon, for a birthday party, or just to take a break. The potential seemed huge, as one could imagine putting a Discovery Zone in every community in America and, at some point, in the entire world! This was going to be a mini-Disneyland with a better return on investment.

The fly in the ointment was predictability. The first sign of smoke was when the company reported a record quarter with earnings growth up nearly 100%. Why was that a problem? Because investors' expectations were slightly higher—they were supposed to deliver exactly 100% earnings growth, and they missed EPS estimates by a penny.

The next morning, Discovery Zone shares were down 50%, and I was having a conversation with a very successful growth investor who sold all of his shares that day. I said, "This is ridiculous. The company still is growing like crazy, almost 100%, and they only missed their earnings by one cent! The potential is still huge! And this management team is world-class." I'll never forget his response: "Mike, if these guys can't find a penny, they are too dumb for me to invest with or their business has other issues."

He was right about at least one of these predictions. Parents would have one birthday party there, but they wouldn't have two. Been there, done that. Kids were getting sick from interacting with a zillion other kids swimming in a sea of plastic, contagious balls. Competitors were knocking them off, with megacorporations such as McDonald's copying them and providing a "fun center" as a way to entice parents to buy more Happy Meals. Discovery Zone was bankrupt within 12 months.

Not great research on my part, no question, but it's hard. How do you distinguish between a fad and a trend? Is it Starbucks or Krispy Kreme? Amazon.com or eToys? The Cheesecake Factory or Boston Chicken? Whole Foods or Webvan? Disney or Discovery Zone?

FAD VERSUS TREND	
FAD	TREND
Atkins diet	Weight Watchers
Crocs	Under Armour
Plastic wristband	The Salvation Army
Boston Chicken	Chipotle

FAD	TREND
Beanie Babies	De Beers
Krispy Kreme	Starbucks
Ride Snowboards	Callaway Golf
TCBY	Whole Foods Market
UGGs	Polo/Ralph Lauren
Pet rock	Pet animals
Eminem	U2

Predictability is a relative term. Some industries and business models are much more predictable than others. An outsourced service provider that has 10-year, noncancelable contracts is much more predictable than a movie production company or a software company that gets 50% of its sales in the last week of the quarter.

The key to determining a company's predictability and its ability to perform against expectations is partially a business model, but also partially a function of the first three Ps: people, product, and potential.

Great managements set expectations that are achievable, and they're fanatical about achieving results. Dell Computer doesn't have the most predictable business model, but the management at Dell is obsessive about delivering against their promises. They are systematic about how they run their business. Winners execute.

Having a product that is exceptional is essential to predictability. The software business is notoriously unpredictable, but if you need an operating system, you buy Microsoft, and if you need a database, you buy Oracle. There is not really a cheaper option because each has a de facto monopoly.

Even looking at a business like Starbucks—which, on the surface, one could say is subject to all the uncertainties of a traditional restaurant, like weather, low switching cost, and consumer fickleness—we see it's actually quite predictable. The average Starbucks customer goes to Starbucks twenty times a month! For $3, a CEO or a secretary can have a world-class cup of coffee (or alternate drink) and have an affordable luxury. Most people I know are really unhappy if they don't get their daily Starbucks experience.

We love businesses that are addictive but don't cause cancer!

Push e-mail services are addictive. Research in Motion's BlackBerry devices have become so addictive they have been called "crackberries."

Potential is critical for predictability because if a company's market isn't growing, its growth is hostage to variables that impact visibility. Even if a company is the leader and taking market share, if the pie is getting smaller, it's challenging to have predictable growth. The institutional brokerage industry, which I'm in, is going through radical structural changes that are decreasing the overall size of the market. Even though our market share has increased significantly and is still growing, it's challenging to have visibility to that growth as the market continues to shrink.

Recurring revenues are the holy grail of predictable, visible growth. A company such as Paychex, which has 80% of its revenues from existing customers, is a great example of this. Business services outsourcing companies, drug companies with patients who need a drug to be healthy, and education companies like Apollo Group who have students in their programs for two to four years are all great examples of companies with recurring revenues. Recurring-revenue businesses almost always have big premiums to their multiples because of their visibility.

One of the biggest positives about on-demand software companies like salesforce.com is that they are selling software as a service. Unlike the license model, on-demand companies charge on a per-user, per-month basis. While their upfront revenue is relatively low, the perpetual nature of the revenue stream is relatively predictable and the value to the customer is compelling.

RECURRING-REVENUE BUSINESSES		
INDUSTRY	COMPANY	HOW MODEL WORKS
Outsourced services	EDS	Multiyear contract based on a combination of services and outsourcing
On-demand software	salesforce.com	Monthly per-user subscription fee
Payroll processing	ADP	Contract to distribute a company's paychecks
Online education	eCollege	Ongoing fees based on student enrollment

It's critical for an investor to create a predictability framework that's appropriate for a specific industry. For example, there are terrific earnings growth opportunities in the biotech sector, where a company won't have revenues for a number of years, but because of the people, the product, and the potential, it could be a compelling investment.

In pre-revenue companies, the first three Ps take precedence, but key *milestones* a company can perform against give investors evidence that it's on track to capture the opportunity. With biotech companies, this could be results and timeliness from phase I, II, and III results with the FDA, a joint-venture partnership with a nanotechnology company, patent approval, or commercial development milestones.

STAR GAZER

BILL CAMPBELL
chairman of Intuit

Bill Campbell has one of the most unique and impressive careers in business. Besides being chairman of Intuit, Bill is on the boards of Apple, Opsware, and Good Technology, and is an advisor to other leading growth companies, including Google and Tellme. During his tenure at Intuit, the company's market value has grown from approximately $700 million to nearly $9 billion as the company continues to establish its position as the clear leader in tax, personal finance, and small-business accounting software.

Michael Moe: *Bill, you're called the Coach of Silicon Valley. How did you get that distinction?*

Bill Campbell: I stepped down as CEO at Intuit and, in 1998, went back in about a year later for another period of time. And since 2000, I have been working with early-stage companies. My goal is to make companies better.

When I first came to Apple in 1983, I had a couple of guys who had a lot of wisdom help me. One was Floyd Kvamme, whom you know as the tech czar for Bush today. When I went to Apple, he was my boss, the executive vice president there; then he went on to Kleiner Perkins.

Regis McKenna ran a public relations firm and was well known as a strategy guy who helped Apple and a lot of other companies in Silicon Valley. What those guys did, for me, was help me tremendously about learning how to adapt to Silicon Valley and what it was going to take to make a company great.

They did that with no remuneration. These guys cared about helping me make Apple better.

I thought when I stepped down as CEO and when I wasn't going to try to chase a buck, that I would try to give back in that same way. So that's what I do. I try to work with companies—I don't take anything, I don't want anything—I just want to make sure that I can help make Silicon Valley companies durable, make companies that have lasting value.

MM: *How do you find the companies that you may want to spend time with or, better said, how do they find you?*

BC: I don't pick them. I let other people do that: my friends in venture capital. What I try to do is see if I can't bring these companies to life. It's what I like to do. I meet entrepreneurs and founders, and determine if I think that they care about making their companies great.

I'm not interested in companies that only want to be high market cap companies. I'm interested in companies that really believe that they can build something of lasting value. If they do, I believe the company will be successful financially as well.

MM: *What companies have you enjoyed working with the most?*

BC: I have had the good fortune to work with great venture capital firms that have introduced me to great companies. I spend most of my time with Kleiner Perkins, Benchmark, and Maveron. There are others, but those are my closest relationships.

I've had good times working with companies like Opsware, Drugstore, Tellme, Good, Google, and Shopping.com. Some huge successes, some modest successes, and for others, the jury's still out.

MM: *Besides a passion to build an enduring enterprise, why did you decide to spend time with those companies?*

BC: Let's start with picking them. I said I don't really pick them, but like everybody else, I've got my own views about success. I think too many people today love an idea. I mean they love the category, they love the market opportunity. But I think the ideas are only as good as the execution.

Great technology people invent things, or can take great technologies and apply them well. But, hopefully, when you're evaluating a founder entrepreneur, you know that they know how to surround themselves with great people who can complement their strengths.

I judge founder/CEOs on their ability to bring in people who are capable of supplementing and complementing their abilities. They mustn't be afraid to surround themselves with strong people who will challenge them. The venture capitalists who I work with really understand this.

MM: *How important are venture capitalists in helping create great companies?*

BC: I think VCs [venture capitalists] have the most clout. Venture capitalists with an operating bias are enormously powerful. Look at ones that have conceptual ability, who understand what market opportunities exist. If they don't complement themselves with people who know how to help run a company, then the company is not going to be successful. Too many venture capitalists aren't good at this, and many of the venture capitalists who are don't market themselves that way.

I think that managing a company to life is an art. I wish it was a science. Watching great VCs do this is wonderful. It does give me comfort that great ideas can become great companies.

Let's go back in time and think about some of the companies that have been legendary. I've always been enamored with what John Doerr did at Macromedia. He helped management put companies together in related fields and watched it emerge as a company that ultimately became hugely successful. Or Dan Levitan and what he did to revive drugstore.com. Or Bill Gurley merging Epinions with Dealtime and turning it into Shopping.com. Take Kevin Harvey working with Tellme. He helped the model change from a consumer voice portal to an enterprise approach to maximize the utilization of that technology. These are just a few.

MM: *What are the key principles for building a foundation for success in a young company?*

BC: Let's go back to my comment that it's an art and not a science. I have my own strong view. I'm not sure that it's universally believed, but let me see if I can start with this. I am a strong believer that you need a strong, experienced management team early. I get arguments from VCs about that all the time.

When I did my first start-up—my own company, Claris—I put together a management team of Donna Dubinsky, Bruce Chizen, Randy Komisar, Yogen Dalal, Dave Kinser, and Dan Mc-Cammon. It was an experienced management team. And that great strength begat strength underneath—it became a very strong company in a very short period of time.

A lot of people didn't think I should get senior people early. I'm not sure what that means. Others thought I should get people who knew how to work in small environments. I'm not sure what that means. My belief is get great people. Find ones who really know how to manage a function, an organization, and great people then will beget great people and hiring will cascade.

When I start to work with a company, the first issue that I deal with is whether the CEO is the right guy. Is the person who founded the company good enough to do that job? I have a bias toward trying to coach people and make them better. So my view is I stick with the CEO until I can ensure that they are good enough to do it. If I coach them every day and assess what kind of response they're providing me about the issues that they face, I know whether they're going to be good or not good, and they'll know it too. You have to recognize the limitations.

My belief is you should try to keep people with great vision in the company to help drive the company to be successful. Scott Cook drove Intuit until it was about $100 million. Just before he stepped down, he agreed to merge Intuit with ChipSoft, about an $85 million company. Scott then brought in a CEO. At that point, Scott Cook was no longer the CEO, but he continued to have great influence. There has never been a more engaged founder. He decided to stay with it. He stayed on the management team and is still active and involved with Intuit today.

MM: *What's the balance between making people better and bolstering the management team?*

BC: It is a fine line. You don't want to jeopardize the company, but giving current management a chance to grow is important. There is no sense in trashing founders, but there is a lot of sense in recognizing if he or she has the ability to be a CEO. Sometimes they need experienced help. Do you remember who worked with Bill Gates in those early days as a COO that guided him toward success? From TI fame, John Shirley, an experienced manager.

MM: *What are the key priorities for the management team?*

BC: Putting great people in place—immediately. I was just talking to a company where the CEO is fighting me hard about putting in a finance person. I don't want just a finance person, I want a CFO. I want somebody who's big-time to be able to come in and do the right things for the company. There is much disagreement about this. There are many times when people say to me, "Oh, you're not going to get those people. If we get the company to cash flow break even, we'll get better people."

I don't believe that at all. I find that there are wonderful experienced entrepreneurs, particularly in Silicon Valley, who are dying for opportunities to come in at an early stage when they can help shape the culture, shape the management team, and make a big difference. It's no different with finance people, certainly no different with CEOs. Go back and think about the probability of Netscape getting Jim Barksdale at the time.

Why not get a great CFO? A CFO can help with everything—operations, financings, legal issues. You can get a lot of young, bright people; they want to do models and planning. But a good CFO can help with operations, and they have good experiences. It's an important function. I can't recall any company that I've worked with through the early stage where the CFO wasn't the single most important person that I brought onto that team.

The second priority, another controversial one, is a product marketing person. Now you'll notice I didn't say "a marketing person." I said "a product marketing person." I've gone around Silicon Valley these last couple of years, and people have been saying, "Why has marketing lost its clout?" I say, "Because it forgot its first name." Its first name is "product." This is the person who helps engineering apply the technology to a market.

I put engineering next. Most often, you'll see the entrepreneurs who come with you are the ones who have the great ideas, who have the technology background, who really are the ones that have conceived of and know how to implement the product. So, engineering management can take the initial implementation and help it grow and scale.

Even Google—when I look at the wonderful, wonderful founder capability that they had from the technical standpoint—when Wayne Rosing went in there to be the vice president of engineering, it made a big difference in terms of structure.

MM: *What else?*

BC: To be successful in engineering management you must focus on hiring and hiring practices. Think about how important they are. Architecture, development plans, schedules. Putting people on teams, breaking ties, scale, and how do we think about that in terms of growth?

MM: *What other characteristics are critical to be a great company?*

BC: After management—I learned this from venture capitalists, who have a lot of courage about these things—don't be afraid to change. Sometimes you've got to make changes. For instance, there may be business-model adjustments or channel adjustments. Take Opsware and think about how they got rid of the full-managed service business and went to a software model. They still used the same technology, but they had to deploy it in a different way. Good Technology had to make some business-model changes. They have gone from a direct sales force to a carrier model.

Some changes are major target-market changes and these take even more courage. Think about Shopping.com going from an advertising portal to cost-per-click. Or Tellme going from a consumer voice portal to an enterprise business. They had people with courage to make those kinds of changes.

If it isn't working, evaluate it and force the change. Even in my coaching days, I used to say that. There's no improvement without change. And believe me, there's no change without trauma.

Next, I really believe strongly that CEOs must start the management discipline early. Be quantitative about everything. If you put a quantitative rigor into your culture, it will last forever. We need to measure everything on a regular basis.

We've got to make sure that measurement is a part of what our company does. As for operating reviews, spend a lot of time with managers, making sure that they understand the responsibilities of each function, where the dollars are spent and how they spend them, how to manage and meet deadlines, what to do about channels and how those things affect the business. Sales targeting is a simple one that people sometimes forget, but it can be quantified.

MM: *If you can't measure it, you can't manage it, right?*

BC: Yes. Have rigorous operating reviews. Force accountability. The companies that I work with do quarterly reviews. Look at midquarter results carefully. What did they say they were going to do at the beginning of the quarter? Where are they at midquarter? What kind of midquarter corrections do we have to make? What results do we have so far? What does that mean for the following quarter? Are we behind? Are we ahead? Should we spend more? Should we spend less?

MM: *What else is in the "Bring a Company to Life" playbook?*

BC: I think another important component is innovation/best practices. There is so much innovation going on in every aspect of business. Not just technology, not just breakthroughs, but every day, are you thinking about what somebody else is doing? Have you seen a best practice? Can we learn from it; can we adapt it?

Now those are the kinds of things from an operational standpoint that I believe make companies come to life. Market size—yep, I'm sure it's important. Right category—sure it's important. Technology appropriate for it—sure it's important. But if they don't operate it, they're going to go out of business.

You can see that I feel very deeply about building the next Apple, the next Intel, the next Intuit. I have great pride in seeing companies go from start-up to some kind of durability. It takes great people, particularly a CEO who can manage, lead, set direction, make changes, and drive a company to both inventiveness and rigor.

Too often we build things with the attitude that "this is a start-up." That means we can be a little less rigorous, we can be a little more slovenly, we can allow 1,000 flowers to bloom. I don't agree. We need to be as rigorous as possible as early as possible.

I've watched many great opportunities go away because of bad management, because of a bad team, because VCs didn't pay attention.

My view for investors is that before they put their dollars anywhere, they should make sure that not only does the company have a vision, but that they also have a rigorous operating structure and philosophy.

→ THE FIFTH P—PROFITABILITY

"Show me the money!"   —ROD TIDWELL IN *JERRY MAQUIRE*

Lou Holtz was my college football coach when I was a *very* backup quarterback at the University of Minnesota. Coach Holtz is an amazing leader and without question would have been a world-class CEO if he wasn't a head football coach. Coach Holtz and I had a conversation about what ThinkEquity was doing. He loved the four Ps, but he had one question: Where are profits? And he could have asked, "How about the sixth P, P/E?"

Profits are critically important for a company to be successful. All companies are ultimately valued on future profits discounted back to today.

I believe that through proper analysis with a disciplined application of the four Ps, an investor can prudently invest in a company when it has negligible profits today or none at all.

Predicting what a company will look like three to five years from now is where art and science converge. While for a business to be successful and valuable, it needs to generate growing and sustainable profits, I think it's possible to invest in a company with the four Ps before profits are self-evident.

As to P/E multiples, while investing in companies with high P/E multiples is risky business and not for widows and orphans, the fastest-growing companies that produce the highest returns over time often have absolutely high P/Es. If we are right about the earnings growth, over time we will be right about the stock. Remember, the average P/E of the top 25 companies from 1995 to 2005 was 18.9x, hardly bargain basement.

The four Ps may seem a bit corny and unsophisticated—they are! But part of the secret to investing success is to make complex things simple and to use a systematic framework to achieve your objectives. The four Ps are the foundation I've built in my effort to identify and invest in the stars of tomorrow.

STAR GAZER

LOU HOLTZ
legendary football coach

Lou is one of the all-time greatest football coaches—with 249 career victories including a national championship at the University of Notre Dame in 1988. He has a track record of taking losing football programs and instantly turning them into champions. Coach Holtz's philosophy of "winning every day" is as applicable to growth companies and life as it is to football.

Michael Moe: *Coach, what are key attributes to winning every day?*

Lou Holtz: When I first went to the University of Notre Dame, Father Joyce said to me, "Coach, I want to cover some things with you that are not negotiable. You're not going to come here to Notre Dame and think you're going to change these things, 'cause these are not going to change while I'm here. We're going to play the most difficult schedule we can find. We expect to compete for the national championship at least once every three years. In addition to that, it's nonnegotiable that the head football coach at Notre Dame is not allowed to make more than the president of the University of Notre Dame. The president's a priest."

That being said, as we walked into a press conference, Father Joyce said, "Coach, I'd appreciate it if you wouldn't mention anything about the salary." I said, "Don't worry, Father. I'm as embarrassed about it as you are. I won't say a word."

But see, he didn't say one thing that would keep us from winning. He presented some obstacles. No matter what situation you find yourself in, there are going to be obstacles, and what I have found is there's usually going to be a solution to things.

Father Hesburgh said to me, "Coach, I could name you the head football coach of Notre Dame, 'cause titles come from above. What I cannot do is name you the leader, 'cause leadership is going to be determined by the people below." And I asked, "Well, Father Hesburgh, what is your definition of a leader?" He said, "A leader is somebody who has a vision and has a plan. That's all leadership is. It isn't about titles."

MM: *Coach, after you left Notre Dame, you went to South Carolina, which had the longest losing streak in Division 1 at the time. Why did you go there?*

LH: When you're down, you have two choices: you get up or you stay down. You can't count on anybody else to pick you up. Georgia isn't going to call and say, "You don't have a quarterback. Let me send you one." Twelve months after I got to South Carolina, a football team that had the longest losing streak in the country went to a Bowl game and beat Ohio State on January 1 the following year, and ended up 17th in the country. The following year, we beat Ohio State again on January 1, and ended up 11th in the country.

The point I'm making is, you're going to be down, you're going to have difficulty, and you can count only on yourself. That's why I hate it when people blame somebody else. I never allowed an athlete to blame somebody else, 'cause when you blame somebody else, you're saying, "I am not in control of my life. I can't get myself out of this situation." And the attitude you have as a leader is by far the most important thing, 'cause that attitude filters down; it doesn't come back up.

To me, the most important thing is an attitude of "I can do things."

MM: *What else does it take to win in sports and in life?*

LH: You have to have a passion for what you're doing. I believe Charlie Weiss is going to be exceptionally successful at the University of Notre Dame, 'cause he has a passion to be there.

I love to be around successful people. You show me a successful parent, businessperson, player, coach—I know the sacrifice they've had to make. Losers call it punishment. People want to be successful without making a sacrifice. You can't. And if you have a passion to do something, you're going to make sacrifices willingly.

MM: *What other key attributes are part of a winner's playbook?*

LH: The great football teams are the ones that can block and tackle. Great students are the ones that learn how to read and write. People get bored with fundamentals. A guy walked into a pet shop, wanted to buy a bird. They had all these birds for $1.25. The salesman told him, "You don't want that bird. I got the ideal bird for you. This bird over here is only $718." The guy said, "Well, the bird looks like the others." The salesman said, "This bird talks and sings." The guy said, "Gee. I'm alone. It's a lot of money, but I'd love to have the company," so he bought the bird.

He came in the next day and said, "I paid $718 for the bird. The bird don't talk or sing." The salesman said, "What did the bird do when he rang the bell?" The guy asked, "What bell?" The salesman said, "Didn't you buy the bell so the bird can get the proper tune?" The guy said, "No." The salesman told him,

"The bird ain't gonna talk or sing unless he can ring the bell, and the bell's only $9."

So he bought the bell and came back the next day, mad as all get-out. He said, "The bird don't talk or sing anything to the gotdog bell." And the salesman said, "That's impossible. I have the same type of bird as you. Just today, my bird got up, rang that little bell, ran up and down that ladder." The guy said, "What ladder?" The salesman said, "Didn't you buy the ladder so the bird can exercise?" He said, "No." "The ladder's $23."

This went on four days. Guy came in the fifth day and said, "I have $819 invested in the bird. Today, the bird finally talked to me just before he died. The bird got up this morning, rang that little bell, ran up and down that ladder, swung on the swing, looked in the mirror at all the things you sold me. Just before he died, he looked over at me and said, 'Did he sell you any bird seed?'"

See, we get caught up in all these fancy things and we forget the basic fundamentals. Another thing about a passion to win is that you get rid of all the excuses while you can. It's unbelievable how many people have an excuse. "We can't do this or this." Look for solutions, not problems.

MM: *What else is part of the plan?*

LH: The third point in the plan is to understand what you are doing. Too many people get confused. See, all you're trying to do is help customers get what they want. I'm not very smart, as I said, but I do have common sense. And all I try to do is simplify things. All I wanted to do was graduate athletes and win. Every decision I made was about how could we graduate and how could we win. Nothing else. It's just common sense.

Common sense. You show me any business that has a future, I'll show you one that's satisfying the needs of the customers.

I happened to be at the University of Arkansas and got to know Sam Walton pretty well. He first started a little store down in Newport, Arkansas, in 1946. His whole philosophy was "If we can buy low, we can sell cheap." He started out in just clothing—predominantly oversized dresses for ladies. He knew what he wanted to do; he knew what the customers wanted.

It's just like Starbucks. You look at any company—are you answering what the customers want?

MM: *You've always been able to adapt to new situations, different areas, teams with different offenses, different strategies.*

LH: You look at the Fortune 500 companies 50 years ago. Compare them with the Fortune 500 today. Not many are on both lists. Why? People's needs change. Are you changing to meet the needs of the people? Then embrace change. Nobody likes change.

I want to tell you, when I was at Notre Dame, when I was at Minnesota, I didn't like to throw the football. I always wanted to run the ball. It's not hard to run the ball. You take it, you turn, and you hand it to Ricky Waters or Jerome Bettis. Anybody can do that. Throwing the ball, now that's hard. You gotta drop back, read the coverage, and throw the ball. That's hard.

So I go to South Carolina. We go to run the ball. First, the quarterback takes the ball, turns to hand the ball, and Ricky Waters and Jerome Bettis aren't there. The guy that is there doesn't want the ball. And we go 0–11. Well, we had to change. We had to go to a shotgun-type offense, spread people out, throw.

Did I want to do that? No. But I had to do it if we were going to win. You have to embrace change as long as you're changing to meet the needs of the customers.

In 1878, they invented the typewriter. The problem with the

typewriter was if you typed too fast, the keys stuck. The guy said, "We'll never sell a typewriter if the keys stick." So he put together a committee to keep the keys from sticking.

The committee came back and said, "We got it solved." The guy said, "How'd you get it to type faster?" They said, "We can't do that. But we can keep the keys from sticking by forcing people to type slower." The guy said, "What do you mean?" They said, "All we have to do is hide the letters on the keypad. We'll put A up here, we'll put B down here, we'll stick C up here, we'll put Q there, we'll put R there, and nobody can type fast. They're going to have to hunt and they're gonna have to peck." Don't you wonder why the letters on the keypad are screwed up? That's so you couldn't type fast. Now today, try to change the letters on the keypad—people say, "Don't change that, see, because I know that." Embrace change as long as you're changing to meet the needs of the customers.

MM: *What else do winners do?*

LH: Winners are dreamers. Great things happen because somebody's a dreamer. One of the 10 greatest speeches known to man was Martin Luther King's "I Have a Dream" speech. Some of the other great ones were John F. Kennedy's, "Ask not what this country can do for you. Ask what you can do for your country," Abraham Lincoln's Gettysburg Address, Winston Churchill's "Never have so many owed so much to so few."

Martin Luther King stood up in Washington in front of 100,000 people. He said, "I have a dream." He motivated and inspired people. Do you think that speech would have that same effect had Martin Luther King stood up and said, "I have a strategic plan about how things are gonna work that I want to share with you"? Strategic plans don't excite anybody, but having a dream does.

There's a rule in life that says you're either growing or you're dying. A tree's either growing or it's dying and so is a business, so is a marriage, so is a person.

It doesn't have a thing to do with age. It has everything to do with whether you have any dreams, whether you have any aspirations. People need four things in life: Number one, you need something to do. Number two, you need someone to love. You need something to hope for. You need something to believe in.

That's what motivates you. It doesn't have a thing to do with age. At age 84, Winston Churchill, after being prime minister of England two different times, is in the House of Commons. And a guy walks up and says, "Happy 84th birthday, Mr. Churchill. Hope I get a chance to wish you a happy 100th. Do you think I'll get a chance to do that?" Winston paused for a minute and thought and looked at him and said, "Yeah. You look pretty healthy to me."

It's that mentality. Remember the word *win*. *Win* stands for *w*hat's *i*mportant *n*ow. You decide what you want to do. Ask yourself 25 times a day, "What's important now?"

MM: *Any more points on winning?*

LH: Evaluating and motivating people is key. People make the difference. You cannot win if you do not have the proper people. Not everybody comes to your organization the right way. I just had three simple rules that I felt enabled me to evaluate people and motivate them to be the best they could be. The three simple rules I've followed all my life are do right, do the best you can, show people you care.

Too many times when we're in a leadership role, we worry about being popular rather than having standards. I love Woody Hayes. I coached for Woody. We won the national championship, and yet Woody was insane. And I'm giving him the benefit of the doubt. But nobody had a greater influence on my life as a coach than Woody Hayes did. Why? 'Cause Woody Hayes believed in his people so strongly that he set that standard here. [Holtz puts his hand above his head.] If you weren't good enough, he wasn't worried about you being happy. He wanted you to be the best you could be and he pushed you and he drove you and he did whatever he had to do in order to get it.

But Woody Hayes believed in Lou Holtz more than I believed in myself. He believed in people; he set a standard. There are too many people who want to lower the standard.

Last, it's good to ask, If you didn't show up, who would miss you and why? If you didn't go home, would your family miss you? And if they wouldn't miss you, why? If your company didn't exist, would anybody miss it? You always want to say, "Am I important? Am I making a difference in people's lives?"

THINK POINTS

→ The four Ps—people, product, potential, and predictability—are the essential characteristics to analyze when investing in tomorrow's megawinners.

→ Price and profits aren't part of the four Ps—not because they don't matter, but many of the huge winners looked expensive on a P/E basis or were losing money when they started.

→ Two other Ps lead to large opportunities—where there are *problems* and where there is *pain*.

7

Valuation Methodology

"In the business world, the rearview mirror is always
clearer than the windshield."

— WARREN BUFFETT

SO FAR, I have spent most of the book evangelizing growth philosophy and providing a methodology on how to spot tomorrow's winners. I have wasted little ink on how to value a growth company even though, for many investors, that's the whole exercise.

It's not that I think valuation analysis isn't important. It's vitally important. But since my objective is to invest in companies that can go up 5 times, 10 times, or even more, my focus is on finding the companies that can have rapid earnings growth for a long period of time.

Having a valuation methodology, however, can provide rigor to analyzing a company's potential. Having a disciplined framework for valuing companies will reduce the risk of chasing a stock that's way ahead of itself without fundamentals to support it.

Whether a company is a high-octane biotech company or a pedestrian farming equipment manufacturer, we determine its intrinsic value in the same way—by calculating all the future earnings of that business and discounting those earnings back to today.

John Williams put forth this methodology in *The Theory of Investment Value,* which offered a formula for determining the intrinsic value of a stock. As Princeton professor Burton Malkiel has written, discounting is "a fiendishly clever attempt to keep things from being simple." Rather than seeing how much money you will have next year (say, $1.05 if you put $1 in a savings account at 5% interest), you look at money expected in the future and see how much less it is currently worth. Thus, next year's $1 is worth only about $.95 today, which could be invested at 5% to produce about $1 a year from now.

Discounted Cash Flow Formula

$$\text{Discounted cash flow} = \frac{CF^1}{(1+r)} + \frac{CF^2}{(1+r)^2} + \cdots + \frac{CF^n}{(1+r)^n}$$

$$CF = \text{Cash flow}$$
$$r = \text{Interest rate}$$
$$n = \text{Number of years}$$

Williams was actually serious about this, and although few people understood it (or perhaps because of that), it caught on in academic circles.

Here's the plain-English way to think about valuation. Let's say your neighbor Jimmy owns a lemonade stand. He wants to take in some investor partners so he has capital to grow. Lo and behold, Jimmy has built quite a lemonade stand. He is willing to sell half of his business for $1 million (valuing the entire business at $2 million).

To determine if that is a good deal, we need some other facts that Jimmy has provided in his private placement memorandum (PPM).

First, it turns out that Jimmy has grown his revenue from his lemonade stand from $100,000 when he started five years ago to $1 million today at a compound annual revenue growth of nearly 60%. Profits, or earnings, have grown even faster, from negligible in year 1 to $200,000 after tax this year. On a static basis, an investor would be paying 10 times earnings (P/E of 10x) to own a part of Jimmy's lemonade stand.

The question is whether this a good deal or a bad one.

Based on historical growth rates of north of 50%, a price of 10 times earnings would seem very cheap. Even based on no growth, an investor in the lemonade stand would get an earnings yield (earnings per share over the past 12 months divided by market price per share) of 10%, which is probably reasonable if 10-year bond yields are below 5%.

The problem is that the right way to value Jimmy's lemonade stand is based on its *future* earnings discounted back to today, not the past.

Let's say Jimmy didn't have plans to open any new lemonade stands and Susie, seeing the success her neighbor has had, decides to open a lemonade stand across the street. A vicious price war takes place and Jimmy's profits get cut in half. While business is not nearly as profitable as it was, both Susie and Jimmy can make a living with the new competition dynamics. Hence, future earnings from Jimmy's lemonade stand are $100,000 a year. With this scenario, an investor is paying a P/E of 20x on future earnings, which is not very compelling unless the discount rate is very low.

A more optimistic scenario is that Jimmy uses the new investment capital to rapidly expand his business. His dream is to be to lemonade what Starbucks is to coffee.

A demographic survey of attractive neighborhoods for new Jimmy's Lemonade stands determines that he can open 50 of them in the next five years and the potential beyond that is open-ended.

Fifty lemonade stands at $2 million per unit generates $100 million in revenue for Jimmy five years out. With a 10% net margin, Jimmy's Lemonade, Inc., is generating $10 million in after-tax profit, or five times more than the value of the entire business just five years earlier!

If we believed this scenario was likely, it would take a ridiculously high discount rate applied to these projected earnings to think Jimmy's Lemonade is not a compelling investment.

While "discounted cash flow" is the academically correct way to determine what a company is worth, it's only as good as the inputs based on future guesstimates. The mistake you often see the MBAs making is they actually believe the guesstimates are *real*.

The investor using the discounted cash flow is making assumptions about revenue growth, margins, and earnings a number of years out, applying a discount rate that may or may not be appropriate, handicapping risk and return, and putting a terminal multiple on those earnings. My point is, despite being the "correct" methodology, it's still at least as much art as science.

Two other valuation methodologies allow a growth investor to triangulate to get a good perspective on the current and correct value of an emerging growth company.

The first, P/E to growth (P/E/G), is the classic way growth investors have valued growth companies. To calculate P/E/G, divide a company's 12-month forward projected price/earnings ratio by the company's 3- to 5-year projected growth rate. So if ABC company's 12-month forward P/E is 20 and its 3- to 5-year estimated EPS growth rate is 20%, its P/E/G ratio is 1 or 100%. If its P/E is 30 and its growth rate is 20%, its P/E/G is 1.5 or 150%. Conversely, a company selling at a P/E of 10 and a growth rate of 20% has a P/E/G of .5 or 50%.

FORWARD P/E	3- TO 5-YEAR GROWTH	P/E TO GROWTH
20x	20%	100%
30x	20%	150%
10x	20%	50%

The rule of thumb is: a normal growth company selling in a normal market environment should trade at a P/E/G of 1 or 100%. The problem with this, of course, is defining *normal.*

The general variables that impact the P/E/G an investor is willing to pay are:

1. *Market cap/liquidity.* The larger the company and the greater liquidity, the greater the P/E/G investors will generally pay.
2. *Visibility of revenues and earnings.* The greater the visibility of future business prospects, the higher the P/E/G investors are willing to pay. Companies with recurring revenues have greater visibility, and generally sell at premium multiples to "normal companies."
3. *Projected growth rate.* The higher the growth rate, the higher an absolute P/E multiple an investor will pay, but the lower

the P/E/G ratio. In other words, the faster a company is expected to grow over the next 3 to 5 years, the less investors believe it and they won't give the company as much credit. The reality is, investors know it's exceedingly difficult to grow at 40 or 50% for any sustainable period. I'll never believe that a company will grow more than 40% over 3 to 5 years as the odds against it are so high. As Peter Lynch has said, "On Wall Street one bird in the hand is worth 10 in the bush."

4. *Interest rates.* In that growth companies are long-duration investments, higher interest rates make future earnings less valuable and accordingly will depress the P/E/G. Lower interest rates should have a positive impact on P/E/G ratios.

5. *General market sentiment.* When investors are bullish on the future, they will give more credit to "futures." If investors are pessimistic on the future and are looking backward, it will have a negative impact on P/E/Gs.

At ThinkEquity, we have created a P/E-to-growth matrix that establishes a framework for analyzing the appropriate P/E for a "normal" company versus its 3- to 5-year growth rate and current 10-year T-bill yield.

Back to my earlier point, the higher the 10-year T-bill yield, the lower the P/E an investor should pay for that growth.

For example, if we expect a company to grow earnings at 25% for the next 3 to 5 years and the 10-year T-bill rate is 5.0%, the P/E matrix shows the appropriate P/E is 24—essentially in line with its 25% EPS growth rate. With a 6.5% 10-year T-bill yield, the appropriate P/E is 17x. With a 3.5% 10 year-T-bill yield, the fair P/E is 38x.

The third technique we use to value emerging growth companies is to calculate a price to sales (P/S) multiple (share price × shares outstanding = market cap, or P in the equation) versus the company's revenue growth rate and its longer-term EBITDA (earnings before interest, taxes, depreciation, and amortization) margins. The higher the revenue growth and the higher the EBITDA margins, the higher the appropriate P/S.

A "normal" company, with an average revenue growth rate and average margins, should sell at a P/S multiple of approximately 1.0x. Normal for us is 10% revenue growth and 10% long-term EBITDA margins.

THINK P/E MATRIX

T-Bill Rate

GROWTH%	2.0%	2.5%	3.0%	3.5%	4.0%	4.5%	5.0%	5.5%	6.0%	6.5%
5%	34	27	22	19	17	15	13	12	11	10
10%	41	32	19	23	19	17	16	14	13	12
15%	50	39	32	27	23	20	18	16	15	13
20%	60	47	38	32	27	24	21	19	17	15
25%	72	56	45	38	32	28	24	22	19	17
30%	86	66	54	44	38	32	28	25	22	19
35%	102	78	63	52	44	38	33	29	25	21
40%	120	92	74	61	51	43	37	33	29	24
45%	141	108	86	70	59	50	43	37	32	28
50%	165	125	99	81	67	57	49	42	36	31

Source: Graham & Dodd's Security Analysis, ThinkEquity Partners.

A growing software company with 30% EBITDA margins might appropriately have a P/S of 3.0 or 4.0x. A moderately growing grocery business with 5% EBITDA margins might appropriately sell at 0.3 to 0.4x P/S.

P/S is a great valuation tool to triangulate the discounted cash flow method and P/E-to-growth-valuation technique.

P/S is particularly useful for emerging companies that aren't yet profitable or are just marginally profitable. P/S gives us a "here-and-now" reference point with current sales and a forecast of future margins that aren't easy to forecast, but certainly no more difficult than calculating future cash flows and growth rates.

I have created a P/S matrix to give investors a reference point for an appropriate P/S multiple versus its revenue growth and long-term EBITDA margins. This was created by analyzing a variety of companies and industries over a period of time. This is not a scientific chart, but it is a useful framework for evaluating high-growth companies, particularly when they have little or no earnings.

For example, a company that is growing its revenues at 25% with long-term EBITDA margins of 25% should sell at a P/S of approximately 3.2x. A company growing revenues at 10% with EBITDA margins of 15% should sell at a P/S of approximately 1.2x.

Factors that influence P/S multiples both positively and negatively include:

1. *Revenue visibility.* As with P/E/G, the more predictable future revenues are, the higher a multiple an investor will pay.
2. *Confidence in long-term margins.* Being able to project a company's long-term margins is a function of its competitive position, barriers to entry, and industry dynamics. Monopolies have predictable long-term margins; most other real companies don't.
3. *Market environment.* When investors are bullish, they will pay a higher P/S multiple and, when bearish, a lower multiple. Typically, the stock market bottoms when credit markets bottom.

I look at all valuation techniques as both art and science. While I believe strongly that the most important element for successful investing

THINK P/S MATRIX

EBITDA MARGIN	Revenue Growth										
	0%	5%	10%	15%	20%	25%	30%	35%	40%	45%	50%
50%	2.5x	3.3x	4.0x	4.8x	5.6x	6.3x	7.1x	7.9x	8.7x	9.4x	10.2x
45%	2.3x	2.9x	3.6x	4.3x	5.0x	5.7x	6.4x	7.1x	7.8x	8.5x	9.2x
40%	2.0x	2.6x	3.2x	3.8x	4.5x	5.1x	5.7x	6.3x	6.9x	7.5x	8.2x
35%	1.8x	2.3x	2.8x	3.4x	3.9x	4.4x	5.0x	5.5x	6.1x	6.6x	7.1x
30%	1.5x	2.0x	2.4x	2.9x	3.3x	3.8x	4.3x	4.7x	5.2x	5.7x	6.1x
25%	1.3x	1.6x	2.0x	2.4x	2.8x	3.2x	3.6x	3.9x	4.3x	4.7x	5.1x
20%	1.0x	1.3x	1.6x	1.9x	2.2x	2.5x	2.8x	3.2x	3.5x	3.8x	4.1x
15%	0.8x	1.0x	1.2x	1.4x	1.7x	1.9x	2.1x	2.4x	2.6x	2.8x	3.1x
10%	0.5x	0.7x	0.8x	1.0x	1.1x	1.3x	1.4x	1.6x	1.7x	1.9x	2.0x
5%	0.3x	0.3x	0.4x	0.5x	0.6x	0.6x	0.7x	0.8x	0.9x	0.9x	1.0x

Source: Graham & Dodd's Security Analysis, ThinkEquity Partners.

in big winners is to be right on the fundamentals—the four Ps—having a rigorous valuation process will benefit investors by providing a disciplined approach to buying a great growth company.

→ **THE SIX Is (AND ONE E)**

"Markets can remain irrational longer than you can remain solvent."
— JOHN MAYNARD KEYNES

One of the characteristics of great investors is that they make complex things simple. How do you make the best returns in the stock market long term? Find the fastest-growing companies with the four Ps, close your eyes, take a deep breath, and hold on for the ride.

That's simple and theoretically correct, but back on planet Earth we have to be at least aware of the short-term realities of the stock market. Ben Graham's voting machine versus a weighing machine is a great analogy to understand how the market works in the short term and how it works in the long term.

In the short term, the market is like a voting machine that reflects the mood of the moment: what's popular and what's not; market sentiment; and the conventional wisdom of the day. In the long term, the market is like a weighing machine and it measures only one thing: earnings.

We win by identifying and investing in companies that generate the most earnings and earnings growth, but the rule is that you must be present to win.

To help understand the near-term influences of stock price movement, I track six variables that I call the six Is. These six Is—*inflation, interest rates, indices (market valuation), investor sentiment, inflows (outflows) to equity funds, and IPO pricing*—impact the near-term direction of emerging growth stock prices.

While these six Is are important because they give me clues to the type of stock environment I am in, I don't want to lose sight of the one E—*earnings*—that ultimately matters. These six Is could effectively be viewed as a weather report to consult before playing a round of golf. It's helpful for me to know if it's windy, rainy, or cold so I know what I'm going to face and can be prepared. If the weather is so bad that it's impossible to go out and play, I can wait in the clubhouse until playing conditions get better. But in the end, all that matters is what the scorecard says after 18 holes!

Inflation

Inflation is an increase in the general level of prices and a fall in the purchasing power of money. The lion's share of value for growth companies is based on their *future* earnings, so inflation, which makes these future earnings less valuable today, has an outsized negative impact for growth companies.

Going back to the concept of "discounting" future earnings, the rate of inflation is a primary driver of the appropriate discount rate.

Inflation also has a direct impact on company profitability. In a low-inflation or deflationary environment, the risk for companies making long-term investment decisions lessens. True growth companies should have disproportionate advantages in low-growth and/or low-inflation environments. Conversely, in periods of high or accelerating inflation, the risk of profitability eroding increases, as does the difficulty in calculating long-term investment outlays. Accordingly, monitoring inflation trends is the most useful in understanding short-term risk for emerging stock prices.

Interest Rates

It makes intuitive sense that the higher the here-and-now interest on CDs or yield on bonds is, the less growth companies' future earnings are worth today. Of course, the reverse is also true. The lower the interest rates are, the more valuable future earnings are today.

Academically, interest rates in their own right don't reflect anything more than the present value of future payments. Sometimes, the relationship between interest rates and stock performance can provide a false picture. If, for example, economic growth is accelerating—which is usually good for stocks—interest rates could rise, devaluing future earnings.

While the perception of risk with higher interest rates may be somewhat overblown, the fact remains that the bulk of a company's earnings

S&P 500: P/E-Inflation Trade-off

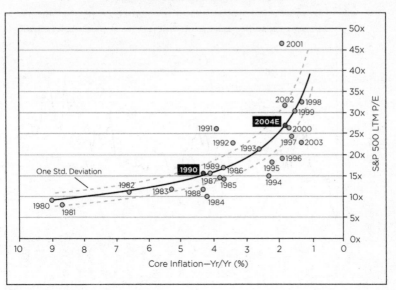

Source: ThinkEquity Partners.

to be received by stock investors is much farther out into the future. The net result of this is that growth companies are more severely impacted by fluctuating interest rates than is the overall market.

By looking inside the current level of interest rates, we can better understand whether interest rates reflect inflationary concerns that have yet to materialize or a rise in equity risk-aversion.

In our equity market valuation model, rather than just comparing 10-year Treasury bond yields to expected earnings, we also look at the "risk-aversion spread," which involves looking at the difference between 10-year AAA corporate yields and 10-year Treasuries to specifically measure the equity risk question.

The effects of heightened equity risk-aversion is very real for growth stocks. For example, in 2002, corporate earnings grew nearly 19%, yet the S&P 500 declined 23%. The decline was a result of a sharp reduction in P/E multiples due to a gigantic equity risk-aversion spread (EPS increase of 19% + P/E decline of -42% = -23% S&P 500).

A simple observation might suggest that the market was overvalued with a P/E of 29x, but what impacted the P/E multiple was the signifi-

Post–9-11 investors are more risk averse

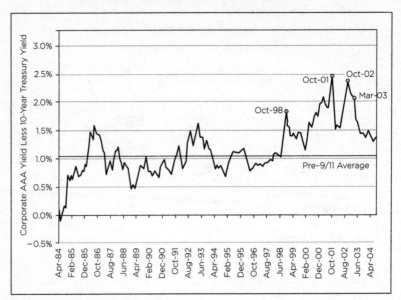

Source: ThinkEquity Partners.

cant increase in investors' equity risk-aversion as evidenced by the spread between Treasuries and AAA.

Bringing this into the real world, if earnings growth is going up and share prices are going down, it generally signifies a long-term buying opportunity.

Indices (Market Valuation)

By understanding the relative valuation of the market versus historic data and in context with the current growth and interest rate environment, we get perspective on near-term risk and opportunity.

Historically, the P/E for the S&P 500 is 14x, and earnings have grown at 7% with a 3% dividend yield, with inflation of about 3%. So, for example, if the P/E for the S&P 500 was 20x and EPS growth was expected to be 5% and inflation was 8%, I would be very worried about the near-term vulnerability of the market. On the flip side, if the P/E was 10x, the EPS growth was 20%, and inflation was 1%, I'd be backing up the truck.

We've developed a simple model that reflects the market's (S&P 500's) historical valuation relative to the core rate of inflation. In using this model, what we hope to glean is whether the market is fairly valued, given our two primary concerns: earnings growth and the rate of inflation.

$$\text{fair value of an index} = [\text{next 12 months EPS estimate} + \text{current quarter dividends} \times 4]/\text{corporate AAA yield}$$

Investor Sentiment

Valuation levels by definition reflect investors' sentiments but leave much to be desired in explaining market moves in the absence of fundamental changes. A classic way to gauge investor sentiment is to simply ask them, "Are you bullish or bearish?"

Investor sentiment polls are fraught with issues, but they are somewhat useful to get a general sense of investor optimism/pessimism with the usefulness driven as a contrarian indicator.

When investors are at bullish extremes, it's generally a warning signal to be cautious. When investors are at negative extremes, it's generally a good time to get more opportunistic. As Warren Buffett famously said, the key to investing is to "be fearful when others are greedy and greedy when others are fearful."

We find put/call ratios, short interest, and cash ratios in mutual funds to be more useful than sentiment polls because they reflect what investors are doing as opposed to what they are saying. Again, the value of analyzing these ratios is as a contrarian sentiment indicator (i.e., heavy shorting in the market is bullish; low levels of cash in mutual funds is bearish, etc.).

Inflows (Outflows) to Equity Funds

At the end of the day, the stock market, like all markets, is a function of supply and demand. Inflows into equity mutual funds are critical to understand the supply and demand fundamentals of the stock market.

Demand is created by cash inflows into equity mutual funds, corporate stock buybacks, and mergers and acquisitions done in cash. Supply is mainly the stock manufactured by Wall Street in the form of IPOs and follow-ons.

Cash inflows or outflows into funds could be looked at as a contrarian indicator, but we have found the correlation to be suspect at best. I look at inflows into equity mutual funds as potential firepower and see outflows as a fundamental drain on demand. Viewing these supply/demand basics is extremely valuable in understanding near-term influences on the market.

Net New Flows into Equity Mutual Funds

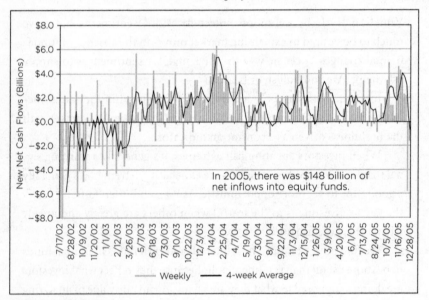

Source: AMG Data.

IPO Pricing

One of the most useful week-to-week indicators of true investor sentiment is IPO pricing relative to a company's filing range. Unlike an "Are you a bull or a bear?" survey, IPO pricing is a real-world indicator of how investors are actually voting—with their cash. Historically, IPO pricing has been an effective tool for measuring the relative strength and health of investor sentiment, by capturing not only how investors are monetizing their sentiment, but also whether they are becoming excessively optimistic or pessimistic.

In a normal market environment we would anticipate that roughly 20% of new IPOs' prices would be above the filing range, 60% within the range, and the remaining 20% below. Additionally, we would expect an IPO to have a "pop"—trading up 10 to 15%. In a frothy market, 50% or more of the IPOs may price above the filing price and the IPO pop may be 25% or more.

In a very pessimistic market, IPO pricing is weak. Very few if any IPOs' prices are above the filing range, there is a minimal IPO pop, and, in fact, many new issues trade down.

When the market gets too hot, something always happens to cool it down. This is the greatest risk with high-multiple, high-octane growth companies.

→ STAR GAZER

DREW CUPPS
president and founder of Cupps Capital Management

Before founding CCM, Drew Cupps managed hedge fund assets and was the growth specialist on the Strong Alternative Investments Team at Strong Capital Management, Inc. Drew has also worked for Driehaus Capital Management. (To read my full interview with Drew Cupps, visit www.findingthenextstarbucks.com.)

I think that probably the best advice [for investors looking for the stars of tomorrow] is to marry a few bits of wisdom. One of them is investing in what you know. Try to find opportunities to invest in what you know and invest in a product that you think fits tomorrow, fits what we will all be doing and thinking and using tomorrow, with a company/stock that's getting validation from the marketplace. Those are probably the three criteria that, when you can fit them all together, will give you your best success.

THINK POINTS

→ Discounted cash flow, P/E to growth, and price to sales
are the three primary valuation techniques for growth
companies.

→ Price to sales is particularly useful for a fast-growing but
unprofitable (or barely profitable) emerging company.

→ Long-term earnings growth is what determines stock
performance, but in the short term, a number of factors
influence share price, including inflation, interest rates,
index valuations, investor sentiment, inflows (outflows)
into mutual funds, and IPO activity.

8

Sources and Resources—
Finding Ideas

"The person that turns over the most rocks wins the game.
And that's always been my philosophy."
—PETER LYNCH

SO WE HAVE A PHILOSOPHY—*earnings growth drives stock price.*
We have some core principles to guide our investment process—the *10
Commandments.* We have a framework for looking at industries that are
benefiting from secular tailwinds—*megatrend analysis.* We have a discipline for analyzing the core fundamentals of a great growth company—
the four Ps. We have a valuation methodology that gives us a perspective
on the relative value of a company—the 6 Is, P/E to growth, and P/S versus margins and growth.

But we still need to find ideas to funnel into our process.

To locate great ideas on where tomorrow's stars will be, you need a
systematic and strategic process, just like you do to analyze these ideas
once you find them. In a world of information overload, what's the best
way to prioritize your time and resources?

There is no getting around it; the harder you work, the more good
ideas you are going to find (the harder I work, the luckier I get)! But it's
important to work smart.

The Internet is the world's most efficient research tool, and Google
is the engine that drives it. In the old days, subscribing to dozens of
regional newspapers and observing magazines was a way to flag ideas
early. Now, Google will push relevant articles onto your desktop.

Reading newspapers and magazines, listening to industry experts, knowing what smart public and private investors are doing, and asking the right questions when doing your homework (who is your toughest competitor and why?) are all part of the idea toolbox.

I read four newspapers a day, including the *New York Times* for the news, *USA Today* to get a pulse on what the average American is thinking, the *Wall Street Journal* to know what the investment community is thinking, and the *San Jose Mercury News* so I'm not clueless in my community (it also has a very good business section). I've tried to read the *Financial Times* for a global perspective, but aside from the famous Lex Column, I find it not worth my time or $1 newsstand price.

I read, or I should say scan, those four papers in no more than 20 minutes. But if I were going to read one newspaper, it would be *Investor's Business Daily (IBD)*. It's 50 times more useful for growth ideas than the four others combined. *Investor's Business Daily* is systematic about providing valuable data that I can use to examine companies and industries that could be of interest.

I first go to the "Daily Graph" section that highlights companies that are experiencing investor interest. Increased investor attention can be an early indicator that something is going positive in a company; good financial numbers often follow.

Next, I look at companies making the "New Highs" list—again a fertile ground for identifying companies whose fundamentals are good and getting better. The "buy cheap stocks" crowd laughs at people like me who are looking at companies that are making new market highs because all the smart people know that "you buy low and sell high." However, my simple brain knows that Wal-Mart, Starbucks, Dell, and Yahoo! were by definition making new highs routinely. Wal-Mart, on its way to a $200 billion market cap, made "new highs" at $500 million, $1 billion, $5 billion, $25 bilion, and so on. Conversely, most of the companies that were in the bargain basement were never heard from again. I agree with Peter Lynch—I don't mind buying high and selling higher.

I then go to the "Earnings News" section, looking for rapidly growing companies, preferably those with accelerating revenue and earnings growth.

Next I read the "New America" section, which often highlights small, emerging companies. The articles on these companies are unlikely to receive a Pulitzer Prize, but "New America" highlights emerging companies well.

The "Internet & Technology" and "Health & Medicine" sections often highlight emerging trends and new leaders. I always review the recent and upcoming IPO table to see what's new and what's hot. IPOs are a gold mine to identify new potential leaders.

The last table I look at daily is the top-performing industry groups. *IBD* ranks 197 industry groups daily with leading groups often signaling strong underlying fundamental growth.

On Friday there is a special "Weekend Section" showing stock charts with fundamental data such as historic earnings growth, relative strength, and earnings momentum for dozens of companies.

Mondays' *IBD* (which you can pick up on Saturday) ranks the 100 strongest growth companies by sales momentum, earnings growth, margins, and ROE.

Does it seem ridiculous that I just walked through how to read a newspaper? The funny thing is, if investors searching for tomorrow's big winners just did what I described in a disciplined fashion, they would have a decent chance for success. All it takes is 20 minutes and $1.25. The online version, investors.com, is good, but I like the actual paper.

Key Features of *Investor's Business Daily*

"NASDAQ Stocks in the News"

"New Highs and Lows"

"Earnings News"

"New America"

"Internet & Technology"

"Health & Medicine"

"Industry Groups"

"Friday's Weekend Graphs"

"Monday's *IBD* 100"

"New Issues"

I get dozens of magazines to get a general pulse for business. Tim Mullaney, who writes on technology trends in *BusinessWeek,* has an excellent nose for ideas.

I think *Newsweek* does the best job of general news reporting, and its "Conventional Wisdom" summary gives an edgy perspective on newsmakers of the day. The political cartoons provide a pulse on what society is thinking.

Fortune has very good business articles, and *Forbes* has some interesting profiles, but it's rare to find anything terribly insightful regarding where the future winners will be.

If I could read only one business or news magazine, there is no question it would be *The Economist,* which is incredible. Besides providing well-written, well-reported global insights on business, politics, and society, *The Economist* has very well researched quarterly industry pieces that are chock-full of great information.

Will we find great investment ideas in any of the general periodicals? Not often, but it helps to create a worldview that ideas need to be filtered through.

Wired and *Business 2.0* provide a forward-looking approach and both often highlight cool new technologies and offer a window to the future.

The blogosphere is without question the place where the best dialogue on tomorrow's winners will take place. The hard part will be to sort through the noise and engage in smart conversation.

I am a contributor and fan of Tony Perkins's *AlwaysOn Open Media.* It's early in terms of the richness in dialogue, but there are already some outstanding contributors and great ideas.

On ThinkEquity's blog (*ThinkBlog*), we link to some of our favorite blogs, which include Bill Gurley's *Above the Crowd* as well as Bill Burnham's blog.

Some of the blogs I love include:

AlwaysOn Network (alwayson-network.com)

Bill Burnham (billburnham.blogs.com/burnhamsbeat)

Bill Gurley (abovethecrowd.com)

Business 2.0 Blog (business2.blogs.com/business2blog)

Canslim Investing (canslim.net)

Capital Spectator (capitalspectator.com)

Engadget (engadget.com)

Gizmodo (gizmodo.com)

Hidden Gems (investorideas.com)

Jonathan Schwartz's Blog (blogs.sun.com/jonathan)

Mark Cuban's *Blog Maverick* (blogmaverick.com)

PIMCO's Investment Outlook from Bill Gross (pimco.com)

Seeking Alpha (seekingalpha.com)

The Big Picture (bigpicture.typepad.com)

The Healthcare Blog (thehealthcareblog.com)

ThinkBlog (thinkequity.com/blog)

VentureBeat (venturebeat.com)

VentureBlog (ventureblog.com)

Wired (blog.wired.com)

I also track leading growth investors and venture capitalists in terms of investments they are making. This may not sound terribly original, but if you'd bought the stocks Warren Buffett listed in the must-read Berkshire Hathaway Annual Report every year, you would have dramatically outperformed the market.

> **STAR GAZER**

RICHARD PERKINS
founder, president, portfolio manager, and director of Perkins Capital Management

Richard ("Perk") Perkins has been investing in emerging growth companies for more than 50 years. Prior to founding Perkins Capital Management, Perk was head of Institutional Sales and Research at Piper Jaffray. Perk started his career as the portfolio manager for the Mayo Clinic Foundation. (To read my full interview with Richard Perkins, visit www.findingthenext starbucks.com.)

> I think the big thing in this business is reading and reading and reading. I read six newspapers a day. And I'm looking at all sorts of things because you never know where you're going to find the idea.

Similarly, tracking what all-star emerging growth portfolio managers have invested in can be a great source of ideas.

Investors we track include Richard Driehaus of Driehaus Capital Management, Joe McNay from Essex, Ron Baron and Cliff Greenberg of Baron Asset Management, Dick Gilder of Gilder Gagnon, Art Samberg of Pequot, Drew Cupps of Cupps Asset Management, and Jack Laporte of T. Rowe Price. These investors have shown a consistent ability to be early and right in many of the big winners in the market.

I track the following public growth investors:

Art Samberg, Pequot

Cliff Greenberg, Baron
  Asset Management

Dick Gilder, Gilder Gagnon

Dick Perkins, Perkins Capital

Drew Cupps, Cupps
  Asset Management

Hans Utsch, Federated
  Kaufmann

Jack Laporte, T. Rowe Price

Jim Callinan, RS

Joe McNay, Essex

Mark Waterhouse, The Hartford

Richard Driehaus, Driehaus
  Capital Management

Rick Leggott, Arbor Capital

Ron Baron, Baron Asset
  Management

Tom Press, American Growth
  Century

It's a bit more difficult to get this information for free, but Yahoo! Finance lists shareholders at no cost and Bloomberg, Thomson, William O'Neil (the publisher of *Investor's Business Daily*), and Big Dough are all services that provide institutional portfolio holdings.

On the venture capital side, there are more than 500 venture capital firms, but relatively few are routinely involved with the huge winners. In venture capital, firms with previous success have an unfair advantage because an entrepreneur with a hot idea will want one of the leading venture groups to invest to give his or her company the Good Housekeeping Seal of approval.

Kleiner Perkins and Sequoia were allowed to invest in Google. Undoubtedly, there were other VCs that may have paid three times the price, but the Google management team wanted the imprimatur of the gold-plated VC firms.

Some of the venture capital firms we focus on are Kleiner Perkins (the New York Yankees of venture capital, with legendary partners John Doerr and Vinod Khosla); Sequoia (the Boston Red Sox, with Michael Moritz and Don Valentine); Benchmark (with Bruce Dunlevie, Kevin Harvey, and Bob Kagle); NEA (with Dick Kramlich); Battery; Bain; Warburg Pincus; MPM; Versant; Redpoint (with Geoff Yang); and Draper Fisher Jurvetson (with Tim Draper and Steve Jurvetson).

By no means is this a comprehensive list of venture firms that have great portfolio companies, but by just monitoring this handful of firms, an investor will be on top of many of the important trends and ideas over the next 10 years—because that's the time frame for which great VCs are investing. Similarly, if I wanted to spot the next blockbuster film, I'd track what Steven Spielberg was working on.

The government puts out some great information as well. The U.S. Department of Labor provides data on where the market job growth is, what cities are booming, hot careers, and good general economic indicators. The U.S. Department of Energy gives great info on alternative energy and initiatives in energy technology. The U.S. Bureau of the Census provides information on everything you could want to know about the U.S. population and demographic trends. The Centers for Disease Control and Prevention (CDC) has tremendous information about health, medical, and safety issues.

VCs WE TRACK

NAME	PAST	FUTURE
Accel	Verilas, Walmart.com, Macromedia, Wiley, Perabit, Polycom, RealNetworks	JBoss, Xensource, facebook.com
Bain	Shopping.com, Web Methods, Taleo Corp	El Dorado Marketing, UGS, M-Qube
Battery Ventures	Akamai	Arbor Networks, Ruckus Network, IP Unity, BladeLogic, Netezza, Aurora Networks
Benchmark	Red Hat, Palm, Jamdat, AOL, Nordstrom.com, eBay	Jamba Juice, Nansolar, Tropos Neworks, Kalido, LogoWorks, Good Technology, Tellme, CollabNet, eBags, Kontiki
The Carlyle Group	Align Technology, Blackboard, ctrip.com, Duratek	Ingenio, Pacific Telecom, Target Media Network
Crescendo Ventures	Ciena, Digital Island, Aljety, Ejasent, Lightspeed	Broadsoft, Esilicon, Envivio, Tropic Networks, Pure Digital
DFJ	Skype, Baidu, NetZero, Hotmail, Focus Media, Overture	Epocrates, Nano Opto, Nanostring, ZettaCore, Ingenio, Technoratti, Zars, Visto, Molecular Imprints, Neophotonics
General Atlantic	MarketWatch, Daksh, E*Trade, Manugistics, Staples.com	SSA Global, Hewitt Associates, webloyalty.com, Lenovo, Zagat.com, ProPay
Kleiner Perkins	Amazon, Google, Genentech, Netscape, Sun, Symantec	Good Technology, Tellme Networks, PodShow, Visible Path, Zazzle, Digital Chocolate, IP Unity, Zettacore, 3VR

VCs WE TRACK

NAME	PAST	FUTURE
Maveron	eBay, Quellos	Cranium, Potbelly's, EOS, Good Technology, El Dorado Marketing
Mobius	Yahoo!	Sling Media, Pay By Touch, Postini, Reactrix, LR Learnings
MPM	Acorda, Idenix, Pharmasset	Affymax, Elixir Pharmaceuticals
NEA	FoxHollow Technologies, Juniper Networks, Salesforce.com, WebEx, WebMD	Ion America, Alien Technology, Glu Mobile, United Platform Tech, IP Unity, Visto
Redpoint	AskJeeves, Foundry Networks, Netflix, Polycom, Sybase, TiVo, MySpace.com, MusicMatch	MobiTV, Fotinet, BigBand Networks, Calix Networks
Sequoia Capital	Apple, Atari, Oracle, Symantec, Electronics Arts, PayPal, Google, Yahoo!	GameFly, Digital Chocolate, eHarmony, FON, LinkedIn, Plaxo, PodShow, WeatherBug, Zappos.com, Netezza, ProSoght
TCV	Altiris, Expedia.com, Netflix, Real Networks, CNet	eBags, eHarmony, Liquidnet, Thinkorswim, TechTarget
Versant	Combichem, Coulter Pharmaceutical, CV Therapeutics, Onyx Pharmaceutical, Symyx, Tularik, Valentis	Jazz Pharmaceuticals, Novacea, Pharmion, Reliant, Salmedix, Syrrx
Warburg Pincus	BEA, NeuStar, Kyphon, Avaya	4GL School Solutions, Aspen Education Group, The Cobalt Group, Kineto Wireless, UGS

9

Think Tomorrow, Today—Hot Areas for Future Growth

"There are no great limits to growth because there are no limits of human intelligence, imagination, and wonder."

—RONALD REAGAN

THUS FAR, WE'VE SPENT most of our time in this book creating a timeless framework to identify and invest in the stars of tomorrow. In this chapter I use this framework to identify 16 investment areas that investors should look at today to find tomorrow's huge winners. Undoubtedly, the shelf life for some of these areas will be short, and my ideas may in hindsight seem silly, but that is the nature of growth investing. And creating these forward-looking scenarios or themes is a critical step in spotting future winners.

→ **WEB 2.0—JOHN DOERR WAS RIGHT!**

When RCA's David Sarnoff introduced television sets at the World's Fair in New York in 1939, people knew it was the beginning of something big, but the early applications were to take what was previously done on the old medium—radio—and put it on the new medium—TV. Families would sit around and watch announcers in front of a microphone (like Don Imus and Howard Stern today!).

The bridge to a new medium almost always starts by taking the old material and processes and transferring them to the new medium. Accordingly, the first phase of the Internet, Web 1.0, was dominated by businesses that tried to put everything and anything on this exciting new medium and companies that created a connection to the Net.

Yahoo!'s early days basically involved putting a yellow pages online. Banner ads swarmed static Web sites. Then brick-and-mortar businesses began webifying themselves. Netscape was the "on-ramp" to the superhighway and AOL helped nontechies get online.

As with going from radio to TV, this new medium was breathtakingly exciting, almost magic, but few people had reconceptualized the true power of the Internet and how new models would emerge to change the game.

BUBBLE VERSUS BOOM AT A GLANCE		
	1999	2006
Who's online	You, but not your parents	Practically everyone
Broadband lifestyle	Huh?	Duh.
Cost to start a company	Super Bowl ads, rooftop parties, Sun servers	Linux, blog buzz, dirt-cheap whatever boxes
Exit strategy	IPO	Yahoo!
Source: Wired magazine.		

Web 2.0, a term coined by Dale Dougherty and Tim O'Reilly, implies that following the dot.com crash, far from being dead, the Web became even more important than before. The companies that survived the nuclear winter were thriving and creating exciting new applications like Wikipedia and BitTorrent.

The key principle behind Web 2.0 is that the Internet has emerged as the fundamental global platform for communications, commerce, information, services, and product development.

Microsoft illustrated the power of a platform with its pre–Web 2.0-era dominance thanks to the Windows operating system. It brilliantly (and arguably unfairly) used its dominant position to bury peripheral competing products to its application suite. Despite having a better product than any Microsoft offered, Lotus 1-2-3, WordPerfect, and Netscape Navigator were all crushed by Microsoft's better business model. Aces beat jacks, and platforms beat products.

The Evolution of the Web

Web 1.0	Web 2.0
DoubleClick	→ Google AdSense
Ofoto	→ Flickr
Akamai	→ BitTorrent
mp3.com	→ Napster
Britannica Online	→ Wikipedia
Personal Web sites	→ Blogging
Evite	→ Upcoming.org and EVDB
Domain name speculation	→ Search engine optimization
Page views	→ Cost per click
Screen scraping	→ Web services
Publishing	→ Participation
Content management systems	→ Wikis
Directories (taxonomy)	→ Tagging ("folksonomy")
Stickiness	→ Syndication

Source: Tim O'Reilly.

The second key concept of Web 2.0 is to tap into the collective intelligence of the Web. James Surowiecki's excellent book *The Wisdom of Crowds* provides compelling examples of how the collective intelligence of many is much more powerful than the opinion of even the smartest individual.

Creating a network effect and leveraging the collective intelligence of the World Wide Web is at the core of many of today's most powerful business opportunities.

Google is unquestionably the poster boy for Web 2.0 and has established itself as the platform to beat. Search is where it all begins, and Google is "at First and Main." Gmail, Google Earth, Froogle, Orkut, and Google News are all strategic in expanding and enhancing its leadership position.

Google's algorithm is made better by more users. Ditto for eBay and Amazon.

My firm was the first on Wall Street to have a blog (www.think equity.blog). Tapping into the collective intelligence of investors in a specific sector or company is extremely powerful and could radically change the way Wall Street research is coordinated.

The reason Zagat in New York City is so amazingly on-target is it has 100,000 people contributing to the opinions it publishes. Wikipedia is a wildly successful online encyclopedia written by users, and anyone who wants to can edit it. Imagine how that model can be applied to stocks.

The key principles of Web 2.0 are:

1. The Web as a platform
2. Collective intelligence
3. Database management
4. The end of software release cycles

As it turns out, John Doerr was right—the Web was underhyped!

Visit www.findingthenextstarbucks.com for information on the following hot companies in the growth area of Web 2.0:

Hot Companies in Web 2.0

51QB	eBags
Alibaba.com	eHarmony
AllConnect	Google (GOOG)
Art.com	inQuira
Baidu	iSold It on eBay
Beijing Lingtu Software	Liquidnet
Bocom Digital	LogoWorks
ChinaHR.com	Progressive Gaming (PGIC)
CollabNet	Ruckus Network

Tropos Networks

Visible Path

WeatherBug

Youbet.com (UBET)

Zappos.com

Zazzle.com

STAR GAZER

RON CONWAY
founding partner of Angel Investors

Ron has been prominent in Silicon Valley since he co-founded Altos Computer in 1979. He focuses on very early stage investments, especially in the wireless, infrastructure, and communications spaces. His home-run investments include Ask Jeeves, Google, and PayPal. I asked Ron if he thinks that Silicon Valley will be as influential in the future as it has been over the past 20 years. (To read my full interview with Ron Conway, visit www.findingthenextstarbucks.com.)

I think for sure Silicon Valley will continue to dominate in innovation in high technology of all kinds: in medical technology, biotechnology, the Internet, software. It's because Silicon Valley has a built-in infrastructure to support start-ups that's unparalleled by any other. We have the accountants, the lawyers, the mentors, the board of directors members all at your disposal in one 50-mile radius to serve entrepreneurs. And there's no other place like that in the world where the infrastructure is so deep and so sophisticated in all areas to support start-up companies.

With the advent of the Internet and search technologies, we're going to be moving the $50 billion advertising market from TV and radio to the Internet, and that's going to produce billions and billions of dollars of growth for Silicon Valley just in the Internet search advertising market. Stem cell research and other medical research are also located right here in Silicon

Valley, with Stanford and UCSF [University of California at San Francisco]. So, I couldn't be more optimistic about the next 20 years.

→ **ONLINE ADVERTISING: ONE-ON-ONE MARKETING**

The old paradigm was that the TV network was in control of what was watched and when it was watched. Television producers constantly interrupted programs to sell you something irrelevant. In the new paradigm, you are in control of getting what you want, when you want it.

Globally, $500 billion a year is spent to inspire purchases, to create awareness, and to build brands. The old advertising truism is that 50% of all money spent on advertising is wasted; we just don't know which 50%! The Net changes this because now we do know.

Traditional network television and cable commercials, historically the preferred channel for advertisers, are being TiVo'd and remote controlled away. Moreover, network TV audience has fallen by one-third since 1985.

Newspapers are under attack on every front, with circulation and challengers impacting local advertising in material ways. By the end of 2004, circulation had declined 14% from 1987. We expect this trend to accelerate with the introduction of more powerful, smaller, and lighter next-generation handsets, PDAs, and notebooks.

Magazine circulation peaked in 2000 and is now at 1974 levels. Traditional radio listenership is at a 27-year low, while commercial-free satellite radio, led by XM and Sirius, is growing in subscribers at a rate of more than 30% per year. Telemarketers are being outlawed (thank God!) with 65 million households now on the national "do not call" registry.

Digitization of media = digitization of advertising and marketing services.

As media becomes digital, all marketing services companies must become digital as well. The principles of targeted marketing, ROI (return on investment), and measurability developed from Internet advertising will become the standard for buying all forms of media.

The new code of advertising will be driven by analytics and metrics, disciplines that are countercultural to the creative-oriented, traditional model.

In 2005, $13 billion was spent on online advertising—which is 4% of all spending on marketing in the United States. While this is up dramatically from historic levels, it is significantly below the percentage of free time that consumers spend online—18%. The Internet's continuing growth in terms of usage vis-à-vis other mediums, fueled in part by the broad adoption of broadband and the dislocation of the other mediums, will provide gigantic growth in the foreseeable future for online advertising companies.

The democratization of media giving consumers more access, choice, and involvement will favor advertisers that provide one-on-one marketing—messages that are highly relevant for *me*.

Blogs represent an emerging threat to traditional media and an opportunity for those who take advantage of them. The self-selection among blog participants is a marketer's dream, especially in very unique, targeted categories. People who blog about flying and private planes are going to be rich targets for groups like NetJet and Cessna.

U.S. INTERNET ADVERTISING ($ BILLION)

	2002	2003	2004	2005	2006E	2007E	2008E	2003–08 CAGR
Keyword search	0.9	2.5	3.9	5.5	7.3	9.2	11.2	34%
Display ads	1.7	1.5	1.8	2.5	3.1	3.7	4.4	24%
Classifieds	0.9	1.2	1.7	2.3	2.8	3.2	3.6	24%
Sponsorship	1.1	0.7	0.8	0.9	1.1	1.2	1.3	13%
Rich media	0.3	0.7	1.0	1.4	1.9	2.4	3.1	34%
Others	1.1	0.4	0.5	0.5	0.7	0.6	0.7	10%
Total U.S. Internet ad spending	6.0	7.3	9.6	13.0	16.9	20.3	24.3	28%
Total U.S. ad spending	239.6	250.9	267.9	282.9	297.2	309.2	321.6	5%
Internet ad spending as a percentage of total	2.5%	2.9%	3.6%	4.6%	5.7%	6.6%	7.6%	

Year-over-Year Percent Change

	2002	2003	2004	2005	2006E	2007E	2008E	2003-08 CAGR
Keyword search	213%	182%	51%	42%	34%	26%	22%	34%
Display ads	-33%	-12%	20%	34%	27%	19%	19%	24%
Classifieds	-22%	37%	40%	30%	24%	14%	13%	24%
Sponsorship	-42%	-33%	6%	17%	17%	12%	12%	13%
Rich media	109%	142%	32%	45%	36%	26%	29%	34%
Others	-6%	-60%	11%	13%	36%	-20%	19%	10%
Total U.S. Internet ad spending	-17%	21%	32%	35%	30%	20%	20%	28%
Total U.S. ad spending	3%	5%	7%	6%	5%	4%	4%	5%

Source: PWC/IAB, ThinkEquity estimates.

The Perfect Ad

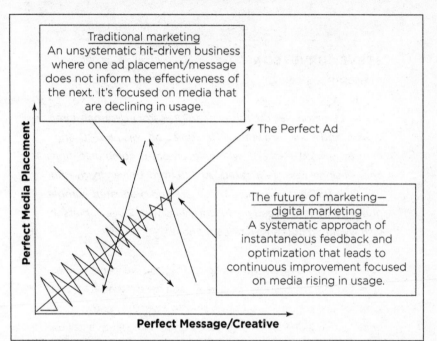

Visit www.findingthenextstarbucks.com for information about the following hot companies in the growth area of online advertising:

Hot Companies in Online Advertising

24/7 Real Media (TFSM)

Adknowledge

Adteractive

Allyes

aQuantive (AQNT)

Blue Lithium

Cobalt Group

Datran Media

Digitas (DTAS)

Double Fusion

DoubleClick

HomeStore (MOVE)

Ingenio

NetBlue

Quigo

QuinStreet

Rapt

Spot Runner

Tacoda

Third Screen Media

Tribal Fusion

ValueClick (VCLK)

Yahoo! (YHOO)

STAR GAZER

STEVE JURVETSON
managing director of Draper Fisher Jurvetson

Steve Jurvetson was the founding VC investor in Hotmail, Inter-woven, and Kana. Previously, Mr. Jurvetson was an R&D engineer at Hewlett-Packard, where seven of his communications chip designs were fabricated. At Stanford University, he finished his BSEE in two and a half years and graduated number one in his class. (To read my full interview with Steve Jurvetson, visit www.findingthenextstarbucks.com.)

We're an early-stage venture capital firm and we invest primarily in technology companies. The reason we do that is that we look for disruption. If you are going to invest in a new enterprise, it really needs to have some unfair competitive advantage, some way they can stir things up and make a difference. It turns out that if you pick any old industry that's well established, it's not usually welcoming of new entrants. Everyone has tricks and techniques for blocking out new ideas.

If you want to enter with a new business, you have to first ask, "What's new, what's different?" Broadly speaking, that could be a new law that just got passed. In the energy domain, it could be a new regulation. It could be a dramatic change in world energy prices. Over the long term, the thing that has perpetually been a source of disruption has been technology innovation.

→ OPEN SOURCE—FREE WORLD

In the beginning, software was free. Then, evil corporations like IBM and Microsoft made software "proprietary" (i.e., it was not to be redistributed, the source code was not available, and users could not modify the programs). Of course, this couldn't last forever, and while there were many programmers who were part of the liberation movement, not until a Finnish computer science student, Linus Torvalds (whose name sounds like a Peanuts character), created Linux, and the advent of the Internet as a collaboration tool, did we see the explosion of the open-source revolution.

Now that the genie is out of the bottle, open source is somewhat inevitable. It returns the control to the customer. The code is open and transparent. Hence, users can see it, change it, and learn from it. Bugs are more quickly found and fixed. If customers don't like what they are experiencing, they can edit the code or choose another application without a ton of hassle or cost.

Freedom!

So you don't think I am a complete moron, I do realize you have to be paid for your product in order to make money. The way open-source models succeed in an economic sense is through monetizing a license relationship with the open-source community.

Web 2.0 provides the platform for collaboration, and the network effect's impact on garnering collective intelligence is what makes open source so potent.

There are now 30 million Linux users worldwide. L.A.M.P. (Linux, Apache, MySQL, PHP/Perl/Python) is a rapidly developing open-source enterprise software stack.

Wikipedia is a multilingual, Web-based, free-content encyclopedia organized by Jimmy Wales in 2001. Wikipedia is written collaboratively by volunteers. Articles can be changed by anyone with access to a Web browser. Wikipedia now has 2,550,000 articles. It's become the second-most-visited reference site on the Web behind dictionary.com.

Blogs are open-source media or, as my friend Tony Perkins (founder of *Red Herring* and the AlwaysOn Network) has coined it, "reality media." There are a zillion guides that tell you where a restaurant in New York City is located, what type of food it serves, and what kind of credit cards it takes. As I said, why Zagat is so powerful is the collective input of more than 100,000 contributors. Blogs take this concept and put it on steroids.

As of February 2006, Technorati, the blogosphere's leading authority, tracked 27.2 million weblogs. The number of blogs continues to double every five months.

Cumulative Weblogs
March 2003–January 2006

Source: Technorati, David Sifry.

The blogosphere is 60 times larger than it was just three years ago, with 75,000 new blogs created every day. That's a new blog every second!

Targeted advertising, subscription blogging services, and other domain/interest-specific blogs will be a hot spot for years to come. The power of tapping into the collective intelligence of the network has profound implications for industries such as all types of research, periodicals, newspapers, and even books.

Visit www.findingthenextstarbucks.com for information about the following hot companies in the open-source growth area:

Hot Companies in Open Source

Alfresco	Pentaho
Apache	Qlusters
CollabNet	Red Hat (RHAT)
Compiere	Six Apart
Digg	SugarCRM
Greenplum	Technorati
Jabber	VA Software (LNUX)
JasperSoft	Virtual Iron
Linux	Wikipedia
Mozilla Firefox	Wind River (WIND)
MySQL	XenSource
Nagios	Zimbra

Note: Apache, Linux, Mozilla Firefox, and Wikipedia are not-for-profit today, but they're cool, and who knows about tomorrow?

➤ STAR GAZER

TONY PERKINS
founder of the AlwaysOn Network

Tony Perkins has been an influential technology journalist and publisher for more than a decade. He co-founded Upside *and* Red Herring *magazines in the early '90s, and he founded the social/professional-networking AlwaysOn Network in June 2002. He is now preparing to publish a print version of AlwaysOn. (To read my full interview with Tony Perkins, visit www.findingthenextstarbucks.com.)*

We now truly live in a globalized world, a global business environment. The term *Silicon Valley* to me no longer describes a geographical location; it describes a business mentality. That business mentality exists all over the planet, which has ramifications in all areas. With my entrepreneur's hat on, I think that on day one when you start a company you need to look out across the planet to create your relationships. The old rule was that until you got to $100 million in revenue, you mainly focused on just building products in America and selling them to Americans.

We're in a period that is fashionably referred to as Web 2.0, and we live in an environment where there's a lot of venture capital money and a lot of information-sharing tools and applications and features out there. The cautionary point would be that a lot of these companies are one-feature companies. But within that world there will be breakaway companies (MySpace is an example) that figure it out just right and become huge. Skype is another example of sitting on top of where consumer behavior is going, but they're doing it in a way that brings several strategies together to make them successful. It's a very fertile time to be an entrepreneur.

The Web 3.0 era will be about data mining and artificial intelligence and stuff like that. So basically in the next 10 years [the focus will be on] your ability to access information, but more important, to quickly understand where those ideas and information are coming from, so that you can move resources and people around initiatives and make things happen.

→ **ON DEMAND—SOFTWARE AS A SERVICE**

"The environment has changed yet again—this time around services. Computing and communications technologies have dramatically and progressively improved to enable the viability of a services-based model. The ubiquity of broadband and wireless networking has changed the nature of how people interact, and they're increasingly drawn toward the simplicity of services and service-enabled software that 'just works.' Businesses are increasingly considering what services-based economics of scale might do to help them reduce infrastructure costs or deploy solutions as needed and on subscription basis."

—RAY OZZIE, MICROSOFT CTO

Just imagine . . . you have to make a few phone calls. But before you can reach out and touch friends and family, you have to purchase and deploy your own telecom infrastructure and software to make that happen. And assuming you get past that enormous complexity and expense, let's pretend that during that first call, the line drops dead. Then what do you do? You write a letter instead.

Luckily, many of our core needs are already being served in an on-demand fashion. We sign up and expect to immediately get connected for phone, for cable, for gas and electric, and for security services, for example, pay small monthly fees and enjoy service uptimes running at 99.9%. On-demand has been all around us in the consumer world, but surprisingly, we're only just kicking off the migration in the world of software.

In 1997 at the Montgomery Tech conference, I heard Larry Ellison of Oracle give a speech articulating the virtues of the thin-computing era, which would ultimately lead to the demise of the traditional software model. The premise made sense: customers pay too much and get too much headache in return during traditional software deployments. Customers were overspending for too many license seats. And that money spent on licenses was overshadowed still by other line items: five times the cost of the licenses for hardware, five times the cost for services and training, and one time the cost annually for maintenance and support. And for what? Only 70% of the promised functionality after a two-year delay for 200% of the original cost projections. No thanks!

Ironically, even though Larry predicted this change, Oracle didn't drive the paradigm shift to fruition and is not yet heavily participating in the movement. In fact, application service provider (ASP) movement crumbled with the dot.com bust, largely because ASP vendors did not design software components from the ground up to fit the model, because they failed to offer customers the functionality that they wanted, and also because the one-off evangelizing by each of the hundreds of VC-funded start-ups drove an irrational performance expectation and a cluttered, noncohesive message that set up the movement for failure.

Ellison protégé Marc Benioff spearheaded the "No More Software" movement with important customer relationship management (CRM) software designed to fit with the on-demand model and with marketing messages both loud and resonating. He homed in on the traditional software model's inefficiencies, which are now breathing furious life into his sails and those of other on-demand vendors. Benioff and others are helping organizations realize that they have better economic and business options than deploying software in the traditional way. They are helping democratize software and are leveling the playing field, giving organizations of all sizes across all geographic regions (anyone with a Web browser) access to the critical business process automation software needed to drive improvements in their businesses, and at a predicable cost.

salesforce.com Subscription Revenue, Subscribers

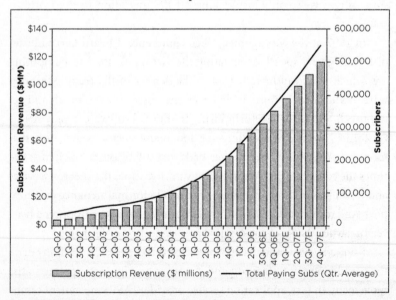

Source: Company Data, Morgan Stanley Research.

Interestingly, what was often cited as the weakness of the ASP model in the late '90s could potentially be a key selling point for customers now. Before, organizations were concerned with potential service breaches: downtime, security lapses, data loss. While still focused on service performance and security, customers are beginning to recognize that with on-demand, they could potentially benefit from the latest and greatest security, load balancing, and fault tolerance mechanisms, all behind the scenes. It is important that in the on-demand world, customers no longer need to moonlight as a software provider and can instead focus on their core business challenges and opportunities ahead.

Obviously, the fruits of the on-demand tree appear to be falling into the laps of the software vendors as well. Premium multiples are justified by growth rates accelerating at 5 to 10 times the rates of the traditional software company with margins that could exceed even the best-run, most competitively dominant software companies—and with unparalleled revenue and earnings visibility to boot. There's a reason why leading VCs and the largest traditional software companies are jumping on the bandwagon. They're going after the early fruit, which I believe is just beginning to bloom.

Visit www.findingthenextstarbucks.com for information about the following hot companies in the growth area of on-demand services:

Hot Companies in On-Demand Services

Arena Solutions	salesforce.com (CRM)
BenefitStreet	SuccessFactors
IP Unity	Taleo (TLEO)
Ketera Technologies	Vcommerce
LivePerson (LPSN)	VurvTechnology
NetSuite	(RecruitMax)
Omniture	WebSideStory (WSSI)
OpenAir	Website Pros (WSPI)
Rightnow Technologies	
(RNOW)	

STAR GAZER

MARC BENIOFF
chairman and CEO of salesforce.com

Marc Benioff founded salesforce.com in March 1999 with a vision to create an on-demand CRM solution that would replace traditional enterprise software technology. Benioff is now regarded as the leader of what he has termed "the End of software," the growing belief that on-demand applications can democratize CRM by delivering immediate benefits to companies of all sizes at reduced risks and costs. Under Benioff's direction, salesforce.com has grown from a groundbreaking idea into a publicly traded company that is the market and technology leader in on-demand CRM. I asked Marc about the future of software and about on-demand. (To read my full interview with Marc Benioff, visit www.findingthenext starbucks.com.)

I think the future of software looks a lot like the Internet today, a stream of heterogeneous services delivered by providers all over the world who are able to integrate their applications to provide composite technology that outpaces and outshines the traditional enterprise software market.

The key features are very low cost, very easy to use, very fast to get going, and very easy to break out of the traditional enterprise software model. This creates lots of unique applications through the concept of a mash-up, which was made popular when craigslist and Amazon.com came together to create apartment rental applications. Now you are really going to see for the first time how these applications are able to come together to create unique Web services delivered to corporations, not just consumers.

Customers have been much more successful with the on-demand model than with the traditional [software] model. You look at a lot of companies, whether it's Merrill Lynch or Cisco or so many of our customers. Thousands of our customers had bought products from Oracle and Siebel and PeopleSoft and Microsoft but never got them running—they were proverbial "shelfware." What our model has been able to do is take that shelfware and get use out of it. Gartner says that only about 18% of SAP's CRM users are actually users. That is, only 18% of the software they sold is in place. There's no other industry in the world with that rate of failure.

Community involvement is important to salesforce.com. We have 1% of our equity, 1% of our profits, and 1% of our employees' time in a 501C3 public charity called salesforce.com Foundation. That gives us the ability to provide a level of community service on a worldwide basis that is unprecedented for a company of our size. In fact, we've won every major award in corporate philanthropy, which is evidence that most companies just don't focus on or care about this idea that we call compassion capitalism. For us, it means that we not only have been able to do a lot of good in the world, but we've created a better company, too. In fact, our ability to recruit people, for example, is much higher than any other company in our class because people want to work for a company that's doing this kind of service work.

→ **JUST-FOR-ME MEDIA**

Sometimes, when I use TiVo, it seems so unbelievable that I wonder if I'm dreaming: 1,000 channels available on my satellite dish, and I can watch whatever show I want to watch when I want to watch it in 70% of the time it would normally take.

I don't have to pay $12 for a CD with only two songs I want. I can go to iTunes and pay 99 cents for each. Now, with my video iPod, I can watch whatever show I want when I want with no commercials and nobody else bothering me. It's just for me!

Podcasting—the convergence of Apple's iPod and broadcasting—is a way of publishing files to the Internet, allowing users to subscribe to a feed and receive new files automatically by signaling an interest in that particular area.

Blogs and video blogs allow you to find and participate in a very narrow interest area. Without the Web, if I lived in Fargo, North Dakota, and I wanted to find other people who were interested in Egyptian tombs, I might have quite a challenge on my hands. Through blogs, RSS feeds, and video blogs, I can find people like me wherever they happen to be.

It's not just me who thinks stuff just for me is cool. Worldwide, digital music downloads were up 169% to 419 million in 2005, and up 20-fold from 2003. Most of this is iTunes-related. Overall, digital music revenue for 2005 was $1.1 billion, up about threefold from $380 million in 2004. Of this, the split was roughly 60–40 between online music and mobile music (mostly ringtones).

iTunes is in 21 countries now, with approximately 42 million iPods sold since inception. In early 2006, there were 3 million songs downloaded from iTunes a day. Since the video iPod's release in late 2005, 8 million videos have been downloaded.

Podcasting is showing explosive growth, with the BBC reporting 2 million podcasts in December 2005 alone. Apple had 2 million podcasts within two days of launching podcast services. About one-third of U.S. adults with iPods have downloaded a podcast.

IKEA, the Swedish überbrand, had a contest for amateurs to create the most effective ways to store home media. Jones Soda lets customers create their own soda labels by submitting their own photos. This level of customization also plays into the just-for-me theme.

Visit www.findingthenextstarbucks.com for information about the following hot companies in the growth area of customized (just-for-me) media:

Hot Companies in Just-for-Me Media

A8	Linktone (LTON)
Apple (AAPL)	Mythic Entertainment
Audible (ADBL)	Pandora
BitTorrent	Photobucket
Bokee.com	Plaxo
Brightcove	PodShow
Convedia	Rock Mobile
DivX	Shutterfly
Facebook	Sina (SINA)
Focus Media	Sling Media
GameFly	SNOCAP
Heavy.com	Turbine Entertainment
Kontiki	VitalStream Holdings (VSHI)
Linked In	YouTube

STAR GAZER

GEOFF YANG
founding partner of Redpoint Ventures

Prior to founding Redpoint in 1999, Geoff Yang was a general partner with Institutional Venture Partners, which he joined in 1987. Geoff is an expert in the systems and consumer media space, where he's found his big winners, including Ask Jeeves, Excite, Foundry Networks, Juniper Networks, MMC Networks, TiVo, and Wellfleet. I asked Geoff what he looks for in companies he invests in and how he quantifies the size of a market opportunity. (To read my full interview with Geoff Yang, visit www.findingthenextstarbucks.com.)

Principally I look for something that can be big. The perennial debate is about what's more important: management or market? While you can make a case for either, I tend to be more on the market side with the philosophy that says, "If the market's big, something can be a big company, and you can hire great people around it." Since we do investments at the earliest stage, I have no problem going and finding people around a great opportunity. The second thing, clearly, is good management, but I feel sometimes even if you have great management, they can only build so big a company if the market can't support the size of a great company. It's almost as if you're throwing a great party and not inviting anybody.

Generally in the venture capital system, you build two types of investments. One is what I call "faster better cheaper." Typically it's characterized by strong engineering and going after existing markets with better solutions. The size of these markets is reasonably easy to quantify, because they're existing, so people are spending money on this type of thing. And you always look at whether you can offer more performance at a lower price or a slightly increased price. Would people go after it? How much market expansion could you have? For us, at the earliest stages, it's often very difficult to quantify with precise accuracy the size of a market other than big, medium, or small. In those instances, I look for proven management, people who have done this type of thing before, who have a credible track record of success doing what you're going to ask them to do.

The other type of investment is a slightly different type of deal that I call "brave new world." You hear terms like *paradigm shift* or *enabling people to do things they've never been able to do before,* and typically it's just characterized by brand-new markets and creating new usage paradigms. Very often in those types of businesses it's very difficult to determine how big a market can be other than by looking at analogies and saying, "Well, this type of thing changed the way people did it, and this is how big that market is, and this is how big that company became." This type of investment is more speculative, and these businesses tend to be more home-run kinds of opportunities, creating a new market category. In those types of businesses, it's harder to find people who've already done what you're asking them to do. So what you look for is people who have done things that are analogous to what you are asking.

→ THE PHONE IS MY LIFE

If you want to understand where the future is going, study your kids.

Watch a group of teenagers hanging out. They all have cell phones. Often they are talking on them or text messaging, many times completely ignoring the other kids in the group huddle.

The cell phone is how many teenagers express who they are. What's the color of the phone? The make? What is the ringtone? What pictures do you have for a background (wallpaper)?

As I said earlier, the cell phone is for kids today what the automobile was for my parents. Increasingly, the cell phone is replacing the computer as kids' means to get information, entertain themselves, and communicate—basically how they live.

My youngest daughter personalizes her phone with fake jewels and changes her ringtones (and mine!) as often as most people change their clothes. Instead of talking, she'll text message with a friend while they're sitting in the same room.

Some people call this the cell phone generation, but I call it the IM (instant message) generation, or always on. It's expected that everyone is instantaneously available always and there is never a moment without stimulation. Web 2.0 as the platform to deliver and update services is the key enabler to be always connected and always on.

Societies like China and India have skipped the whole migration from a world with cords because those countries weren't encumbered by preexisting infrastructure and a mindset of protecting it. They were able to leapfrog to the future and have started with the cell phone being the phone, the computer, the game system, and more. China is already the number-one cell phone market in the world with more than 350 million in use.

The ubiquitous BlackBerry Smart Phone by Research in Motion (RIMM) has more than 4 million "crackberry" addicts—with expectation that smart phones will see more than a tenfold increase in users within 10 years. BlackBerry is the undisputed leader in smart phones, but Good Technology, Seven, and Microsoft will all be competitors providing smart phone software. Motorola, Palm, Apple, and others will be competitors on the hardware side.

MOBILE LEADS INTERNET IN MOST MARKETS

COUNTRY	MOBILE USERS (MILLION)	INTERNET USERS (MILLION)	MOBILE PHONE TO INTERNET USER RATIO	INSTALLED PCs (MILLION)
China	363	100	3.6:1	53
U.S.	177	211	0.8:1	207
Japan	88	78	1.1:1	55
Germany	69	51	1.4:1	39
UK	54	37	1.5:1	26
Italy	54	32	1.7:1	16
South Korea	37	32	1.2:1	27

Source: Euromonitor, CNNIC, World Bank, Morgan Stanley Research (July 2005).

A variety of phone services and the importance of a single universal phone number (10% of people in the United States have *only* a cell phone number) and e-mail address highlight the power of NeuStar and VeriSign's franchises. VeriSign through its JAMBA product has a complementary franchise in ringtones and wallpaper.

Visit www.findingthenextstarbucks.com for information about the following hot companies in the growth area that I call "the phone is my life"—cell phone technology:

Hot Companies in Cell Phone Technology

BridgePort Networks	MobiTV
BroadSoft	Motricity
Cbeyond (CBEY)	NeuStar (NSR)
Clearwire	Palm (PALM)
Digital Chocolate	QUALCOMM (QCOM)
Global IP Sound	Research in Motion (RIMM)
Glu Mobile	Skype (owned by eBay)
Good Technology	Synchronoss (SNCR)
Kineto Wireless	Tellme Networks
MetroSpark	UP Technologies
Mobile 365	VeriSign (VRSN)

→ STAR GAZER

BRUCE DUNLEVIE
general partner at Benchmark Capital

Bruce is a seasoned veteran of venture capital with more than 15 years of experience in high tech investing. His investments include Accept.com (acquired by Amazon.com), Collabra Software (acquired by Netscape Communications), Encompass (acquired by Yahoo!), Good Technology, Handspring (acquired by palmOne), Matrix Semiconductor, and Palm Computing (acquired by 3Com). (To read my full interview with Bruce Dunlevie, visit www.findingthenextstarbucks.com.)

A lot of what we do is very early stage, so the notion of investing in a company, or even in a business plan, is probably worth challenging since so much of what we do has nothing going for it at the time we look at it: three guys, hopefully a good idea; sometimes one person and the proverbial back of a napkin. In that context, much of the judgment is predicated on our assessment of the entrepreneur, which includes the recruitment of a lot of other high-quality people and the ability to deliver against some hoped-for product and set of schedules. Certainly the notion of business model comes into play, but I honestly think a lot of what we do is bereft of any clear business model. It's more a question of hoping that one will emerge as the entrepreneur (who, by definition, is an attractive person), figures it out as he goes along. That is to say, one important characteristic is the ability to do rapid midcourse correction because predicting the future is very difficult and no entrepreneur at time zero is able to do that with much accuracy.

→ THE ABCs (AND THE THREE Gs) OF BIOTECH

An aging population is a powerful backdrop for the health-care industry—in particular for health-care companies that are solving big problems. Biotech has been the land of hopes and dreams for 25 years, but now, it's the land of opportunity. After spending tens of billions of dollars on researching and developing new drugs, the industry is now at a point where it's actually able to sell new products.

In looking for tomorrow's winners, we don't focus on what's in our grandparents' medicine cabinets—we're trying to anticipate what we want in ours and what will be in those of our children. When describing an investment opportunity, people say it's like a cure for cancer. Many leading biotech companies literally are finding cures for cancer—and heart disease, Alzheimer's, AIDS, and diabetes, to name a few.

The convergence of science and technology, combined with Wall Street raising $200 billion for biotech companies, has resulted in a wave of exciting innovation. With traditional pharmaceutical companies investing its R&D dollars in more pedestrian areas, the true innovation is occurring in the biotech industry.

Not only are these companies creating cures, they are also creating products that improve the outlook for those stricken with diseases. People with cancer, diabetes, heart disease, and most other life-threatening diseases live longer after diagnosis than they did 30 years ago, and they are able to maintain a normal life for longer as well.

OBJECTIVE OF BIOTECH PRODUCTS: SHRINK THE MARKET		
DISEASE	NUMBER OF U.S. CITIZENS AFFECTED	NUMBER OF NEW CASES PER YEAR
Heart disease	71 million	1.2 million
Alzheimer's	4.5 million	447,000
Cancer	10.1 million	1.3 million
Diabetes	20.8 million	1.4 million
HIV/AIDS	1.7 million	40,000

Source: American Heart Association, American Cancer Association, American Diabetes Association, Avert.org, Alzheimer's Association.

The aging population is an early sign that society will soon be faced with dramatically increasing incidence of age-related diseases such as Parkinson's and Alzheimer's. These diseases cannot yet be cured, but biotech companies are beginning to capture this huge market opportunity with treatments to improve the quality of life for these patients. Biotech companies will continue to focus on treating nonfatal diseases and disorders and tapping into these large markets.

The ABCs (and three Gs) of biotech are to invest in Amgen, Biogen, and Celgene coupled with Genentech, Gilead, and Genzyme—the blue-chip growth companies for the future—leaving the Mercks and Pfizers for investors who wish to invest in the heroes of yesteryear.

ESTIMATED COST OF SEQUENCING A GENE	
1974	>$100,000,000
1998	$150
2005	<$8.75

Source: Michael Milken; David Agus, M.D.; Cedars-Sinai Medical Center.

An important investment theme will be smaller biotech companies that have a single potential blockbuster product being acquired by the ABCs or traditional pharma companies to fill our medicine cabinets and augment growth. The target population for these products, particularly in the United States, Europe, and Japan, is growing older, with a direct correlation between age and demand for medicine.

There are hundreds of "publicly traded products" that benefit from being acquired by a more substantial organization that can use its distribution and clout to accelerate sales.

Visit www.findingthenextstarbucks.com for information about the following hot companies in the growth area of biotechnology:

Hot Companies in Biotech

Abrika Pharmaceuticals

Acorda Therapeutics

Aegera Therapeutics

Affymax

Agensys

Alnylam (ALNY)

Amgen (AMGN)

Anormed (AOM)

ARYx Therapeutics

Axial Biotech

Bayhill

BioCryst (BCRX)

Biogen (BIIB)

Biomimetic Therapeutics
  (BMTI)

Cardiome (COM)

Celgene (CELG)

Chelsea Therapeutics (CHTP)

ChemoCentryx

CoTherix (CTRX)

Depomed (DEPO)

Emisphere (EMIS)

FibroGen

GeneCure

Genentech (DNA)

Gentium (GENT)

Genzyme (GENZ)

Gilead (GILD)

InSite Vision (ISV)

InterMune (ITMN)

Jazz Pharmaceuticals

MetaMorphix

Momenta (MNTA)

Omrix Biopharmaceuticals
  (OMRI)

Osiris Therapeutics

Paratek Pharmaceuticals

Questcor Pharmaceuticals
  (QSC)

Reliant Pharmaceuticals

Replidyne

Repros Therapeutics (RPRX)

Tengion

Vertex (VRTX)

VIA Pharmaceuticals

ViaCell (VIAC)

Xencor

Xenoport (XNPT)

Zars

ZIOPHARM Oncology
  (ZIOP)

STAR GAZER

SAM COLELLA
co-founder of Versant Ventures

Sam Colella specializes in biotechnology investing. Over the course of his career, Sam has had 20 years of successful operating experience in the high technology industry and more than 21 years of investing experience in the health-care sector. Prior to founding Versant, he established one of the first life science-focused investing groups in the industry as a general partner with Institutional Venture Partners (IVP). (To read my full interview with Sam Colella, visit www.findingthenext starbucks.com.)

People ask me all the time, "What were the big winners?" The companies that I really like to identify may not have had the biggest multiples of return. But I consider them to be successes because they're going to last. I try to build great and lasting companies. That's my theory on venture capitalism. If you build a great company, you'll get a great return. I've never been a very good stock picker. There are other VCs who will look at a company and say, "Yeah. I can take this company, invest in it, and in three years, I can flip it and get 10 times my money." That's not my style because my background's in operating.

→ **DIGITAL DOCTOR**

Maria Lelis was a nurse who got just a bit confused. In October 2005, she mixed up the records for two of her patients at Rochdale Infirmary: one who had died, and one who was supposed to be discharged. The undertakers were a bit taken aback when the "dead" patient sat up in her bed.

It's estimated that as many as 98,000 people die every year due to medical errors—many because of poor communication or mix-ups. Mistakes in medical records can result in the wrong arm being amputated, not knowing about allergies, and going into the hospital sick and coming out sicker—all this amid what is called the best health care in the world!

It's an age-old truism that doctors have illegible writing, and yet today, it's estimated that only 13% of hospitals and at most 28% of physician practices use electronic records. Also remarkable is that patients' health histories are not aggregated among their different hospitals and physicians.

Given the enormous quantity of information for health care, the increased strains on the system, the need for consistency and aggregation, and the fact that tools now exist to make it happen, there will be an explosion of products and services for the digital doctor.

Hand-held record-keeping and patient information systems, records that can provide better information for care, and other products to provide superior health-care services and lower cost will be part of this future.

The government, under President George W. Bush, has put $150 million into the research and development of uniform digital medical records over the next 10 years. Today there is no uniform system to make the dozens of software programs and patient databases link together.

RFID (Radio Frequency Identification) tags are becoming standard not only in manufacturing and retailing, but also in livestock and even in pets. The technology is simple: a device the size of a grain of rice is inserted under the skin and functions as a barcode. The RFID tag gives off a number, which, when entered into a standardized database, links to all available medical information for the patient. RFID technology will be a key enabler to improve patient care.

This technology could have a profound effect in human medicine, particularly for people who have difficulty remembering their own medical histories (elderly people and those with Alzheimer's, for example). It could literally be life saving in emergency situations. Privacy concerns are a notable hindrance at the moment, but improvements in security and regulation will likely reduce this dilemma. Companies currently perfecting RFID tags in animals are well positioned to burst onto the medical scene.

Visit www.findingthenextstarbucks.com for information about the following hot companies in the growth area of digital medicine:

Hot Companies in Digital Medicine

Drugs.com

drugstore.com (DSCM)

Electro-Optical Sciences
   (MELA)

Epocrates

FoxHollow (FOXH)

Intuitive Surgical (ISRG)

Quality Systems (QSII)

UnitedHealth Group (UNH)

WebMD (WBMD)

→ HEALTHY, WEALTHY, AND WISE

In 1900, there were fewer than 5,000 million-dollar households in the United States. Today, there are 8 million. Of the 691 billionaires in the world, 346 live in the United States.

THEN VERSUS NOW		
	1900	2005
Million-dollar households	<5,000	8 million
Billion-dollar households	0	346
Male life expectancy	48	76
Percentage of U.S. population with a high school degree	13%	85%
Percentage of U.S. population with a college degree	3%	24%

	1900	2005
Percentage of U.S. jobs in farming	38%	<2%

Source: U.S. Census Bureau.

In 1900, a male born in the United States had a life expectancy of 48 years. Today, it's 76 years—effectively double the 38 years' life expectancy of a male born in 1850.

In 1900, 38% of all jobs were farming-related, just 13% of the U.S. population had high school degrees, and only 3% had college degrees. In 2005, 85% of U.S. adults had a high school degree and 24% had a college degree.

With a population that's getting older, is more affluent, and is more knowledgeable as a nation, there will be booming opportunities for service and product companies that help people feel younger.

Fitness centers and spas, personal trainers, nutritionists, and plastic surgeons all benefit from this theme. Chinese traditional medicine (CTM)—using natural ingredients and thousands of years of knowledge—is experiencing growth. A full 16.5 million people practice yoga in the United States, up 43% since 2002, according to *Yoga Journal. Time* magazine reported that 10 million American adults meditate daily, up 100% in 10 years. There's a convergence of holistic medicine with people wishing to feel younger and live longer.

A society that is growing in its affluence needs tailored financial services such as wealth management, tax planning, and money management. Family offices (offices set up to handle the financial affairs of a wealthy family) historically were realistic only for the Rockefellers, Gettys, and their ilk, but will be made available for a growing part of the population.

People living longer and getting richer, and globalization making the earth a smaller place, will enable travel services to flourish. Cruise ships providing entertainment and knowledge exploration as well as specialty travel providers such as Backroads that offer unique travel experiences are on-trend. Boutique hotels such as Kimpton and high-end branded hotels like The Four Seasons that make travelers feel at home benefit as well.

Historically, a person graduating from college and then working for an employer until retiring at age 65 was considered normal. Today, the average person coming out of college will have 12 employers before retirement. It is typical for someone retiring today to live another 20 to 30 years. What happens when people routinely live to be 100? Well, things might not change too much considering there's a growing trend of people retiring in their seventies or later. Why? It's due to financial reasons such as the elimination of pensions, and people being more active and healthy well into their seventies.

No longer can people graduate from school and "drive off" to life— they will need to continue to fill up their knowledge tank throughout their careers to stay relevant in the job. Lifelong learning will be a core fundamental to anybody in business in the future. Continuing education will be part of this, but learning new skills and adapting to a global marketplace in a knowledge-based economy will be critical to survive and thrive.

Online learning and training providers will continue to enjoy tremendous growth. Conferences and knowledge networks will be integrated into workers' ongoing job programs.

Visit www.findingthenextstarbucks.com for information about the following hot companies in the growth area of general health and fitness:

Hot Companies in Healthy, Wealthy, and Wise

Amvescap (AVZ)	Jamba Juice
Blue Nile (NILE)	KnowFat!
Cranium	Life Time Fitness (LTM)
Curves	Lifeway Foods (LWAY)
Disney's Little Einsteins	Lush
Eaturna	Pharmaca Integrative
eCollege.com (ECLG)	Pharmacy
Four Seasons Hotels (FS)	Quellos
Gaiam (GAIA)	Space.NK.apothecary
Glacéau (Vitamin Water)	Whole Foods Market (WFMI)
GOL Airlines (GOL)	

STAR GAZER

WILLIAM SAHLMAN
professor at Harvard Business School

William Sahlman is the Dimitri V. d'Arbeloff-class of 1955 professor of business administration at Harvard Business School. The d'Arbeloff chair was established in 1986 to support teaching in and research on the entrepreneurial process. His research focuses on the investment and financing decisions made in entrepreneurial ventures at all stages in their development. He is a member of the board of directors of several private companies. (To read my full interview with William Sahlman, visit www.findingthenextstarbucks.com.)

Large companies get stuck in a mode where they have this [unchanging] mental image of what they should be doing or how they're improving their products. They're always vulnerable to people who completely redefine what's going on. Look, for example, at the software business. The software business was always done in a traditional way, where you had a direct-sales force, a high average selling price, a big site license, and an annual update fee. So that would be Siebel.

And then guys came along and said, "Well, no, why don't we just have it be on the server? And why don't we sell you only what you need? And why don't we view our customer as the salesperson who's going to use this stuff, as opposed to the IT manager?" And so salesforce.com and RightNow Technologies are massacring Siebel.

I'm involved in a company called Aspen Aerogels. It's got insulation that's three to four times as good as any insulation in the world. They cracked the code on how to get its cost down to the point where it will be a very, very important, widely available product, at just the time when we need better insulation in everything from cars to refrigerators to homes.

I believe it's early, but stem cell technologies have the ability to cure diseases, rather than just provide symptomatic treatments. In the interim, they're going to provide lots of diagnostic tests and ways to improve understanding of what happens in individuals. So I think there are going to be lots of interesting products coming out of that domain.

→ EDUCATION IN THE KNOWLEDGE ECONOMY

"If you think education is expensive, try ignorance."

—DEREK BOK, FORMER PRESIDENT
OF HARVARD UNIVERSITY

Many of the early investors in the education market were previously investors in health care. This is no coincidence, as we see the education industry today as the health-care industry of 30 years ago. Health care and education are both critical human services, but even beyond that, the similarities are striking. While the comparison is not perfect, it is instructive and provides perspective on the opportunity for the education-and-training industry.

In 1970, health care was a huge market, 8% of GDP, but a highly fragmented cottage industry. Critics questioned not only whether you *could* make money, but whether you *should* make money in it. Characterized by limited professional leadership, low technology, and high cost, the industry had few large companies. From an investor's standpoint, while health care was a large component of GDP, the market capitalization of the sector represented just a fraction of total U.S. capital markets. Wall Street firms that covered the sector typically had just one analyst

HEALTH CARE IN 1970 AND 2005	
1970	2005
Huge market—8% of GDP	Huge market—16% of GDP
Highly fragmented cottage industry	Segmented by category
High cost	Consolidating
Low technology	Strong R&D and technology focus
Lack of professional management	Strong management controls and accountability
Negligible market capitalization (less than 3% of total)	16% of U.S. capital markets
Human essential service	Human essential service

who was responsible for writing research on the group, exploring everything from medical devices to health-care services and pharmaceuticals.

Fast forward the clock to today. Health care is an even larger market, upwards of 16% of GDP. Segmented by category (medical devices, pharmaceuticals, biotechnology, health management organizations, etc.), the industry is showing a growing level of sophistication, is technologically advanced due to significant capital investments, and has generally implemented strong management controls and accountability. The influence of market forces in health care since 1970 has created a dynamic industry, one that is the most technologically advanced in the world. It's not a perfect system, but if you are sick, the United States is where you would want to be. From an investment standpoint, the health-care industry represents 16% of U.S. capital markets.

Similarly, the education-and-training industry is a huge market (more than 16% of GDP), but it's a highly fragmented cottage industry with 100,000 schools and 15,000 school districts, inefficient, with limited professional management, and characterized by limited use of technology. Debate in some circles questions whether for-profit enterprises have a role in education. In addition, education-and-training companies account for less than 1% of U.S. capital markets.

Education has become critical for both individuals and employers. In a knowledge economy, a four-year degree is a prerequisite to participating in the industries of the future. As the result of technology innovations such as the Internet, video conferencing, and satellite systems, an idea economy has emerged, driven by knowledge and information.

The educational needs of the knowledge economy, contrasted with the current system's inability to fill those needs, provide innovative companies with open-ended opportunities for growth. The classic "big in-

EDUCATION TODAY
Huge market—8% of GDP
Highly fragmented cottage industry: 100,000 schools in 15,000 districts
High cost: $10,000 per student per year in K–12, more than $30,000 is typical for postsecondary schools
Relatively low technology
Lack of professional management
Negligible market cap (less than 1% of U.S. capital markets)
Human essential service

vestment opportunity" is a company that has a solution to a problem; the more significant the problem, the larger the investment potential. There is not, in my view, a bigger problem in the United States today than the need to better educate our populace, and hence, I think the investment potential in this sector is tremendous.

Businesses are saying they can't employ the students coming out of our schools—graduates can't read or write. Corporations are spending billions of dollars on remedial education, investing tens of billions on corporate training, and making large contributions to education reform.

Americans need look no further than their own paychecks to see the importance of education in today's economy. In 1980, the pay difference

UNEMPLOYMENT RATE IN 2003	EDUCATION ATTAINED	MEDIAN WEEKLY EARNINGS IN 2003
2.1%	Doctoral degree	$1,349
1.7%	Professional degree	$1,307
2.9%	Master's degree	$1,064
3.3%	Bachelor's degree	$900
4%	Associate's degree	$672
5.2%	Some college, no diploma	$622
5.5%	High school graduate	$554
8.8%	Some high school, no diploma	$396

Source: U.S. Bureau of Labor Statistics.

between someone who had a high school education and a college education was 50%. Today it is 111% and growing.

Put another way, a 30-year-old male with only a high school degree makes less than two-thirds what he made in the 1970s. This becomes even more striking when you take into account that only 24% of the U.S. adult population has a bachelor's degree or better.

The "push" from employers demanding relevant skills and the "pull" from employees seeking better jobs has created a fertile growth environment for postsecondary providers, as well as redefined who the students are. Twenty-five years ago, 25% of the students in postsecondary schools were 25 years or older. Today, nearly 50% are 25 years or older.

The problem is, most colleges and universities are set up for 18- to 22-year-old students in terms of classes during the day, semesters or quarters starting two or three times a year, no parking, dormitories, football team, and marching bands. But these are now totally irrelevant to nearly 50% of the student population.

An unfortunate irony is that at precisely the time that education has become crucial to economic success, it has also become unaffordable to many people because tuition is on the rise. Technology has the opportunity to "democratize" education. With broadband delivery able to give students access to classrooms and curricula around the world, technology can lower the cost, improve the access, and in some cases even improve the quality of a college education.

In this new world of anytime, anywhere education, content providers —educators and schools—need to find ways to facilitate the needs of the market. During a panel discussion in which I participated, the head of training at a major telecommunications company told the audience of content providers (universities like University of Pennsylvania, Stanford, and University of Minnesota), "We spend $150 million a year on training, and I've got a message for all of you. We're done putting people on airplanes. You have to figure out a way to deliver the content we desperately want and need when we want it and where we want it."

In an economy with less than 5% unemployment, an underdegreed adult population, and nearly 70% of new jobs created requiring higher skills, corporate training has never been more important. A half century ago, a man could learn how to drive a tractor and have that job skill for

40 years or more. Today, a person learns a software program and has that current skill for maybe 18 months before the available technology changes enough to adopt a new program.

The highly fragmented $110 billion corporate and government learning market provides huge opportunity. The corporate learning market is going through dynamic changes as education and training become increasingly critical in our knowledge-based global economy and as in-house corporate learning falls to the megatrend of outsourcing.

The K–12 market is the largest segment of the education industry, with approximately $510 billion spent annually, which amounts to $10,000 per year per child. Despite the size, the K–12 market is the most problematic to invest in today. Entrenched bureaucracies and personal and political interests contribute to the challenges facing this sector. Parents—alarmed by studies showing that this generation of children will be less educated than the previous one for the first time in this country's history—are demanding change. Businesses are increasingly recognizing that without systematic education reform, their competitive

K–12: Investing in a Market Evolution

Drivers of Change		The Market Is Changing	Barriers to Change
No Child Left Behind is driving assessment, transparency, flexibility, and teacher quality.			State and local resistance to NCLB lawsuits, and/or seeking compliance, rather than systematic change.
Widespread social support of assessment and accountability (as evidenced by state and local programs that predate NCLB).	Threat of outsourcing is increasing the value of education.		Schools lack a clear vision of a future with ubiquitous technology.
The emergence of equitable K-12 education as a key, timely, civil rights issue draws focus and a sense of immediacy to the problem.	Threat of global competition is galvanizing the business world to make U.S. workforce better prepared.		Teachers, principals, superintendents, school boards, and state agencies typically have different appetites for change and often conflict when change is implemented.
Increasing consumer behavior in K-12 education; Armed with choice, parents and students are thinking and behaving more like customers.	A teacher retirement bubble in the next five years may evolve the U.S. teacher base into younger, more tech-savvy change agents.		Teacher colleges have not significantly updated curriculum to include a meaningful and incorporated use of technology.
Increased funding (from state and federal sources) will allow for flexibility and the tools to implement change.	Superintendents and principals are coming from alternative backgrounds (business, law, military, etc.) and are increasingly change agents.		Education leadership/ administration degree programs (e.g., for principals and superintendents) are often dated.
Key business figures are publicly advocating real systematic change (e.g., Bill Gates, Craig Barrett).	Recent studies and press on the antiquated nature of education degree programs may spark degree program updates and changes.		The press often focuses on conflicts and crisis, which can stymie change agents in political positions.

Source: ThinkEquity Partners.

positions will look dim 10 years in the future. Politicians from both sides of the aisle have acknowledged that the education status quo is unacceptable and have passed dramatic legislation enabling charter schools, school choice, vouchers, and state takeovers. The entrenched status quo says, "Give us more time, give us more money, and we'll fix it." The good news is that the American people are saying that 200 years is long enough, and we need to fix the system today. Increased accountability and parental involvement have created significant demand for supplemental tutoring for kids, increased testing, and teacher training. Moreover, dramatic reforms are being initiated throughout the country.

Charter schools are leading the way. In 1992, there wasn't one charter school. Today, there are more than 3,500. Charter schools, school choice, private management of public schools, and voucher initiatives all contribute to the dynamic opportunities in the K–12 school market.

The key to understanding both the problems and the opportunities in the K–12 area is to examine how the money is spent. Of the $510 billion or $10,000 per student, only about 50% of the money is spent in the classroom. I can't think of another service industry where 50 cents out of every dollar is spent outside of where the service is rendered.

Technology can bring American schools into the 21st century, but first we need to bring our schools into the 20th century. While technology has become so important to American business that IT captures more than 50% of capital expenditures, in schools IT spending represents less than 2% of total spending.

Last, although it probably should be first, is early education. Early-childhood education and child care are at the foundation of the education puzzle. When looking at how we can solve the problems in our education system, one comes to the conclusion that you can't solve the K–12 problem until you solve the "0–5 problem." In today's society, both parents are employed in 60% of families with children under six. Sixty-two percent of married mothers with children under the age of six now work outside the home, compared with 19% in 1960.

Studies now empirically show, however, that what children learn when they are one, two, and three years old is linked to how they do when they enter school. And how a child does in the first grade is correlated with his

Percentage of Women with Children under Age 6

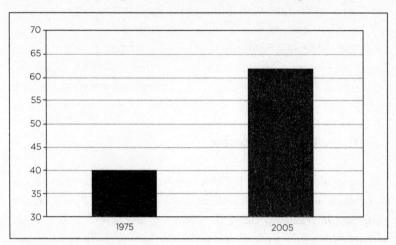

Source: U.S. Census Bureau.

or her success in the 11th grade, and in the 11th grade, in life. The concern is that the learning a child historically received in the home is being "out-sourced" to a child-care provider. Thus, the need for educationally en-riched, high-quality, and affordable child care has never been more important. Conditions are in place for a boom in the demand for education and train-ing as well as a rethinking of the way in which that education is delivered.

Visit www.findingthenextstarbucks.com for information about the following hot companies in the growth area of education:

Hot Companies in Education in the Knowledge Economy

4GL School Solutions

American Public University

Apex Learning

Apollo Group (APOL)

Aspen Education Group

Blackboard (BBBB)

Bridgepoint Education

Cambium Learning

Capella University

Carnegie Learning

eChalk.com

eCollege.com (ECLG)

Eduventures

Fairfield Language Tech-
    nologies (Rosetta Stone)

High-Tech Institute

K12

New Oriental Group

PRCEDU

Regency Beauty Institute

SchoolNet

Scientific Learning (SCIL)

TetraData

The Learning Annex (LGAX)

Tutor.com

U.S. Education

Virginia College

Wireless Generation

→ **THE POWER OF WOMEN**

On September 20, 1973, at the Houston Astrodome, more than 50 million people watched Billie Jean King destroy 55-year-old Bobby Riggs in three sets in what was called the "Battle of the Sexes." This followed Helen Reddy's 1972 number-one hit "I Am Woman," both events inspiring to the women's movement. Margaret Thatcher's ascent to being a very powerful prime minister in the United Kingdom showed women they didn't have to take a backseat to anybody in their careers.

These events were significant catalysts for 30 years of dramatic change in women's roles in society, business, and politics. The shift has been staggering. In 1970, women comprised 42% of the undergraduate college population. They now comprise 57%! Medical schools, business schools, and law schools all show the same shift.

In 1981, the NCAA began sponsoring championships in women's sports. Today, more than 150,000 women compete each year for NCAA championships in 20 sports. In women's basketball, fewer than 10,000 spectators attended the 1982 Division I championship, but in 2004, the Women's Final Four attracted a sellout crowd of more than 28,000, despite a ticket price of $150 apiece!

Women's issues will be getting more CEO attention, legislative funding, and societal support. In business 15 years ago, a woman CEO was very unusual; today, nearly 16% of Fortune 500 executives are women, and in 2002, women owned nearly 30% of all businesses. In terms of new companies, women are starting businesses 2-to-1 over men.

Politically, women have earned places in the presidential cabinet and the U.S. Supreme Court, and almost 19% of Congress members are

EDUCATIONAL ATTAINMENT

High School Graduate or Higher

AGE GROUP	TOTAL	MEN	WOMEN
25–34 years	84%	82%	86%
35–44 years	85%	83%	87%
45–64 years	83%	83%	83%
65 years and over	66%	66%	65%

Bachelor's Degree or Higher

AGE GROUP	TOTAL	MEN	WOMEN
25–34 years	28%	26%	29%
35–44 years	26%	26%	26%
45–64 years	26%	29%	24%
65 years and over	15%	21%	12%

Source: U.S. Census Bureau, 2005.

women, up from only 7% in 1995. It could be expected that by 2050, 50% of Congress will be women. Talk of a female presidential candidate has even reached a dull roar as people ponder the likelihood that Hilary Clinton or Condoleeza Rice will run.

Technology allows businesspeople to be productive without being tethered to a traditional office environment, working 9 to 5. While this benefits everyone, it has a particularly positive impact on women. JetBlue Airlines and Home Depot are leaders in "homesourcing," allowing many employees, and women in particular, to work exclusively from home offices.

While women are increasingly influential in all kinds of companies, they dominate the health-care and social-services fields. In 2002, one in three women-owned firms were in health-care or social assistance. Over 72% of social-assistance businesses are owned by women, as well as more than 50% of nursing and residential care facilities. With more women at the helm, I believe the environment and clean energy will benefit, as will children's issues, education, child care, and special-needs programs.

Having more women in the workplace increases the need to outsource services traditionally provided by stay-at-home moms, from housekeeping and tutoring to home-cooked meals. Special services to make a time-challenged woman's life easier will win big.

Visit www.findingthenextstarbucks.com for information about the following hot companies in the growth area of women's role in the economy:

Hot Companies in the Power of Women

Bright Horizons Family Solutions (BFAM)	Let's Dish!
	Lucy Activewear
Dream Dinners	Martha Stewart Living (MSO)
Educate (EEEE)	Super Suppers
Knowledge Learning	Trader Joe's

→ SIMPLY THE BEST—PREMIUM BRANDS

"The consumer isn't a moron. She is your wife."   —DAVID OGILVY

It became obvious to me when my assistant, who was struggling to make ends meet, treated herself to a café latte every day that Starbucks had "legs" to its opportunity. Standing in line to get your caffeine fix, you see people wearing anything from hard hats to pinstripe suits. From CEO to secretary, for $3.50, you can have the best cup of coffee in the world.

One of my distinct pleasures was to know Ely Callaway and write research on Callaway Golf. Mr. Callaway was fanatical about manufacturing a superior golf club. I don't believe a Big Bertha is worth three times the price of a normal driver and it certainly didn't improve my score threefold, but Callaway became the number-one golf club manufacturer in the world because golfers thought it was the best. The security of the Callaway headquarters was so tight you would have thought you were visiting the CIA.

Premium wine and premium beer sales continue to grow at a fast pace, while the overall industry's growth is flat to declining.

I remember when Horst Rechelbacher put avocado and other strange concoctions in my mom's hair back home in Minneapolis as he was experimenting to develop what became Aveda. Aveda is now a $1 billion enterprise providing "natural" high-quality self-care products. An eight-ounce bottle of clove shampoo costs about $10 versus $2 for Head & Shoulders. Kiehl's started as a New York City pharmacy in 1853 and is now a provider of high-quality, unique beauty care products. It's a booming business that is benefiting from the same trend.

The Cheesecake Factory, P. F. Chang's, and California Pizza Kitchen are all doing very well by providing customers the best product and service in their categories. The Cheesecake Factory overwhelms patrons with selection, quantity, and, of course, out-of-this-world cheesecake. P. F. Chang's delivers hip Chinese cuisine (even to people who don't like Chinese food). California Pizza Kitchen is the category killer for upscale, gourmet pizza.

In-N-Out Burger has a cult following in California, with its freshly made french fries, never-frozen meat, and delicious shakes. Potbelly's in

Chicago has developed an equal passion among its customers by delivering a high-quality product, great service, and a fun environment.

One of the hottest holiday gifts has become a Graeter's ice cream gift thermos. Based in Cincinnati, Ohio, Graeter's has developed unbelievably devoted followers with its "French Pot" process.

Consumers are ready, willing, and able to buy products and services that they believe are without peers.

Visit www.findingthenextstarbucks.com for information about the following hot companies in the growth area of premium brands:

Hot Companies with Premium Brands

Bliss World (subsidiary of Starwood Hotels & Resorts)	Kona Grill (KONA)
	MAC
Blue Holdings (BLUE)	NapaStyle
California Pizza Kitchen (CPKI)	Peet's Coffee & Tea (PEET)
	People's Liberation (PPLB)
Castle Brands (ROX)	Potbelly's
Coach (COH)	Sephora
Design Within Reach (DWRI)	Starbucks (SBUX)
Eos Airlines	True Religion (TRLG)
Frederic Fekkai	Under Armour (UARM)
GoSMILE	Urban Outfitters (URBN)
Iconoculture	Vineyard Vines
Jones Soda (JSDA)	Volcom (VLCM)
Kerzner (KZL)	Yankee Candle (YCC)
Kiehl's	Zumiez (ZUMZ)

STAR GAZER

BRYANT KIEHL
CEO of Potbelly's

Some notable investors have said that Potbelly's is going to be the next Starbucks. I sat down with Bryant Kiehl and asked him about Potbelly's organization, how the company began, why it's successful, and where it's going. (To read my full interview with Bryant Kiehl, visit www.findingthenextstarbucks.com.)

As was most of Chicago, I was a big fan of the original Potbelly's shop on Lincoln Avenue. I became a die-hard regular. I remember the day that I first met the owner. He was burning cardboard in the Potbelly stove during the middle of Saturday lunch. I asked him why he hadn't opened more shops, and he responded that he hadn't yet met the right person. My response to him was "You have now." The rest is history.

Our vision is to stay true to the Potbelly brand while growing smartly. We want to preserve the simple recipe that made us successful and constantly get better at what we do. At present, we are focusing on augmenting our cult following as we expand into new markets. We want to prove that you can be big and good simultaneously. There are not many corporations left that are considered good. We want to be one of the few.

The key ingredients behind the company's phenomenal success are:

- A simple but incredibly good menu that allows us to serve great-tasting food to our customers.
- Striving to maintain a consistently good product while constantly improving it as well.
- A fun and interactive experience with the customers.

- Quality of service that is always quick and thoughtful.
- A really well-priced product that is of the highest quality (we give 'em a bang for their buck).
- Having a brand that people want to be a part of because it is authentic and real and it means something to everyone who is a part of it.
- Always striving to keep all of the above as simple and consistent as possible.

Potbelly's doesn't franchise because it's incredibly difficult to stay true to the brand if we franchise. Smart growth does not necessarily equate with rapid growth, which can often mean inconsistent operations and incredibly varied levels of service and quality in each franchise. We want our brand to be uniquely ours—from the top down—and we want our customers to count on the consistency of our brand.

We have performed well financially and have awarded our investors with greater value because of our fantastic product. We do not want to give up control over the quality and soul of the brand. We are not franchise-driven. We are in the restaurant business, not the real estate business. We have a single, united vision, purpose, and focus, which has led us to make decisions for the company based on what is right for the entire brand, for the right reasons. Simplicity is paramount. There is no soul in many of the franchised shops out there. Walk into one of those and then walk into a Potbelly's. The differences between the two are drastic, from the shop design to the ambient noise, all the way down to the scent in the air. Our is fresh, it's real, and we intend to keep it that way.

→ **MINORITY TO MAJORITY**

Hawaii's majority population has always been a minority within the overall U.S. population. California, Texas, and New Mexico are now minority/majority states, and by 2010, Georgia and New York are expected to be.

Latinos are not only the largest minority within the United States (some 40 million strong), but they are the fastest growing. The Latino population more than doubled from 1980 to 2000, from 15 million to 35 million, and grew another 14% to 40 million by 2004, according to the Pew Hispanic Center. It's expected that the Latino population will grow to 60 million by 2020, or approximately 20% of the U.S. population.

A U.S. SNAPSHOT: POPULATION BY RACE AND ETHNICITY

	POPULATION	DISTRIBUTION
Hispanic	40,424,528	14%
Native-born	22,381,207	7.7%
Foreign-born	18,043,321	6.2%
Non-Hispanic white	194,876,871	68%
Non-Hispanic black	34,919,473	12%
Non-Hispanic Asian	12,342,486	4%
Non-Hispanic other	5,717,108	2%
Total population	288,280,465	100%

Source: Trends 2000.

A key fact: With a median age of 27, the Latino population is much younger than the overall U.S. population (whose median age is 40). A full 36% of the Latino population is under the age of 18.

As an additional window to the future, Latino immigrants have double the birthrate of the rest of the United States. This will have a profound influence on our schools and workplaces. In fact, between now and 2020, Latinos are expected to account for half of the growth in the U.S. labor force.

The shift in the great American melting pot from a white majority to a much more diverse population led by Latinos provides challenges and opportunities for products, services, and marketers. According to the communications firm Ketchum, 89% of Latinos feel very proud of their Hispanic background and want to pass that cultural tradition on to their children. Seventy-nine percent believe that television programs and commercials should be directly targeted to the Latino community; 69% of the Hispanic market gets more information from advertisements in Spanish than in English; and they are 10% more likely than the general U.S. population to buy products that are the latest technology.

Latinos spent $500 billion in the United States in 2005, and it's expected this will grow to $1 trillion by 2020.

The growing population of Latinos will be the growth driver for many of the consumer trends in the United States, from restaurants to clothes, to music and entertainment, to financial services. Targeted media such as Univision and focused marketers have a huge tailwind for the next 50 years.

Visit www.findingthenextstarbucks.com for information about the following hot companies in the growing Latino market:

Hot Companies in the Latino Market

Bravo Group	Spanish Broadcasting
Chevy's	System (SBSA)
Chipotle (CMG)	Target (TGT)
Dieste & Partners	Telemundo
El Dorado Marketing	Univision (UVN)
MultiCultural Radio Broadcasting	

→ SAFE AND SECURE

The events of September 11, 2001, permanently changed the way I look at the world and the opportunities within it. Before 9/11, the role of government was to get out of the way so we could get business done. Now, the first question people ask is, "Is it safe?" National security is being taken more seriously than ever before by government agencies and companies alike.

The Internet is one area being closely watched, as Web 2.0 is a platform not only for legitimate businesses, but also for terrorism, crime, and fraud. Organizations are finding themselves continuously defending their enterprises against nonstop attacks from viruses, trojans, worms, and spyware. In a 2005 FBI report on computer crime, 87% of the organizations surveyed had experienced some type of security attack within the past 12 months.

According to International Data Corporation (IDC), the worldwide IT security market was $27.4 billion in 2004 and is expected to be $60 billion by 2009 for a CAGR of 20%. Worldwide security software expenditures came to $10 billion in 2004 and are expected to be $419.2 billion by 2009.

With the government becoming a major driving force and client, 9/11 has spawned a lot of new business around "physical" security. Examples include biometrics, X-ray technology, MRI, and chemical sensing, to name just a few. Additionally, technologies to support emergency workers have seen a lot of momentum, such as CAD/CAM software to map public spaces like buildings and train stations with the highest amount of granularity for emergency plans and scenario management. In addition, the new needs of homeland security have created many new requirements for the integration and interpretation of enormous amounts of data across historically separated government silos.

Computer systems touch upon nearly every aspect of the economy and our personal lives. Unfortunately, their significance has attracted the attention of parties who want to disrupt them to exploit the resulting publicity and damage for their own purposes. Currently, a lot of cyberattacks originate with hackers who consider hacking a competitive sport in which they try to defeat large technology companies like Microsoft and Symantec.

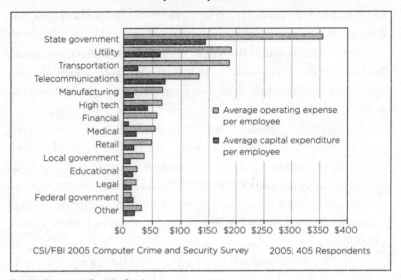

Average Reported Computer Security Expenditure/Investment per Employee by Industry Sector

Source: Computer Security Institute.

Larger coordinated attacks that can include full-blown cyberwars have been discussed and cannot be dismissed at this point. Technologies that guarantee the continuous "always-on" nature of computer systems will continue to be in hot demand. With antivirus protection and firewalls having become standard, the focus has moved to more sophisticated traffic flow analyses, authentication and authorization, and the overall convergence of security and network management to make computer systems infallible. Return on investment is the key metric organizations use to determine the value of a security solution.

Phishing attacks (phony e-mails intended to troll for the credit card or account numbers of unsuspecting victims) happen daily at most organizations, with the richest targets being financial institutions and their customers. Not surprisingly, organized crime and the FBI are meeting head on in cyberspace as some of the most sophisticated scams are being orchestrated by the Mafia.

The number of spam messages *daily* was 28 billion in 2005 (five for every man, woman, and child on Earth) and IDC expects it will grow to 45 billion by 2009.

In the world of convergence, some of the greatest security problems and opportunities will involve new applications such as VoIP, Web services, and storage networks. As these new applications grow in popularity, they will become more attractive targets for attack.

In a mobile world, wireless security grows more and more important. Just as it becomes more challenging to protect American citizens when they move outside U.S. borders, the security around always on knowledge workers will present challenges.

Last, as security increases in sophistication, defenses will move from detection to prevention. The transition will be from alerting you that you have a security problem to the higher-value preventing it from happening in the first place. While Symantec, IBM, and Microsoft are the gorillas in this market and have been consolidators, this space is ripe for new, innovative companies.

Security Technologies Used

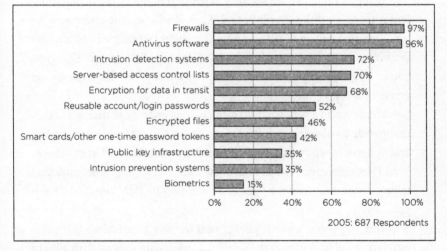

Source: CSI/FBI 2005 Computer Crime and Security Survey

Visit www.findingthenextstarbucks.com for information about the following hot companies in the growth area of security:

Hot Companies That Keep Us Safe and Secure

3VR Security	Network Intelligence
Arbor Networks	Oakley Networks
CipherTrust	Opsware (OPSW)
Cisco (CSCO)	Pay By Touch
CyberTrust	RSA Security (RSAS)
Elemental Security	ScanSafe
Fortify Software	VASCO Data Security (VDSI)
InfoBlox	Websense (WBSN)
Intergraph (INGR)	

→ HERE COMES THE SUN—ALTERNATIVE ENERGY

As I've said, great investment opportunities are frequently found where there is a problem. The bigger the problem, the bigger the opportunity.

Whether oil prices are $60 or $20 per barrel, the fundamental problem is there is a finite amount of oil. And oil will become uneconomical long before it runs out. It's also a fundamental fact that oil pollutes our environment in a way that's not sustainable. In Beijing and Shanghai, you can't go jogging because the air quality is so bad. This will only get worse unless it's addressed now.

Moreover, in a very volatile world, oil prices of more than $60 a barrel provide an obscene cash flow to countries such as Iran, Saudi Arabia, and Venezuela, which can use that wealth in ways that are harmful to us. Tom Friedman says, "Green is the new Red, White, and Blue," meaning taking action that makes us less dependent on foreign sources for oil is patriotic.

And the problem is only going to get worse. China is already the second largest oil importer in the world and represented more than 30% of the annual increase in oil consumption in 2005. Over the past five years, the growth in oil consumption in China has outpaced economic growth. With China's domestic oil production expected to decline starting in 2009, how will the world supply the oil China needs?

The key to solving this problem can't be found in the heated debate on whether we should drill for oil in Alaska. (I think we should. Anybody

AS PRICES RISE, TECHNOLOGIES EMERGE	
LONG-TERM OIL PRICE PER BARREL	ENERGY SOURCES UNLEASHED
$20–$30	**Ultradeep offshore wells** Futuristic gear for tapping formerly inaccessible deposits **Gas to liquid** Natural gas converted into diesel fuel **Tar sands** A sludgy mélange of petroleum and gravel **Digital oil fields** Networked drilling rigs and remote-controlled wells
$30–$70	**Natural gas** Conventional compressed methane (clean, efficient, and explosive) **Coal to liquid** An abundant energy resource transformed into diesel **Biodiesel** Vegetable oil pressed from soybeans and palms **Ethanol** Gasoline-compatible alcohol fermented from corn, sugar, and cellulose
ABOVE $70	**Methane hydrates** A crystalline amalgam of methane and frozen water **Hydrogen** The most common element in the universe (a superclean energy source) **Plug-in hybrids** Grid electrons propelling cars for short trips **Oil shale** High-grade petroleum melted out of sedimentary rock

Source: Wired magazine, December 2005.

who disagrees hasn't been to Alaska.) That's only a Band-Aid to the problem. The real issue is how to create a sensible long-term energy plan.

For the better part of a century, cheap oil has been a disincentive to developing and investing in alternative energy and energy technology. Now, a confluence of factors including the economics of $60-plus a barrel, security, environmentalism, scarcity, and breakthrough technologies all make alternative energy a megainvestment theme for the next 50 years. Renewable energy such as wind, solar, biofuels, and hydro is key to this theme, as are fuel cells and biomass.

The chief drawback of renewables is their cost compared with conventional sources of energy. The cost of generating electricity from wind turbines is at least 5 cents per kilowatt hour (kWh), for example. Solar or wave power cost is at least 18 or 20 cents per kWh. In contrast, the cost of electricity from conventional sources like oil, gas, and coal is typically much lower—as little as 3 to 5 cents per kWh.

Nevertheless, a close look at the renewable energy landscape reveals that it has regulatory, commercial, and technological trends on its side, all of which are working to close the cost gap with conventional sources. Taken together, they promise a far more sustainable, market-driven basis for investment in renewables than yesterday's faith in high oil prices.

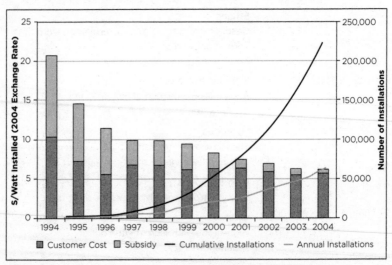

Residential Solar Market Transformation in Japan

Source: National Renewable Energy Laboratory.

Wind farms currently can provide enough energy for 1.6 million homes. By 2020, it will be 10 times that number.

Solar power is a permanent solution for as long as we have the sun, and when we don't, it won't matter anyway. President Bush's legislation to give homeowners using solar power a $2,000 tax credit is a start. And, experience in Japan has shown that long-term incentive programs are a great way to stimulate a self-sustaining industry. After 10 years of declining subsidies, the Japanese solar industry no longer needs subsidies to be cost effective. Germany is following in Japan's footsteps, as is California.

OIL VERSUS HYDROGEN VERSUS ETHANOL			
FACTOR	OIL	HYDROGEN	BIOFUELS
Energy security risk	High	Low	Low
Cost per mile	Medium	Medium–high	Low
Infrastructure cost	Very low	Very high	Low
Technology risk	Very low	Very high	Low
Environmental cost	Very high	Medium–low	Low
Implementation risk	Very low	Very high	Low
Interest group opposition	Very high	High	Low
Political difficulty	?	High	Low
Time to impact	—	Very low	Low

Source: Vinod Khosla, Kleiner Perkins Caufield & Byers.

With biofuels, we can literally grow our energy needs with corn and sugar cane. Ethanol has been around since Henry Ford used it in the first model T, but now it is at the forefront of viable solutions to the energy problem. Chemically, ethanol is identical to the grain alcohol that spiked the punch in college. Engines that run on ethanol cost less than gasoline engines and have almost no emissions that cause global warming.

Compared to hydrogen fuel cells, ethanol is compelling as an immediate solution since the switch to a flex-fuel car (one that could use either gasoline or ethanol) would require a minimum investment from the automakers because little change in the infrastructure would be needed to provide ethanol versus gas and the switchover could take place very quickly, in 3 to 5 years versus 10 to 15 years for hydrogen cars.

Brazil is already showing how this can work. In Brazil, 75% of all cars are flex-fuel versus a miniscule number in 2000. And, 40% of Brazil's light transportation fuel comes from ethanol. The conservative Department of Energy estimates that 30% of fuel consumption will be ethanol by 2030. With five million flex-fuel cars already operating in the United States and compelling reasons for change, this should be a big opportunity fast.

Using biotechnology and process technology, yields of crops can be increased dramatically. The "food-and-fuel" option can turn America's heartland into an economic powerhouse like Saudi Arabia.

Hydropower, mainly from dams, could rise 30-fold by increased retrofitting of the 95% of dams that aren't used for electricity.

Fuel cell technology has advanced with commercial portable generators you can use for your home. The Toyota Prius is the new BMW for some celebrities, many technogeeks, and, especially, the "green group." There are special primo parking spots in parking garages and downtown for hybrid cars in Palo Alto.

The International Energy Agency (IEA), a quasigovernmental agency not known for excessive greenery, forecasts that more than $1 trillion will be invested in nonhydro renewable technologies worldwide by 2030. By then, the IEA predicts, such technologies will triple their share of the world's power generation to 6%. In some regions, such as western Europe and California, the share could top 20%.

Green is good both for our world and for investment opportunities.

Biomass Will Make a Difference

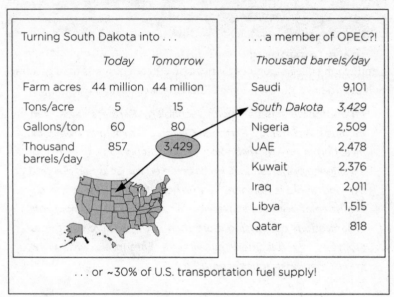

Turning South Dakota into . . .				. . . a member of OPEC?!	
	Today	*Tomorrow*		*Thousand barrels/day*	
Farm acres	44 million	44 million		Saudi	9,101
Tons/acre	5	15		*South Dakota*	*3,429*
Gallons/ton	60	80		Nigeria	2,509
Thousand barrels/day	857	3,429		UAE	2,478
				Kuwait	2,376
				Iraq	2,011
				Libya	1,515
				Qatar	818

. . . or ~30% of U.S. transportation fuel supply!

Source: Vinod Khosla, Kleiner Perkins Caufield & Byers.

Visit www.findingthenextstarbucks.com for information about the following hot companies in the growth area of alternative energy:

Hot Companies in Alternative Energy

Altra

Archer-Daniels-Midland (ADM)

CoalTek

Evergreen Solar (ESLR)

First Solar

GreenFuel

Imperiuim Renewables
(Seattle Biodiesel)

Iogen

Ion America

Miasole

NanoSolar

Pacific Ethanol, Inc. (PEIX)

Renewable Energy
Corporation (REC)

Rentech (RTK)

Sasol (SSL)

SunPower Corporation
(SPWR)

SunTech Power (STP)

VeraSun

Vestas (VWS)

STAR GAZER

IRA EHRENPREIS
general partner at Technology Partners

Ira Ehrenpreis has been with Technology Partners since 1996. Ira leads Technology Partners' Cleantech investment practice, investing in energy technology, water technology, and materials science opportunities. He has worked for Goldman, Sachs & Co. and Juniper Partners venture capital firm. Ira is the co-chairman of both the VCNetwork and the YVCA, two nonprofit organizations comprising more than 1,000 venture capitalists. (To read my full interview with Ira Ehrenpreis, visit www.findingthenextstarbucks.com.)

I have three primary drivers as to what excites me about clean tech. The first of these really relates to the venture asset class. The way I look at venture capital, it's all about finding the inefficiencies in the asset class. That's what private equity is supposed to be about. It's not about momentum investing. It's not about investing along the efficient frontier. It's supposed to be about finding the next new big thing and doing it in a way that takes advantage of the private market. The first driver is that we believe clean tech remains one of the few underserved areas in the venture asset class. Number two, venture capitalists always look for big markets, and the energy and the water market, and for that matter the materials science areas, are really among the biggest markets in the world. Driver number three is we're always looking for a place where early-stage companies can have a profound impact on how the ecosystem works.

Probably the most important thing to understand when we look at the term *clean tech* is that clean tech is not monolithic.

In other areas when venture capitalists invest, when we use a sector terminology, there's a relatively standard meaning of that sector, that business model. But in clean tech, that's not the case. *Clean tech* is an umbrella term for the three pillars that define it. The first pillar is energy technology, the second pillar is water technology, and the third is materials science. In the energy space alone, there are hardware deals, there are software deals, there are services deals, there are companies that are a combination thereof. There are companies that focus on the electricity aspect; there are companies that focus on the solar aspect or the storage aspect; there are coal technology companies. There is a wide range of kinds of companies and, therefore, kinds of business models that represent great stuff. For me, that's one of the exciting things.

I think that if you look forward, we're going to find that 2006 and 2007 will be the years of biofuels. It will be the beginning of new kinds of petroleum substitutes or ways of attempting some form of energy independence. We've already seen the beginnings of that with some initial filings of companies that look like they will be going public in the latter half of '06, and I think we'll continue to see that trend into '07. So I'm excited about biofuels, which means both ethanol and biodiesel opportunities.

I think we're going to see coal technologies become an increasingly important area of innovation. The fact remains that the United States is the Saudi Arabia of coal. We have 26% of the entire world's coal reserves here. Over 50% of our entire electricity generation is based on coal-fired plants. There are technologies that help to make coal cleaner and increase the efficiency of burning coal.

→ NANOTECHNOLOGY—THE MINI-ME REVOLUTION

"Imagination rules the world."   —NAPOLÉON BONAPARTE

Nanotechnology will be at the forefront of innovation and progress in information technology, communication, health care, energy technology, and consumer lifestyles for the next 50 years.

Futurist K. Eric Drexler coined the term *nanotechnology* in his 1981 classic *The Engines of Creation*. *Nano* means "little men" or "dwarf" in Greek. *Nano* is also the designated prefix for a billionth of a standard measure (such as meter, gram, or liter) in the metric system.

How small is small? In terms of length, a nanometer is one billionth of a meter. A single nanometer is so small that 10 hydrogen atoms could span the distance. Contrary to popular belief, the extremely cool, extremely small iPod Nano doesn't employ any nanotechnology.

Nanotechnology, according to the National Science Foundation, is "working at the atomic, molecular and super-molecular levels, in the length of scale of approximately 1 to 100 nanometer range, in order to understand and create materials, devices and systems with fundamentally new properties and functions because of their small structure."

Ultimately, nanotechnology is tiny technology that fundamentally changes the rules of science. Through nanotechnology, convergence of distinct disciplines of chemistry, biology, and physics can create applications and solutions previously unimaginable. Applications of nanotechnology such as stain-resistant clothing and high-performance tennis racquets are cool, but offer only a glimpse of the more exciting opportunities to come.

By 2010, nanotechnology will significantly influence information and communication technology, health care, consumer markets, and energy technology. Hundreds of companies, from start-ups to Fortune 500s, are working around the clock (and around the world) to commercialize nanotechnology.

Information technology and communication will significantly benefit from nanotechnology as Moore's Law is being challenged to meet future demands for computer speed, efficient power usage, and device storage. Today, all of the big-chip manufacturers, including Intel and Transmeta of Santa Clara, California, and Advanced Micro Devices (AMD)

Targets of Large-Company Nanotechnology Development

Company	Devices	Displays	Computing	Sensors	Health care	Energy	Materials	Defense
Intel	●							
IBM	●		●					
HP	●		●					
3M					●		●	
DuPont		●					●	●
GE	●	●			●	●	●	●
Samsung	●	●						
Hitachi	●	●				●		

Source: ThinkEquity Partners.

of Sunnyvale, California, are producing parts with nanoscale features. Beyond the simple nanoscale miniaturization, these companies and several start-ups are exploring a completely new approach that takes advantage of quantum-scale effects. If a logic chip could be made this way, it would hold tens of billions of logic elements, compared with 50 million on existing chips.

Nanotechnology will play an important role in creating new approaches to diagnosing and curing disease. The convergence of "wet" (biology) and "dry" (nanotechnology) will significantly enhance the opportunities in biotech.

Nanoparticles are being developed to deliver drugs and genes to patients, allowing medicines to be taken in a more convenient form. Another application for nanoparticles could be the enhancement of medical imaging. For example, iron particles might improve the quality of MRI scans.

Energy technology will benefit from nanotechnology, both through its more efficient use (particularly in lighting) and through more effective ways of generating electricity. Nanoscale particles used in new solid-state lighting could cut the electricity used for illumination by up to 50% by 2025. Ordinary light bulbs would be replaced with improved

NANOTECH-ENABLED PRODUCTS
TODAY AND TOMORROW

2004	2008	2012 and Beyond
Consumer Goods		
Sunscreen/ cosmetics	"Smart" paints/coatings	Self-cleaning fabric
Self-cleaning fabrics	Nonprecious catalysts	Solid-state refrigeration
Stain-resistant clothing		
Sporting goods		
Composite parts		
Information and Communications		
CMP slurries	Nonvolatile memory	Quantum computing
Optical components	Flat-panel displays	Flexible ICs
LCD displays	OLEDs	Dip-pen lithography
Nanolithography	Spintronics memory	Biomolecular devices
Inkjet printers (MEMS)	All optical devices	
Hard-drive disk heads	Ultra-high-density storage	
Health Care/Life Sciences		
Burn and wound dressings	In vitro diagnostics	In vivo diagnostics
Sensors (MEMS)	Gene expression arrays	Drug delivery
Microarrays (MEMS)	Biosensors	Prosthetics
MRI agents	Synthetic bone	Gene therapy

2004	2008	2012 and Beyond
Energy and Environment		
	Felixible photovoltaics	Solar arrays
	Nanostructured catalysts	Remediation
	Miniature fuel cells	Solid-state generation
	Nanostructured magnets	

Source: ThinkEquity Partners.

versions of light-emitting diodes (LEDs) that emit bright white light. Companies such as Color Kinetics are already commercializing such technology. Nanotechnology is also helping to bring energy technologies such as fuel cells to market. Cheap and efficient solar cells look within reach, using newly developed materials to replace the fragile and expensive silicon-based wafers currently in use.

Governments are the leading nanotech investors in the world, funding R&D to the tune of about $3.5 billion a year (about $1 billion in the United States). Venture capitalists are still relatively small participants, but leading VCs such as Draper Fisher Jurvetson, Venrock, and Harris & Harris have invested hundreds of millions in nanotechnology to date.

Given the newness of the industry, there are very limited ways to participate in the public markets today. Options include investing in companies such as FEI and Veeco providing research instrumentation—"picks, pans, and shovels" for the "prospectors." These include imaging tools (small-scale cameras and microscopes), manufacturing tools (for building and cleaning nanodevices), and building blocks (physical, biological, and chemical matter). Harris & Harris got involved as a business development company with a portfolio of "tiny-technology" private investments.

There are significant implications for established companies such as DuPont, Intel, GE, IBM, and HP, which are making bets in order to participate in the disruptive changes nanotechnology will bring forth.

Visit www.findingthenextstarbucks.com for information about the following hot companies in the growth area of nanotechnology:

Hot Companies in Nanotechnology

Altair Nanotechnologies (ALTI)

Apollo Diamond

Ceres (CERG)

Color Kinetics (CLRK)

Harris & Harris (TINY)

InPhase Technologies

Molecular Imprints

Nanofilm

NanoOpto

NanoString

Nanosys

Nano-Tex

Nantero

Terracycle

XDx

ZettaCore

Zyvex

→ **STAR GAZER**

CHARLIE HARRIS
chairman of Harris & Harris

Harris & Harris Group, Inc., is a publicly traded company that operates as a venture capital firm. It invests in tiny-technology-enabled companies, including nanotechnology, microsystems, and microelectromechanical systems (MEMS) technology firms. (To read my full interview with Charlie Harris, visit www.finding thenextstarbucks.com.)

In 1994, I looked at a venture capital deal called NanoPhase that was built on a cornerstone of nanotechnology and intellectual property. I had never looked at a nanotechnology deal before, but in the course of doing the due diligence on this opportunity, I got more and more intrigued and realized that nanotechnology would change the world.

We quickly realized that, number one, nanotechnology was very early in its development cycle, but in the long run, this was going to be revolutionary in the most literal senses of the word, that it was going to give mankind a totally new tool kit from which to operate and from which to build things. So we invested in NanoPhase, and, as good luck would have it, it went public three years later in 1997. We were fortunate enough to make some money on that investment, but the main thing we got out of it was the beginnings of an education.

Starting in 1994, I looked at every deal that I could identify that was based on nanotechnology, but back then, most of what we saw was essentially a series of science experiments that weren't really ready for commercialization. By early 2001, we realized that a pipeline of opportunities was building up that met the characteristics of classical early-stage venture capital investments. We made our second investment ever in a nanotech company in the middle of 2001. It was a spinout from Harvard University called Nantero. Whereas NanoPhase is a materials company, Nantero wanted to make memory devices based on utilization of carbon nanotubes—a complex exercise and one that, if successful, promised much greater rewards because it was addressing a very large market. Nantero's technology would enable memory devices to be instant-on so that there would be no time wasted in booting up computing devices with this memory device, along with its other potential advantages. If successful, Nantero's memory could replace all existing forms of memory devices.

We realized that because nanotechnology (which is really just sets of enabling technologies) eventually was going to be part of almost any field that we could identify, we would wind up with a lot of economic diversification in our portfolio because we would be investing in many different products addressing many different markets.

10

Case Studies

"I wonder why we hate the past so?"
—W. D. HOWELLS TO MARK TWAIN

"It's so damn humiliating."
—TWAIN'S REPLY

IN ATTEMPTING to identify and invest in the stars of tomorrow, it's often instructive to analyze the characteristics of the big winners of the past, and also, companies that had promise, but faltered.

→ CASE STUDY COMPARISON: BEST BUY VERSUS CIRCUIT CITY

BEST BUY   **TICKER: BBY**

YEAR FOUNDED: 1966   YEAR OF IPO: 1985

FOUNDED IN ST. PAUL, MN, BY RICHARD SCHULZE

CURRENT CEO: BRADBURY ANDERSON

COMPANY FUNCTION: LARGEST RETAILER OF
CONSUMER ELECTRONICS, HOME OFFICE SUPPLIES,
SOFTWARE, AND MORE

Folk Story

Richard Schulze sold brand-name stereo equipment as a manufacturer's representative for six years before he decided to start Sound of Music. Initially, the store sold only stereo components, but expanded into other electronic goods. In 1981, a tornado destroyed all but the storeroom of the company's largest store. Schulze responded to the catastrophe by holding a huge sale in the parking lot. This led to the idea of a superstore. In 1983, the company changed its name to Best Buy and opened the first Best Buy store.

Best Buy's business model combines the specialty retailer with the big-box merchant by selling name brands at discount prices. Best Buy's products are all sold on the floor, so customers can see their purchases firsthand. In addition, salespeople are not paid on commission, which helps customers get knowledgeable assistance without pressure. This sales strategy was so popular with consumers that Best Buy's revenues increased 1,000% between 1989 and 1994.

The Four Ps

People: Best Buy traditionally valued long hours and personal sacrifice from employees. Now, recognizing trends toward quality work from home as well as corporate burnout, 50% of its employees are allowed to work on their own schedules, with performance measured in progress toward company goals. Insiders own 16.3% of stock.

Product: Best Buy sells brand-name consumer electronics and office supplies at competitive prices. They have a strong brand represented by the yellow tag.

Potential: Best Buy has 25% market share in the electronics/appliance stores industry. This $83 billion industry is expected to grow 10%, in comparison to Best Buy's expected growth of 17%.

Predictability: Best Buy has met or exceeded Wall Street expectations in 16 of the 20 quarters from 2001 to 2005. The industry is well established and cyclical in nature.

MAJOR TRENDS THAT BENEFIT BEST BUY: Consolidation, demographics, Internet, brand

SECRET TO SUCCESS: Best Buy delivers quality at affordable prices and approaches new opportunities early on and in practical ways.

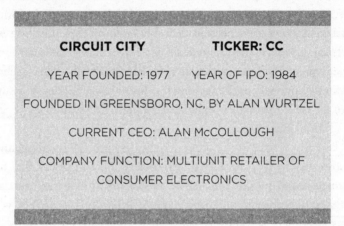

CIRCUIT CITY   TICKER: CC

YEAR FOUNDED: 1977   YEAR OF IPO: 1984

FOUNDED IN GREENSBORO, NC, BY ALAN WURTZEL

CURRENT CEO: ALAN McCOLLOUGH

COMPANY FUNCTION: MULTIUNIT RETAILER OF
CONSUMER ELECTRONICS

Folk Story

Circuit City got its start long before it became Circuit City. Samuel S. Wurtzel founded Wards, an acronym for Wurtzel and his family members Alan, Ruth, David, and Sam, in 1949 in Richmond, Virginia. The original Wards TV sold televisions out of a tire shop and grew to include the sale of home appliances. In 1961, Wards had four stores and made its initial public offering. Wards expanded into more areas of consumer electronics and also into appliances and furniture through various acquisitions.

In 1970, Sam Wurtzel retired, and his son Alan Wurtzel replaced him as head of Wards. The idea for Circuit City as a retailer of top-name brands with in-store service, convenient pickup, and knowledgeable sales personnel emerged, and Circuit City stores began replacing other Wards retailers. In 1981, Circuit City stores became superstores. It began trading on the NYSE as Circuit City Stores, Inc., in 1984. Circuit City introduced PCs in 1989, a year after competitor Best Buy, and stopped selling appliances in 2000. Circuit City remains a competitor in the consumer electronics space.

The Four Ps

People: Circuit City has a relaxed corporate atmosphere with casual dress and conveniences such as dry cleaning and sports fields on site. Their salespeople have been paid hourly since 2003, eliminating pressured sales. Insiders own 1.8% of stock.

Product: Circuit City is a consumer electronics and office supplies retailer. It is similar to Best Buy, except it often introduces the same concepts later—for example, computers in 1989 versus 1988, and hourly pay in 2003 versus 1989.

Potential: Circuit City has 3.5% market share and is expected to increase its earnings at 14% versus the industry's projected 10% growth rate.

Predictability: Circuit City has met or exceeded Wall Street expectations in 11 of 20 quarters from 2001 to 2005. The electronics/appliance stores industry is well established and cyclical in nature.

MAJOR TRENDS THAT BENEFIT CIRCUIT CITY: Consolidation, demographics, Internet

SECRET TO SUCCESS: Circuit City has pursued a variety of markets since its creation.

By the Numbers

	BBY	CC
Market cap at IPO	$28 million	$182 million
Market cap today	$24 billion	$4 billion
Earnings growth	26%	−7%
Stock CAGR	33%	15%
Estimated growth rate	17%	14%

	BBY	CC
Operating margin	5%	1%
2005 revenue	$29 billion	$11 billion
Value of $1 today	$301	$21

Best Buy versus Circuit City

Source: FactSet, ThinkEquity Partners.

Both Best Buy and Circuit City have been successful, but Best Buy has been spectacularly so. Best Buy's management constantly has shown the ability to be an innovator, while Circuit City has been a follower since the mid-1990s. Insider ownership remains material at Best Buy and is meaningless at Circuit City. In the notoriously difficult retail sector, Best Buy met or beat quarterly Wall Street estimates 16 times and Circuit City did only 11 times from 2001 to 2005.

→ **CASE STUDY COMPARISON: INTEL VERSUS ADVANCED MICRO DEVICES (AMD)**

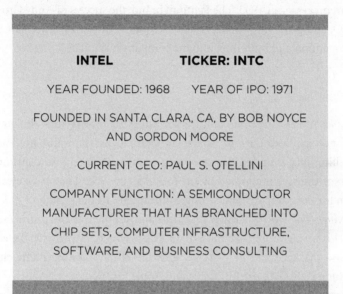

INTEL   **TICKER: INTC**

YEAR FOUNDED: 1968   YEAR OF IPO: 1971

FOUNDED IN SANTA CLARA, CA, BY BOB NOYCE
AND GORDON MOORE

CURRENT CEO: PAUL S. OTELLINI

COMPANY FUNCTION: A SEMICONDUCTOR
MANUFACTURER THAT HAS BRANCHED INTO
CHIP SETS, COMPUTER INFRASTRUCTURE,
SOFTWARE, AND BUSINESS CONSULTING

Folk Story

In 1968, Fairchild Semiconductor founders Bob Noyce and Gordon Moore (creator of Moore's Law, the theory that processing power will double every 18 months) left Fairchild to join a highly innovative new venture named NM Electronics. Financed with $2.5 million by famous venture capitalist Arthur Rock (the first Intel chairman), NM later in that year purchased the rights to use the name Intel from a company called Intelco. In 1969, Intel launched the world's first example of a semiconductor RAM and the "dropped-e" Intel logo was adopted. It became one of the most highly recognized brands in the world. Throughout the next decade, Intel pioneered the development of microprocessors and read-only memory. In 1981, it won an important IBM PC microprocessor supplier account, paving the path for future success.

Despite nearly a decade of a PC recession and the sudden death of their founder Bob Noyce in 1990, Intel continued to press on, breaking the supercomputing record in 1991 and releasing the wildly successful Pentium processor in 1993. The Pentium brand, the success of Andy Grove as CEO, and growth in their processors continued to push Intel past their competition and built Intel into the company it is today.

The Four Ps

People: Intel's corporate culture continues to inspire new design and technology. Both current Chairman Craig R. Barrett and CEO Paul S. Otellini have long tenures in management with Intel and continue to pursue the vision adopted by the founders in 1968. They have clear vision for the company and strong commitment to the product.

Product: The world's largest producer and supplier of microprocessors, Intel is inside more than 85% of all PCs produced worldwide. Intel has 12.5% market share in a market growing at 20%. Its big-name clients include Dell, Gateway, IBM, HP, and Apple.

Potential: Intel is in a market that seems relatively mature, but enjoys consistent growth in the international marketplace. It competes with such giants as AMD, Fairchild Semi, and National Semiconductor. Intel also faces data storage competition from Scandisk and IBM.

Predictability: Market maturity in the semiconductor sector, questionable ability to expand into other regions, and comparably high prices of R&D are concerns for Intel, but they lead the sector in both R&D and acquisitions, which could correlate to future earnings growth. Intel has met or exceeded Wall Street expectations in 16 of the past 19 quarters. "Intel Inside" has successfully created brand value, which converts visibility into profitability.

MAJOR TRENDS THAT BENEFIT INTEL: Internet, globalization, knowledge economy

SECRET TO SUCCESS: Heavy investment in R&D enables Intel to be an innovator that leads by example.

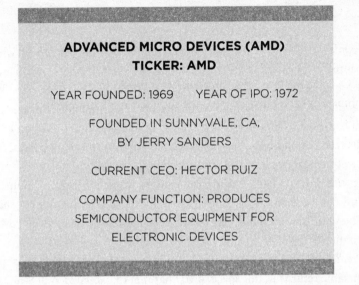

ADVANCED MICRO DEVICES (AMD)
TICKER: AMD

YEAR FOUNDED: 1969   YEAR OF IPO: 1972

FOUNDED IN SUNNYVALE, CA,
BY JERRY SANDERS

CURRENT CEO: HECTOR RUIZ

COMPANY FUNCTION: PRODUCES
SEMICONDUCTOR EQUIPMENT FOR
ELECTRONIC DEVICES

Folk Story

Lore has it that in the 1960s, Jerry Sanders wore a pink suit to a meeting with IBM executives. He denies it, but the story lives on, probably because in the semiconductor industry Sanders is a visible legend for his flair and style. In 1969, Sanders was working at Fairchild Semiconductors when six other employees grew disgruntled because of management changes. They decided to break free, and Sanders went with them on the condition that they elect him president. They agreed, and he was president and CEO of AMD for the next 33 years.

AMD started as an integrated circuits and transistors manufacturer, but has since branched into microprocessors, Flash memory devices, and processors. They strive to innovate to the needs of consumers, not for the sake of innovation itself. AMD has strong ties to IBM and Microsoft as a significant supplier of processors. The legendary Sanders retired as CEO in 2002 and replaced himself with Dr. Hector Ruiz. Since taking the helm, Dr. Ruiz has introduced the 50/15 initiative for 50% of the world to have affordable access to the Internet by 2015, and continues to innovate in search of more efficient and affordable technologies.

The Four Ps

People: AMD has a team-oriented, nonhierarchical climate in which people are viewed as the most important asset. Insiders own a mere 0.2% of stock.

Product: AMD produces microprocessors, Flash memory devices, and silicon-based solutions for the computer and consumer electronics industries. In addition, they market their interest in selling products to meet the real needs of real consumers in the real world today.

Potential: AMD has a 2% market share in the semiconductor industry, and battles industry giant Intel for domestic and global market share. The semiconductor industry is estimated to grow at 20%, versus AMD's predicted 15%.

Predictability: Competitive and innovative pressures lead to unpredictable returns in this space. AMD has met or exceeded Wall Street expectations only nine times in the past five years.

MAJOR TRENDS THAT BENEFIT ADVANCED MICRO DEVICES (AMD): Globalization, Internet

SECRET TO SUCCESS: AMD innovates to the needs of consumers.

By the Numbers

	INTC	AMD
Market cap at IPO	$60 million	$781 million
Earnings growth	21%	1%
Stock CAGR	15%	8%
Estimated growth rate	17%	16%
Operating margin	31%	1%
2005 revenue	$39 billion	$6 billion
Value of $1 today	$109	$14

Intel versus AMD

Source: FactSet, ThinkEquity Partners.

Intel and AMD have both achieved success, but Intel has been one of the most successful companies in the world. Intel's culture of rigorous innovation and building a brand have contributed to its outsized success.

→ **CASE STUDY COMPARISON: DELL VERSUS GATEWAY**

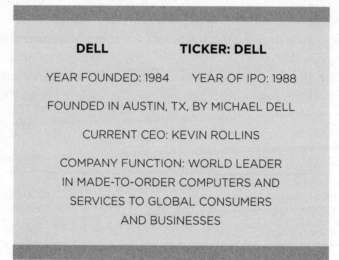

DELL   **TICKER: DELL**

YEAR FOUNDED: 1984   YEAR OF IPO: 1988

FOUNDED IN AUSTIN, TX, BY MICHAEL DELL

CURRENT CEO: KEVIN ROLLINS

COMPANY FUNCTION: WORLD LEADER
IN MADE-TO-ORDER COMPUTERS AND
SERVICES TO GLOBAL CONSUMERS
AND BUSINESSES

Folk Story

Not many undergraduate students can boast about dropping out, but Michael Dell is an exception to that rule. At 18, Dell started selling custom-made computers from his dorm room, and at 19 he dropped out, using $1,000 in start-up capital to formally begin Dell Computer Corporation. In 1992, at 27, Dell became the youngest CEO ever to make the Fortune 500 list of the world's largest companies.

Dell's company sold 10 million computer systems by 1997, and its success has continued into the 21st century. It makes more than $50 million in online revenue each day. Technical services make up 30% of the company's revenues. Dell printer sales reached 33% market share in just 18 months, despite predictions that Dell could not succeed in printers without retail stores. In 2005, Dell was ranked "America's Most Admired Company" by *Fortune*.

The Four Ps

People: Dell is a flat organization, with the entrepreneurial, fast-paced climate more typical of a start-up company. People at any level are welcome to make decisions that will benefit operations. Management owns 9.8% of stock.

Product: Dell was an early adopter and innovator in manufacturing and virtual storage online, just in time to leverage the power of the Internet. Dell's computers are made to order and delivered quickly. Dell is also regarded as one of the best global brands.

Potential: Dell has 35% market share in the computer processing hardware industry. The industry is currently valued at $232 billion and has an expected long-term growth rate of 16%. Dell is expected to grow at 19%.

Predictability: Dell's business is dependent on global computer sales and the popularity of electronic devices. Convergence of products in the digital home is a trend in their favor as they continue to improve on integration of their goods. Dell met or exceeded Wall Street expectations in 13 quarters from 2001 through 2005.

MAJOR TRENDS THAT BENEFIT DELL: Internet, globalization, demographics, convergence, brand

SECRET TO SUCCESS: Dell has a commitment to meeting customer demands quickly and at low cost.

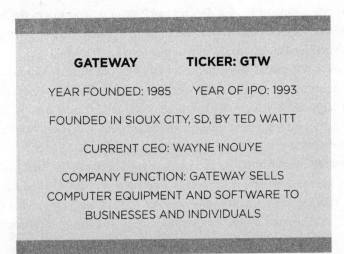

GATEWAY   **TICKER: GTW**

YEAR FOUNDED: 1985   YEAR OF IPO: 1993

FOUNDED IN SIOUX CITY, SD, BY TED WAITT

CURRENT CEO: WAYNE INOUYE

COMPANY FUNCTION: GATEWAY SELLS COMPUTER EQUIPMENT AND SOFTWARE TO BUSINESSES AND INDIVIDUALS

Folk Story

Founded in 1985 in an Iowa farmhouse, Gateway has grown into one of America's best-known brands with millions of customers. With $10,000 from Grandma, a rented computer, and a three-page "business plan," Ted Waitt turned Gateway into a company whose innovations have helped to shape the technology industry.

Despite nearly a decade of steady growth, a successful acquisition of eMachines, and continuous expansion into the home media sector, Gateway has recently seen a slowing in their consumer PC sales and a steady decline in their stock price due to these slower sales as well as losses reported as a result of the exploration of retail outlets. With Wayne Inouye (a seasoned executive who turned around eMachines) behind the wheel, the future is uncertain for Gateway. Despite recent downturns, Gateway remains focused on its core businesses and recently received a breath of fresh air with a winning bid as computer supplier for the state government of California.

The Four Ps

People: With several decades of senior executive experience at prominent retail companies, Inouye orchestrated the successful turnaround of eMachines, Inc., culminating in its acquisition by Gateway in March 2004. Management and insiders control 29% of shares outstanding with Ted Waitt as the single largest shareholder. Gateway prides itself on its diversity in terms of people, ideas, customers, and products.

Product: With solid computers, monitors, home theater components, and customer support, Gateway offers solutions for consumers, small and large enterprises, and government and educational groups. They also have a strong brand image with the cow box reflecting their farmhouse heritage.

Potential: Despite a market cap of just over $1 billion, Gateway has less than 1% market share in the computer processing hardware industry. It has suffered from negative growth rates in previous years and is currently not covered by any Wall Street analysts. The computer industry is expected to grow at a rate of 16%, but Gateway will need to garner market share to benefit from this growth.

Predictability: Gateway faces stiff competition from industry giants such as Dell and Apple. The computer industry is maturing and Gateway needs innovative products to compete. It has met or exceeded Wall Street expectations in only 8 of the previous 20 quarters.

MAJOR TRENDS THAT BENEFIT GATEWAY: Internet, globalization, brand
SECRET TO SUCCESS: Gateway has a memorable brand image, but needs to set its product above competitors.

By the Numbers

	DELL	GTW
Market cap at IPO	$212 million	$1 billion
Market cap today	$72 billion	$1 billion
Earnings growth	35%	NM
Stock CAGR	41%	−2%
Estimated growth rate	16%	No estimate
Operating margin	9%	0%
2005 revenue	$54 billion	$4 billion
Value of $1 today	$339	$1

Dell versus Gateway

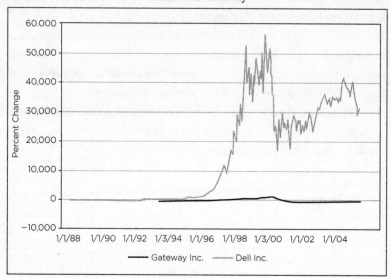

Source: FactSet, ThinkEquity Partners.

Though they were started within a year of each other by young rebels with a similar cause, the evolutions of Dell and Gateway couldn't be more different. Under Michael Dell's leadership, Dell evolved from a commodity maker of PCs to an undisputed leader in manufacturing, distributing, and creating a global brand. Gateway, under Ted Waitt's leadership, stayed in a time warp in a dynamic and increasingly competitive domestic PC market.

→ **CASE STUDY COMPARISON:**
STARBUCKS VERSUS KRISPY KREME

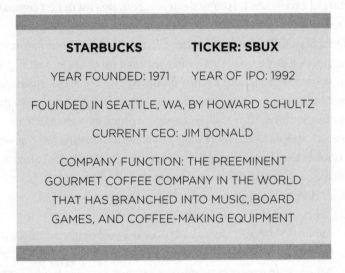

STARBUCKS   TICKER: SBUX

YEAR FOUNDED: 1971   YEAR OF IPO: 1992

FOUNDED IN SEATTLE, WA, BY HOWARD SCHULTZ

CURRENT CEO: JIM DONALD

COMPANY FUNCTION: THE PREEMINENT
GOURMET COFFEE COMPANY IN THE WORLD
THAT HAS BRANCHED INTO MUSIC, BOARD
GAMES, AND COFFEE-MAKING EQUIPMENT

Folk Story

In 1971, Starbucks was born as a small, whole-bean coffee retailer as committed to coffee beans as wineries are to their grapes. The original founders, Jerry Baldwin, Zev Siegel, and Gordon Bowker, were inspired by Dutch immigrant Alfred Peet, who had established a loyal customer base in Berkeley, California. Peet instructed the three in the fine intricacies of coffee roasting, and as they mastered it, their popularity in Seattle grew. Named after the coffee-loving first mate in *Moby-Dick*, Starbuck, the company became an aromatic icon.

Howard Schultz discovered Starbucks in 1981, and he was forever changed. He loved the quality and passion that the owners imparted in their coffee, and he believed Starbucks could become the most valued coffee brand in the world. He set about reaching this goal, undaunted by the year it took to even be hired at Starbucks. Inspired by the Italian coffee bar, and committed to every employee in memory of his late father, Schultz eventually became CEO of the company now known as Starbucks Corporation.

The Four Ps

People: Eligible full- and part-time employees receive full health benefits. Starbucks has an extensive training program for employees and a culture of excellence. It is consistently on *Fortune*'s list of best companies to work for in the United States. Insiders own 2% of stock.

Product: Starbucks sells quality coffee differentiated by unique flavor, products, and cup design. They also offer seasonal products and retail goods such as games, music, and kitchen products. The Starbucks experience is meant to be a part of one's day. They even have WiFi! Each store's unique décor has Starbucks' flair while incorporating local customs and traditions.

Potential: Starbucks has more than 11,000 units globally, 2,872 of which are outside the United States. They plan to expand to 15,000 units in the United States and 15,000 more internationally. Much of their international unit growth is planned for China, which currently has only 179 units. Their expected growth rate is 22%.

Predictability: Starbucks has indeed become a part of its customers' days, with the average customer coming 16 to 20 times per month. The company achieved 164 months of positive same-store sales results through August 2005.

MAJOR TRENDS THAT BENEFIT STARBUCKS: Brand, demographics, globalization

SECRET TO SUCCESS: Passion for quality product and customer service.

KRISPY KREME   TICKER: KKD

YEAR FOUNDED: 1937   YEAR OF IPO: 2000

FOUNDED IN WINSTON-SALEM, NC, BY VERNON RUDOLF

CURRENT CEO: STEPHEN F. COOPER

COMPANY FUNCTION: A DOUGHNUT RETAILER THAT TOUTS FRESHLY MADE HOT ORIGINAL GLAZED DOUGHNUTS MADE IN A "DOUGHNUT THEATER"

Folk Story

In 1937, Vernon Rudolph bought a doughnut recipe from a French chef in New Orleans and started selling the doughnuts to local grocery stores in Winston-Salem, North Carolina. Fans started asking for hot, fresh doughnuts, so he cut a hole in the wall of his store and opened a retail branch. Over the next several decades, Krispy Kreme grew into a small Southeastern chain. Vernon wanted to ensure quality and consistency, so he developed a doughnut-making process that became today's doughnut theater.

In 1973, Vernon passed away, leaving a chain of doughnut stores, a loyal customer base, and a secret recipe. Revenues slowed, however, and the chain was sold to Beatrice Foods in 1976. The original franchisers purchased the chain in 1982. By then, nationwide expansion was well underway. Scott Livengood, a Krispy Kreme loyalist and longtime employee, became CEO in 1998 and took the company public in 2000. After a $21 IPO and a period of huge growth, with shares topping $50 at their peak, prices crashed to as low as $6 and the company came under scrutiny in 2004 for questionable bookkeeping. Livengood retired and in 2005, Krispy Kreme hired Stephen F. Cooper, an interim recovery CEO for such companies as Enron, Laidlaw, and Morrison Knudsen, to help generate a turnaround.

The Four Ps

People: The legendary founder died in 1973 and the company floundered. CEO Scott Livengood was a fan of the product and a longtime company employee, but had no experience as a chief executive. Cooper is a veteran recovery specialist, but he has little experience in restaurants. Company culture varies significantly between franchises.

Product: Great doughnuts, but a majority of marketing focuses on the doughnut theater (which loses its intrigue after a few visits) and impulse buys due to the HOT DOUGHNUTS NOW sign (which has limited visibility even in the best conditions). The product also runs counter to the wellness megatrend.

Potential: There are 368 Krispy Kreme franchises in 45 U.S. states and six countries. Many grocery stores and gas stations sell Krispy Kremes as well, decreasing novelty and leading to a sense of ubiquity. Individual store revenues have been decreasing despite growth at the corporate level, and franchises have been shutting down more quickly than they have been opening.

Predictability: Doughnuts are a long-standing treat, but they run counter to low-calorie, low-carb diets characteristic of the current wellness trend. The franchise faces significant competition from Dunkin' Donuts. A turnaround seems possible but unlikely.

MAJOR TRENDS THAT BENEFIT KRISPY KREME: Brand

SECRET TO SUCCESS: Hot, fresh doughnuts and a doughnut theater set Krispy Kremes apart from competitors.

By the Numbers

	SBUX	KKD
Market cap at IPO	$216 million	$262 million
Market cap today	$24 billion	$337 million
Earnings growth	48%	NM
Stock CAGR	30%	1%
Estimated growth rate	22%	19%
Operating margin	11%	NA
2005 revenue	$7 billion	$700 million
Value of $1 today	$30	$1

Starbucks versus Krispy Kreme

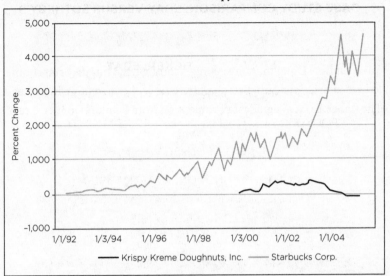

Source: FactSet, ThinkEquity Partners.

When Krispy Kreme went public, bulls said this was the next Starbucks. Enthusiasts pointed to the long lines at Krispy Kreme stores, the
sensational unit economics, and the ubiquitous brand. The problem
was, despite Krispy Kreme's having been around since 1937, its raging
popularity was a fad (how many doughnuts could you eat per week?) and
the company wasn't built to sustain the hypergrowth it was achieving.

Contrary to Starbucks, which was extremely careful about overex-
posing its brand and diluting it with poor associations, Krispy Kremes
started showing up everywhere, from grocery stores to gas stations. Starbucks believed that it had to own and operate its stores to control quality; Krispy Kreme rapidly franchised its units. (Dunkin' Donuts and
McDonald's are two examples of companies' successfully franchising
their concepts, but they did so thoughtfully over decades.)

→ **CASE STUDY COMPARISON: EBAY VERSUS SOTHEBY'S**

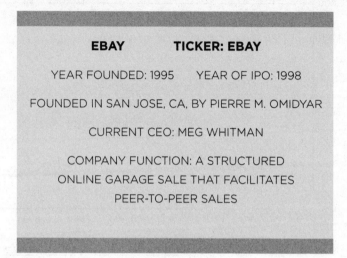

EBAY   TICKER: EBAY

YEAR FOUNDED: 1995   YEAR OF IPO: 1998

FOUNDED IN SAN JOSE, CA, BY PIERRE M. OMIDYAR

CURRENT CEO: MEG WHITMAN

COMPANY FUNCTION: A STRUCTURED
ONLINE GARAGE SALE THAT FACILITATES
PEER-TO-PEER SALES

Folk Story

In 1995, Pierre M. Omidyar's then fiancée was having difficulty finding other Pez candy dispenser collectors. This problem, others like it, and the emerging potential of the Internet gave rise to eBay. Omidyar recognized an untapped peer-to-peer marketplace in which the exchange of millions of goods could take place using the Internet and emerging secure money-transfer technologies such as PayPal.

Omidyar hired Jeff Skoll as the company's first full-time employee, and the two developed the online auction giant. Today, eBay consumes more shopping time than any other online retailer, and its markets serve more than 23 countries on all continents except Africa. Millions of items are listed on the average day, and consumers can view everything from used cars to home electronics to toast bearing a likeness of the Virgin Mary's image. The customer is the number-one focus for CEO Meg Whitman, who personally went so far as Guatemala to enable craftswomen to sell on eBay. More than 724,000 people report eBay as their primary or secondary source of income.

The Four Ps

People: Meg Whitman is an expert in branding, having overseen global marketing for Playskool and Mr. Potato Head. eBay's corporate culture focuses heavily on customers' needs. Insiders hold 25% of stock.

Product: eBay is an Internet-based secondary marketplace for virtually everything. It is essentially the ultimate online garage sale. Sales volume is increasing, but the rate slowed to 32% in 2005, compared to over 40% in 2004.

Potential: eBay became the largest used-car retailer after only four years in the market. eBay is striving to leverage more than 212 million Internet users in China. The first mover tends to get disproportionate spoils on the Internet, so to continue rapid growth, eBay must continue to be innovative.

Predictability: eBay has met or exceeded Wall Street expectations in all but one quarter since its IPO.

MAJOR TRENDS THAT BENEFIT EBAY: Internet, demographics, globalization, brand

SECRET TO SUCCESS: eBay facilitates trustworthy consumer transactions between peers.

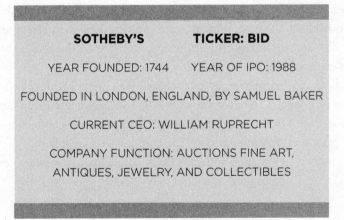

SOTHEBY'S   TICKER: BID

YEAR FOUNDED: 1744   YEAR OF IPO: 1988

FOUNDED IN LONDON, ENGLAND, BY SAMUEL BAKER

CURRENT CEO: WILLIAM RUPRECHT

COMPANY FUNCTION: AUCTIONS FINE ART, ANTIQUES, JEWELRY, AND COLLECTIBLES

Folk Story

The auction house's first-ever sale occurred under Baker's name in 1744. Well more than two centuries later, Sotheby's sold a single book, *The Gospels of Henry the Lion*, for more than £8 million. Today there are more than 100 Sotheby's offices throughout the world, and the company reports just over $500 million annually in sales. Sotheby's has preserved its corporate mission to handle premier auction items with great panache and showmanship for 225 years.

Sotheby's Holdings, Inc., together with its subsidiaries, operates as an auctioneer of fine art, antiques, decorative art, jewelry, and collectibles.

The Four Ps

People: Over the past two centuries, Sotheby's has continued to hire leaders with visions not only to expand the auction house's extensive clientele, but also to preserve its brand/reputation as the world's premier auctioneer. Insiders own a paltry 0.5% of stock.

Product: Acting as an auctioneer includes identification, evaluation, and appraisal of works of art; stimulating purchaser interest; and matching sellers and buyers through the auction process.

Potential: Sotheby's offers a tailored, world-class service comparable to no other auction house. With arts sales growing more than 12% internationally, Sotheby's is nicely positioned to compete in this unique niche. It is expected to grow at 15%.

Predictability: Sotheby's met or exceeded Wall Street earnings expectations in 7 out of 12 quarters between 2001 and 2005. The auction market is linked with the health of the economy and consumer confidence.

MAJOR TRENDS THAT BENEFIT SOTHEBY'S: Demographics

SECRET TO SUCCESS: Sotheby's provides quality auction services for an elite selection of products.

By the Numbers

	EBAY	BID
Market cap at IPO	$715 million	$450 million
Market cap today	$64 billion	$1 billion
Earnings growth	77%	1%
Stock CAGR	80%	5%
Estimated growth rate	30%	16%
Operating margin	33%	21%
2005 revenue	$5 billion	$500 million
Value of $1 today	$62	$2

eBay versus Sotheby's

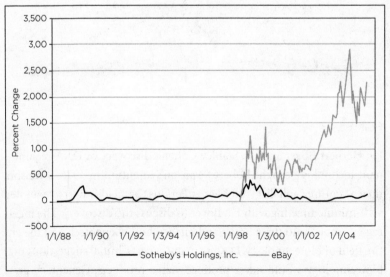

Source: FactSet, ThinkEquity Partners.

eBay utilized the emerging megatrend of the Internet to match up buyers and sellers of everything from Pez dispensers to automobiles. Its auction format automates what Sotheby's has done manually for more than 200 years. Combining the "reach" only the Internet can provide with the "richness" provided by its millions of contributors, eBay has a market value more than 60 times greater that Sotheby's' despite eBay's having existed for little more than a decade.

→ **CASE STUDY COMPARISON:**
  GENENTECH VERSUS PFIZER

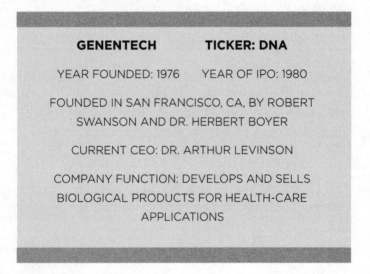

GENENTECH	TICKER: DNA
YEAR FOUNDED: 1976	YEAR OF IPO: 1980

FOUNDED IN SAN FRANCISCO, CA, BY ROBERT
SWANSON AND DR. HERBERT BOYER

CURRENT CEO: DR. ARTHUR LEVINSON

COMPANY FUNCTION: DEVELOPS AND SELLS
BIOLOGICAL PRODUCTS FOR HEALTH-CARE
APPLICATIONS

Folk Story

Dr. Herbert Boyer and Dr. Stanley Cohen's discovery of DNA recombinant technology caught Robert Swanson's attention in 1976. Swanson, then a venture capitalist with Kleiner Perkins Caufield & Byers, requested a 10-minute meeting with Dr. Boyer to discuss the discovery. The meeting expanded into three hours and birthed both Genentech and the entire field of biotechnology. Despite many experts' initial suggestions that biotechnology would never produce viable products, Genentech grew quickly and marketed its first recombinant DNA drug, human insulin, in 1982.

Its first IPO in 1980 was at an offering price of $35, but the stock ran up to $88 only an hour after it opened on the market. This was the first in a chain of record-breaking stock offerings, including a second IPO in 1999 when Roche Holding, Ltd., exercised its option to make Genentech redeem all of its outstanding shares not owned by Roche. After a month off the market, Genentech's second IPO shot from $97 to $127, and is considered the largest IPO in the history of health care. Today, Genentech continues to deliver innovative drugs to the market.

The Four Ps

People: Fortune repeatedly ranks Genentech as one of the best companies to work for in the United States. It is also among the top-ranked companies by women and working mothers. Insiders still own 55.6% of stock.

Product: Genentech created the biotechnology industry. Today it markets biologically based treatments for many life-threatening diseases. It has at least 30 products in development phases.

Potential: Genentech has a 9% market share in the biotechnology industry, which has an expected growth rate of 26%. Genentech is expected to grow at 33%.

Predictability: Biotechnology is heavily dependent on the regulatory environment, but despite this, Genentech has met or exceeded Wall Street expectations in 17 of the past 20 quarters. Multiple products create diversity within the brand, which increases visibility of revenue and earnings growth.

MAJOR TRENDS THAT BENEFIT GENENTECH: Convergence, demographics

SECRET TO SUCCESS: Genentech invented the biotechnology industry and has continued to lead with innovation and quality.

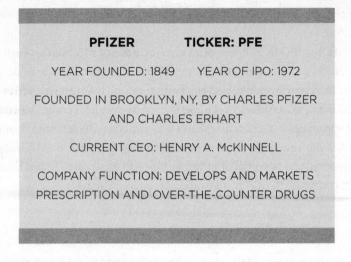

PFIZER   TICKER: PFE

YEAR FOUNDED: 1849   YEAR OF IPO: 1972

FOUNDED IN BROOKLYN, NY, BY CHARLES PFIZER
AND CHARLES ERHART

CURRENT CEO: HENRY A. McKINNELL

COMPANY FUNCTION: DEVELOPS AND MARKETS
PRESCRIPTION AND OVER-THE-COUNTER DRUGS

Folk Story

Charles Pfizer, a chemist, and his cousin Charles Erhart, a confectioner, left Germany in 1849 with $2,500 borrowed from Pfizer's father. Their goal was to introduce new chemicals to the U.S. market. The company's first pharmaceutical product was almond toffee–flavored santonin, a candy-flavored treatment for intestinal worms, which was a common affliction in 1849. Pfizer spent the next century developing chemicals that corresponded to American needs, such as wound medicines in the Civil War, citric acid for use in such products as Coca-Cola and Dr Pepper, penicillin in World War II, and many human and animal medicines in later parts of the 20th century.

Pharmaceuticals became the chemical of choice, and Pfizer donates $2 million every working day to provide medicine and health care to people in need throughout the world. It is known for Benadryl, Listerine, Neosporin, Rogaine, Sudafed, Visine, and more. Pfizer's prescription arsenal includes Lipitor, Viagra, and Zoloft.

The Four Ps

People: Pfizer is frequently voted one of the best companies to work for in the United States. Its culture centers on integrity, respect for people, teamwork, performance, and leadership, among other things. Pfizer has established these values over more than 150 years. Insiders hold less than 1% of stock.

Product: Pfizer is valued as one of the top global brands. It is striving to help people live longer, healthier, and happier lives through such products as Lipitor, Benadryl, Listerine, and Rolaids.

Potential: Pfizer has 16% market share in a $1.2 trillion market expected to grow at 10%. Pfizer is expected to grow at 8%.

Predictability: Pfizer has been within three cents of earnings expectations for all quarters in the past five years. They fell short of earnings expectations four times, but only once by more than one cent. Despite this solid earnings history, the pharmaceutical industry is heavily dependent on the regulatory environment and is subject to lawsuits.

MAJOR TRENDS THAT BENEFIT PFIZER: Brand, demographics, convergence

SECRET TO SUCCESS: Pfizer has delivered quality products tailored to the needs of the population for more than 150 years.

By the Numbers

	DNA	PFE
Market cap at IPO	$263 million	$7 billion
Market cap today	$104 billion	$157 billion
Earnings growth	31%	15%
Stock CAGR	22%	10%

	DNA	PFE
Estimated growth rate	33%	7%
Operating margin	16%	28%
2005 revenue	$5 billion	$51 billion
Value of $1 today	$142	$24

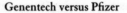

Genentech versus Pfizer

Source: FactSet, ThinkEquity Partners.

The first biotech IPO in 1980, Genentech has consistently been an innovator in life sciences and technology, placing itself at the forefront of the convergence megatrend. Pfizer has profited historically from a robust pipeline of new drugs. But increasingly its products remind me of the contents of my grandparents' medicine cabinets, whereas Genentech is developing drugs for today's and tomorrow's populations.

→ CASE STUDY COMPARISON:
APOLLO GROUP VERSUS EDISON SCHOOLS

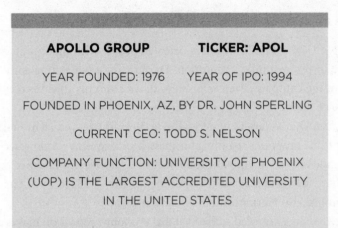

APOLLO GROUP   **TICKER: APOL**

YEAR FOUNDED: 1976   YEAR OF IPO: 1994

FOUNDED IN PHOENIX, AZ, BY DR. JOHN SPERLING

CURRENT CEO: TODD S. NELSON

COMPANY FUNCTION: UNIVERSITY OF PHOENIX
(UOP) IS THE LARGEST ACCREDITED UNIVERSITY
IN THE UNITED STATES

Folk Story

Dr. John Sperling did not learn to read until he was on tour with the Merchant Marines, but he overcame his childhood of poverty to ultimately achieve a PhD from Cambridge University. As a professor at San Jose State University, he participated in research that concluded that traditional universities were disinclined to meet the educational needs of working adults and that ongoing-education degree programs often required twice as much time for working adults to finish compared to their full-time student counterparts. Dr. Sperling left San Jose State to begin Apollo Group, which has become the leading provider of education for working adults.

Called McUniversity by the cynics, UOP has produced respected executives for leading companies such as Intel, General Motors, and AT&T. At UOP, adults who were once invisible on the traditional campus can pursue applicable professional education in order to change careers or improve their standing in the professional world. Dr. Sperling believed that all people, independent of age and ethnicity, deserve access to high-quality education. Today, Apollo Group remains committed to the growing population of adults seeking advanced education. UOP has an enrollment of more than 295,000 students, approximately 30% of whom are enrolled online. The average age of online students is 36.

The Four Ps

People: UOP is run by business-oriented people with significant experience in postsecondary education. Dr. Sperling's pioneering spirit lives on in the company, even as he steps down from his role. Insiders hold 18% of stock.

Product: UOP offers 18 undergraduate, 39 graduate, and 18 professional certificate programs spanning business, health care, counseling, technology, and education. Apollo Group operates University of Phoenix, the Institute for Professional Development, the College for Financial Planning, and Western International University.

Potential: In a knowledge-based global economy, education makes a difference in how individuals and companies perform, but only 24% of adult Americans have a bachelor's degree or higher. Supply effectively induces demand, so the potential for UOP's product is great domestically and greater internationally. Today, there are 90 campuses and 150 learning centers in 39 states, Puerto Rico, Vancouver, and British Columbia.

Predictability: Apollo has a highly predictable business model with students enrolled in programs for two to four years. The company has significant operating leverage, with 2% in 1994 increasing to 25% today. Apollo has met or exceeded Wall Street expectations in every quarter from 2001 to 2005.

MAJOR TRENDS THAT BENEFIT APOLLO GROUP: Knowledge economy, demographics, Internet, brand

SECRET TO SUCCESS: Early mover recognizes trends and needs of the working population.

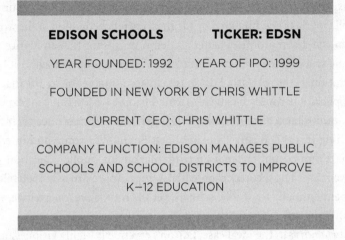

EDISON SCHOOLS   **TICKER: EDSN**

YEAR FOUNDED: 1992   YEAR OF IPO: 1999

FOUNDED IN NEW YORK BY CHRIS WHITTLE

CURRENT CEO: CHRIS WHITTLE

COMPANY FUNCTION: EDISON MANAGES PUBLIC
SCHOOLS AND SCHOOL DISTRICTS TO IMPROVE
K–12 EDUCATION

Folk Story

In Chris Whittle's 30-plus years in business, he has been both a media darling and a goat. Started when he was a 20-year-old University of Tennessee student, Chris's 13/30 media company grew 30% a year for 20 years. Chris, a man of big ideas, first envisioned Edison Schools amid dinner conversation in the Hamptons. Edison's objective is to reinvent the K–12 public education system.

Edison Schools operates charter schools, administers school districts, and runs a host of after-school and tutoring programs. Edison is contracted to help underperforming schools or districts improve test scores, which is cause for controversial performance statistics. Edison has reported both success and failure. Seeking to grab market share and proliferate its brand name, Edison entered into some high-profile but unprofitable contracts that ultimately led to sustained investor losses. Meanwhile, the education community criticized Edison for growing too quickly, with more concern for shareholders than students, in the years it was publicly traded. In all, Edison overpromised and underdelivered.

The Four Ps

People: Edison attracted widely acclaimed academic experts, teachers, and business leaders. They struggled in large part because they fell short of expectations. These shortcomings were exacerbated by the scrutiny of public markets and hindered by the most entrenched union in the world.

Product: Edison promises better academic results for the same price as a public school. However, it is difficult to deliver a program without total operational control. Also, Edison is held accountable for results that are complex to measure.

Potential: Charter schools have expanded into 40 states since their first opening in 1991. Bush's "No Child Left Behind" program and international competition create a growing market for public education improvements. The theoretical potential is huge. Approximately $500 billion is spent annually for public schools, yet the results are, on average, very poor.

Predictability: In the ideal case, Edison's revenue is highly visible since it can secure three- to five-year contracts. The reality, however, is that the for-profit stigma can discourage new contracts, and ultimately that all contracts can be broken.

MAJOR TRENDS THAT BENEFIT EDISON SCHOOLS: Knowledge economy, demographics

SECRET TO SUCCESS: Edison challenges conventional wisdom in public education.

By the Numbers

	APOL	EDSN
Market cap at IPO	$118 million	$760 million
Market cap today	$13 billion	No longer publicly traded
Earnings growth	49%	N/A
Stock CAGR	52%	N/A

	APOL	EDSN
Estimated growth rate	21%	N/A
Operating margin	32%	N/A
2005 revenue	$2 billion	N/A
Value of $1 today	$99	$0

Apollo Group versus Edison Schools

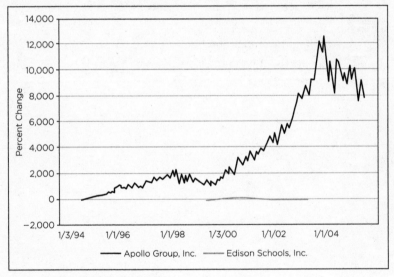

Source: FactSet, ThinkEquity Partners.

On the surface, Edison Schools and Apollo Group would appear to have had similar opportunities. Both were delivering educational services for profit and were leaders in their respective segments. The turbocharged politics inherent with K–12 education contributed to Edison's being a poor investment. Edison's management DNA of overpromising and underdelivering was a stark contrast to Apollo's earned reputation of underpromising and overdelivering.

THINK POINTS

→ Learn from past winners to spot new future winners.

→ You can learn as much from investment losers as winners.

→ Applying the megatrend framework with the 4 Ps is the recipe for identifying the stars of tomorrow today.

APPENDIX

PRELIMINARY GROWTH STOCK ANALYSIS

THE PRELIMINARY GROWTH STOCK ANALYSIS (PGSA) is a company "fact finder" I've developed over the past 20 years. The purpose is to have a systematic due-diligence framework to evaluate emerging growth companies. I've borrowed ideas from many sources in business and investing to compile the PGSA. I believe this is a great start to finding companies with the four Ps and the stars of tomorrow, today.

Fisher Analysis (Taken from Phil Fisher's
Common Stocks and Uncommon Profits)
1. What is the current size of the market/source? What is the market potential? At what rate is the industry growing? Assess megatrends (knowledge economy, globalization, Internet, brands, outsourcing, convergence, demographics, consolidation).
2. Does management have the vision and commitment to develop new products to allow for growth once present opportunities are exploited? Where is the company going to be in five years, and how are they going to get there?

PRELIMINARY INFORMATION

Company name:_____   Industry:_____

Date:_____

Analyst:_____   Symbol:_____

Met with whom:_____   Growth rate:_____

Investor contact:_____   Price: $_____

Phone number:_____   Market cap:_____

Web site:_____

Headquarters:_____   Shares outstanding:_____

1. What does the company do? Explain so a second grader can understand. What are the major profit drivers in each line of business?

2. What is the industry's stage of development (life-cycle position)?

---

3. How committed is the company to research and development? What percentage of revenue is spent on R&D versus sales? What are major R&D initiatives? How many people are in R&D?

4. How good is the sales organization? (Consider experience, depth, and incentive structure.)

5. Does the company have a worthwhile profit margin? (Consider trends, margins versus compeitition, gross/operating margins.)

6. What is the company doing to maintain or improve margins?

7. Does the management have good personnel and labor relations? (Consider strikes, middle-management turnover, stock ownership of employees, option programs.)

8. Does the company have outstanding executive relationships? (Consider turnover at the top, compensation structure, depth, experience, culture, industry/business relationships.)
9. How good are the company's cost analysis and accounting controls? (What are the systems and controls?)
10. What is the most important aspect to success particular to this industry? (Consider trends. Who is the best competitor and why?)
11. Does the company management have a long-range or short-term view on profits? (What investment is the company making in personnel, advertising, R&D, training, etc.?)
12. Will the company need continued financing support for growth?
13. Does the company management communicate well with the Street? Do they clam up under duress?
14. Is management's integrity unquestioned?

Porter Analysis (from Michael Porter's *Competitive Strategy*)

1. Ease of entry of new competitors? What are barriers to entry (scale, product, branding, capital, etc.)?
2. Threat of substitutes (commodity versus proprietary product)? Are substitutes available? What is pricing structure in the industry?
3. Bargaining power of buyers?
4. Bargaining power of suppliers?
5. Rivalry among existing competitors? How cutthroat is it?
6. Government? What are the current and potential legislative environments?

Company-Specific Industry Position

Who are the competitors?

Name   Public/Private   Size   Strength   Weakness

What is the company's position and role within the industry? (Leader?)

Growth Potential

1. Sales and EPS estimates for the year? (First Call.) What is current revenue growth? Organic? Acquisition?
2. Estimates by division/product (if appropriate)?
3. Industry market share? Chief competitor's market share?
4. International operations? (What is its percentage of operations? What is the potential?)
5. New-product research (trend as a percentage of sales)?

Accounting and Financial

1. Degree of recurring revenue? Earnings visibility?
2. Any weird stuff on the balance sheet?
3. What is the ROE? (Be detailed.)

General

1. Who owns the stock? Five largest shareholders?
2. Who covers the stock?
3. Investment bankers?
4. What are its relative strength and EPS rankings in *Investor's Business Daily*?

Outside Contacts

1. Largest customers
2. Competitors' salespeople

3. Independent industry visionaries (2)
4. One customer who was lost

Class Growth Stock Scorecard (from Jim Broadfoot's *Investing in Emerging Growth Stocks*)

Visibility/recurring revenue (What percentage? 50% is good.)	15
Maturity (early-stage or mature?)	12
Competition (monopoly or cutthroat?)	12
Distribution (direct is best)	10
Momentum (growth accelerating or stable?)	10
Return on equity (over 20% is good)	7
Balance sheet strength (under 25% debt to capital ratio)	7
Cash flow (operating?)	7
Growth rate (20% is good)	10
Accounting (reputation of internal and external)	10
	100

Four Ps Scorecard

People	50
Product	15
Potential	20
Predictability (visibility plus profitability)	15
	100

ThinkEquity Questions (for the company's management)

1. What are the three most important things for the company to achieve in the next six months? In the next three years?
2. Without making a prediction or a forecast, but being an optimist, what do you think this company could look like in five years?
3. What things could happen to screw it up?
4. What businesses do you admire?
5. What do the smart people ask that we haven't?

Megatrend Scorecard

	✓ **if yes**
Knowledge economy	☐
Globalization	☐
Internet	☐
Demographics	☐
Convergence	☐
Consolidation	☐
Brands	☐
Outsourcing	☐
	(max = 8)

→ DISCOUNTED CASH FLOW (DCF) ANALYSIS

When performing a discounted cash flow analysis, as the name suggests, I'm interested in the actual cash that the business generates so I can calculate the present value of those cash inflows.

In the scenario on page 337, Jimmy wants to sell half of his lemonade business to an investor, who will take the money out of his bank account and give it to Jimmy. In turn, the investor will receive half of the cash the lemonade stand generates. Therefore, the investor will be interested in the amount that can be deposited into his bank account over the years.

The important thing to understand is that net income does not equal the amount of actual cash a company generates. This is due to the fact that (a) when calculating net income in the income statement, depreciation and amortization (D&A) are included as an expense even though there is no cash payment associated with them; (b) capital expenditures are cash investments to sustain or grow a business's fixed assets, though they are not captured on the income statement; and (c) as a business grows, it will require more and more working capital (to fill in the time gap between paying for inventory and receiving cash payment from customers).

Looking at the lemonade stand's future financial performance, this is how it works:

Assuming that Jimmy adds 10 new stands a year and revenue per

LEMONADE STAND DISCOUNTED CASH FLOW MODEL

(DOLLARS IN THOUSANDS)	YEAR 1	YEAR 2	YEAR 3	YEAR 4	YEAR 5
Number of lemonade stands	10	20	30	40	50
Revenue per stand	$2,000	$2,000	$2,000	$2,000	$2,000
Revenue	$20,000	$40,000	$60,000	$80,000	$100,000
Net income	$2,000	$4,000	$6,000	$8,000	$10,000
Net margin	10.0%	10.0%	10.0%	10.0%	10.0%
Additional stands	9	10	10	10	10
Capital expenditures ($10/stand)	$90	$100	$100	$100	$100

Depreciation and amortization are negligible; changes in working capital are not taken into account.

Free cash flow (FCF) (= net income − cap ex)		$1,910	$3,900	$5,900	$7,900	$9,900

PV of FCF = FCF / $(1+r)^t$		$1,661	$2,949	$3,879	$4,517	$4,922

Terminal value

Terminal value based on perpetuity growth = Year 5 FCF (1+LT growth rate) / (weighted average cost of capital − LT growth rate) $77,677

PV of Terminal value $38,619

= Terminal value / $(1+r)^n$

Sum of PVs of free cash flow and terminal value	$56,547

Weighted average cost of capital (WACC)	15.0%
Long-term growth rate	2.0%

PRESENT VALUE SENSITIVITY ANALYSIS

		PERPETUITY GROWTH RATE				
		1.0%	1.5%	2.0%	2.5%	3.0%
	11.0%	$79,618	$83,051	$86,864	$91,127	$95,922
	13.0%	$64,278	$66,477	$68,877	$71,506	$74,397
Discount Rate	15.0%	$53,437	$54,935	$56,547	$58,289	$60,176
	17.0%	$45,401	$46,466	$47,602	$48,817	$50,118
	19.0%	$39,227	$40,010	$40,840	$41,720	$42,655

stand is $2 million, total revenue will increase by $20 million a year. We know that net income is 10 cents on each dollar of revenue so we can calculate net income and see that it grows from $2 million in year 1 to $10 million in year 5.

Before discounting these earnings, we have to make some of the adjustments that I mentioned above.

Buying 10 new lemonade stands each year costs Jimmy money. In fact, it costs $10,000 for each of them, in cash. However, it is not captured on the income statement, so Jimmy has to use part of his profit to make these investments. Therefore, we subtract these investments from the net income each year to get to a number that will actually be a pure cash amount that can be deposited in a bank.

In this example, we assume depreciation and changes in working capital are negligible, so we won't worry about them. (For those interested in how one would account for them: add D&A to net income to cancel the effect of a noncash expense on the income statement; and subtract the difference between next year's and this year's working capital.)

By making these adjustments to net income, we get to a number called free cash flow—the amount of cash that the business generates.

The next step is to discount the annual free cash flows to get their present value—the amount they are worth today. That's the same formula we discussed in chapter 7, "Valuation Methodology."

The most important factor is choosing the discount rate, or a range, to use in discounting the cash flows. The average is 12% for public companies in the United States. The discount rate has to reflect the risks associated with the investment and may be hard to estimate for a private company. That's why it is useful to apply a range.

One last thing we have to worry about is that so far we have only forecasted Jimmy's financial performance for the next five years, even though his business will, we hope, run longer than that. To capture the cash flow–generating power of the business after year 5, we assume his business will grow at a rate of 2% forever after—this is called the terminal value based on perpetuity growth. Jimmy's business, when looking at it from year 5 to forever, will be worth $77.677 million in year 5. So we need to discount back this amount to today (getting $38.619 million) and add it to the summation of the five present values of the free cash flows we calculate based on the operations of the first five years. The sum of these present values gives Jimmy's business's worth: $56.547 million.

THINKLIBRARY

To be a great investor, you have to be a curious person and always looking for opportunities to learn. Investing is part art, part science, and the books you read will significantly influence the type of investor you are. I've shared my "library" to provide a summary of what I feel are noteworthy books on investing, business, trends, and culture.

Broadfoot III, James W. *Investing in Emerging Growth Stocks: Making Money with Tomorrow's Blue Chips.* John Wiley & Sons, 1989. Some of the material is dated, but this is still an excellent framework for investing in emerging growth companies.

Bronson, Po. *The Nudist on the Late Shift: And Other True Tales of Silicon Valley.* Random House, 1999. Fun and insightful.

Buffett, Warren E. *Annual Reports.* Berkshire Hathaway, Inc. A must-read for every investor.

Christensen, Clayton M. *The Innovator's Dilemma: When New Technologies Cause Great Firms to Fail.* Harvard Business School Press, 1997. The reason why big and radical ideas rarely come from established companies.

———. *Seeing What's Next: Using the Theories of Innovation to Predict Industry Change.* Harvard Business School Press, 2004. Core systematic ways to think strategically ("This fits that objective").

Citrin, James M. *The 5 Patterns of Extraordinary Careers: The Guide for Achieving Success and Satisfaction.* Esaress Holding, 2003. A great headhunter provides an insightful framework to success in building a career.

Clissold, Tim. *Mr. China: A Memoir.* Robinson, 2004. Read everything available to understand China better.

Collins, Jim. *Good to Great: Why Some Companies Make the Leap . . . and Others Don't.* HarperCollins, 2001. Jim Collins is the best at analyzing core business principles and making a science of them.

Collins, Jim, and Jerry I. Porras. *Built to Last: Successful Habits of Visionary Companies.* HarperBusiness, 1994. Enduring business principles for growing companies.

Drucker, Peter F. *Innovation and Entrepreneurship.* Harper & Row, 1985. Anything by Peter Drucker should be read.

Ellis, Charles D., with James Vertin. *Classics: An Investor's Anthology.* Richard D. Irwin, 1989. A collection of the most enduring writing on investment theory and practice, *Classics* offers invaluable insights from the industry's leading thinkers.

———. *The Investor's Anthology: Original Ideas from the Industry's Greatest Minds.* John Wiley & Sons, 1997. A wonderful collection of essays from some of the investment industry's best minds.

Fisher, Kenneth L. *Super Stocks: The Book That's Changing the Way Investors Think.* McGraw-Hill, 1984. A great student of the market, Fisher introduces the concept of price to sales.

Fisher, Philip A. *Common Stocks and Uncommon Profits.* Harper & Brothers, 1958. One of the deans of growth investing provides ways to invest in great growth companies.

Friedman, Thomas. *From Beirut to Jerusalem.* Farrar, Straus and Giroux, 1989. Everything by Friedman is great. This excellent book makes sense out of the sometimes senseless events of the Middle East.

———. *The Lexus and the Olive Tree: Understanding Globalization.* Farrar, Straus and Giroux, 1999. Tom Friedman is the guru on globalization.

———. *Longitudes and Attitudes: Exploring the World After September 11.* Farrar, Straus and Giroux, 2002. Tom Friedman is the best journalist in terms of global observations and perspectives.

————. *The World Is Flat: A Brief History of the Twenty-first Century.* Farrar, Straus and Giroux, 2005. The best Friedman book yet, it's the key to understanding future influences of globalization.

Gilder, George. *Microcosm: The Quantum Revolution in Economics and Technology.* Touchstone, 1989. Gilder is a big thinker, but not always right.

————. *Telecosm: The World After Bandwidth Abudance.* Touchstone, 2000. I read everything that George Gilder writes, even if I don't understand half of it.

Gladwell, Malcolm. *Blink: The Power of Thinking without Thinking.* Little, Brown, 2005. The power of first impressions and gut reactions.

————. *The Tipping Point: How Little Things Can Make a Big Difference.* Little, Brown, 2000. An important book that helps us understand inflection points.

Godin, Seth. *Purple Cow: Transform Your Business by Being Remarkable.* Portfolio, 2003. Simple, fun, and effective.

Goodspeed, Bennett W. *The Tao Jones Averages: A Guide to Whole-Brained Investing.* Penguin, 1983. Short but smart, it helps you understand the artistic side of industry.

Graham, Benjamin. *The Intelligent Investor: The Definitive Book on Value Investing.* HarperCollins, 1973. A must-read by the dean.

Graham, Benjamin, and David L. Dodd. *Security Analysis.* McGraw-Hill, 1934. Still the bible of security analysis.

Grove, Andrew S. *Only the Paranoid Survive: How to Exploit the Crisis Points That Challenge Every Company.* Currency, 1996. Getting inside the mind of one of Silicon Valley's legends.

Kawasaki, Guy. *The Art of the Start: The Time-Tested, Battle-Hardened Guide for Anyone Starting Anything.* Portfolio, 2004. I love Guy and his manual for entrepreneurs.

Kelly, Kevin. *New Rules for the New Economy: 10 Radical Strategies for a Connected World.* Penguin, 1998. He's an original and forward thinker.

Kessler, Andy. *How We Got Here: A Slightly Irreverent History of Technology and Markets.* Collins, 2005. Fun and interesting.

Komisar, Randy, with Kent Lineback. *The Monk and the Riddle: The Art of Creating a Life while Making a Living.* Harvard Business School

Press, 2000. Putting the fun back into funerals, it's a witty and insightful read that speaks to the soul of business.

Lefèvre, Edwin. *Reminiscences of a Stock Operator.* George H. Doran, 1923. The story of Jesse Livermore, despite its real-life tragic ending, is cute, fascinating, and instructive.

Lewis, Michael. *Liar's Poker: Rising through the Wreckage on Wall Street.* W. W. Norton, 1989. A classic in demystifying Wall Street—and with Michael Lewis there are always broad lessons.

———. *Moneyball: The Art of Winning an Unfair Game.* W. W. Norton, 2003. It's all about thinking differently and getting the odds on your side.

———. *The New New Thing: A Silicon Valley Story.* W. W. Norton, 2000. Michael Lewis tells the story of serial entrepreneur Jim Clark in a way that captures the DNA of Silicon Valley.

Lindstrom, Martin. *Brand Sense: How to Build Powerful Brands through Touch, Taste, Smell, Sight, and Sound.* Kogan Page, 2005. A holistic approach to brand building.

Lynch, Peter, with John Rothchild. *Beating the Street.* Fireside, 1993. The second part of the Peter Lynch trilogy.

———. *Learn to Earn: A Beginner's Guide to the Basics of Investing and Business.* Fireside, 1995. As with Warren Buffett and Peter Drucker, read everything Peter Lynch writes.

———. *One Up on Wall Street: How to Use What You Already Know to Make Money in the Market.* Fireside, 1989. The best book ever on investing for the general public.

Mackay, Charles. *Extraordinary Popular Delusions & the Madness of Crowds.* Harmony Books, 1980. Understanding bubbles and crowd behavior. Human nature hasn't changed since the beginning of time.

Malkiel, Burton G. *A Random Walk down Wall Street.* W. W. Norton, 1973. This classic is an easy read written by a big brain.

Marvin, Carolyn. *When Old Technologies Were New: Thinking about Electric Communication in the Late Nineteenth Century.* Oxford University Press, 1988. The more things change, the more they stay the same.

Moore, Geoffrey A. *The Gorilla Game: Picking Winners in High Technology.* HarperBusiness, 1998. An important book for anyone interested in innovation.

————. *Inside the Tornado: Strategies for Developing, Leveraging, and Surviving Hypergrowth Markets.* HarperBusiness, 1995. Great book to help you understand the strategies of innovation.

Naisbitt, John. *Megatrends: Ten New Directions Transforming Our Lives.* Warner Books, 1982. The original and a classic.

Naisbitt, John, and Patricia Aburdene. *Megatrends 2000: Ten New Directions for the 1990's.* William Morrow, 1990. Understanding megatrends is key to growth investing.

Neff, Thomas J., and James M. Citrin. *Lessons from the Top: The 50 Most Successful Business Leaders in America—and What You Can Learn from Them.* Currency, 1999. A detailed review of what made the best CEOs tick. Hint: the common denominator is passion.

Negroponte, Nicholas. *Being Digital.* Alfred A. Knopf, 1995. A classic framework to understand the new digital world.

Norman, Donald A. *The Invisible Computer: Why Good Products Can Fail, the Personal Computer Is So Complex, and Information Appliances Are the Solution.* MIT Press, 1998. An important book on the future of technology.

O'Neil, William. *How to Make Money in Stocks: A Winning System in Good Times or Bad.* McGraw-Hill, 1994. O'Neil is founder and publisher of *Investor's Business Daily*. This book is a systematic framework for investing in growth stocks.

Packard, David. *The HP Way: How Bill Hewlett and I Built Our Company.* HarperBusiness, 1995. It all started in a garage. What a story.

Perkins, Anthony B., and Michael C. Perkins. *The Internet Bubble: Inside the Overvalued World of High-Tech Stocks—and What You Need to Know to Avoid the Coming Shakeout.* HarperCollins, 1999. Tony nailed this.

Peters, Thomas J., and Robert H. Waterman, Jr. *In Search of Excellence: Lessons from America's Best-Run Companies.* HarperCollins, 1982. A timeless classic on the principles of great companies.

Pink, Daniel H. *Free Agent Nation: The Future of Working for Yourself.* Warner Books, 2002. A fun read with good insight on the new, independent knowledge worker.

Popcorn, Faith. *The Popcorn Report: Faith Popcorn on the Future of Your Company, Your World, Your Life.* Doubleday, 1991. A guru on understanding consumer trends.

Rosenberg, Jr., Claude N. *Stock Market Primer: The Classic Guide to Investment Success for the Novice and the Expert.* Warner Books, 1962. Instructive and timeless on fundamentals of investing.

Schwager, Jack D. *The New Market Wizards: Conversations with America's Top Traders.* John Wiley & Sons, 1992. Some excellent interviews with leading investors.

Schwartz, Peter. *The Art of the Long View: Planning for the Future in an Uncertain World.* Currency Doubleday, 1991. A little boring, but it's the best "how to" guide on creating scenarios.

———. *Inevitable Surprises: Thinking Ahead in a Time of Turbulence.* Gotham Books, 2003. Updated scenarios for thinking about the future.

Schwartz, Peter, Peter Leyden, and Joel Hyatt. *The Long Boom: A Vision for the Coming Age of Prosperity.* Perseus, 1999. A brilliant framework for thinking about how the future may look.

Schwartz, Peter, and James A. Ogilvy. *Next Leap: Scenarios for China's Future.* Hardwired, 1998. Peter Schwartz is the best at scenario analysis.

Siegel, Jeremy. *Stocks for the Long Run: The Definitive Guide to Financial Market Returns and Long-Term Investment Strategies.* McGraw-Hill, 1994. Professor Siegel nails the science part of investing.

Silverstein, Michael J., and Neil Fiske. *Trading Up: The New American Luxury.* Portfolio, 2003. Boston Consulting Group thinkers discuss the importance of premium brands.

Sperling, John. *Rebel with a Cause: The Entrepreneur Who Created the University of Phoenix and the For-Profit Revolution in Higher Education.* John Wiley & Sons, 2000. Apollo Group was the top-performing stock from 1994 to 2004. Enough said.

Staley, Kathryn F. *The Art of Short Selling.* John Wiley & Sons, 1997. There aren't many good books on short selling, but this is one. Working with Dick Gilder (whom I view as one of the best growth investors ever) helps.

Surowiecki, James. *Wisdom of Crowds: Why the Many Are Smarter Than the Few and How Collective Wisdom Shapes Business, Economies, Societies and Nations.* Doubleday, 2004. An important book for understanding the power of the Internet and the network effect.

Swisher, Kara, with Lisa Dickey. *There Must Be a Pony in Here Some-*

where: The AOL Time Warner Debacle and the Quest for a Digital Future. Three Rivers Press, 2003. A good reminder that smart people can do dumb things.

Toffler, Alvin. *Future Shock.* Random House, 1970. Definitely ahead of his time, but still stimulating.

Train, John. *The Midas Touch: The Strategies That Have Made Warren Buffett "America's Preeminent Investor."* Harriman House, 2003. In my view, the best book on how Warren Buffett does it.

———. *The New Money Masters: Winning Investment Strategies of Soros, Lynch, Steinhardt, Rogers, Neff, Wanger, Michaelis, Carret.* Harper-Collins, 1989. It's always instructive to study what makes the best investors tick.

Wanger, Ralph. *A Zebra in Lion Country: The "Dean" of Small-Cap Stocks Explains How to Invest in Small, Rapidly Growing Companies Whose Stocks Represent Good Values.* Simon & Schuster, 1997. If you're standing in a bookstore by the personal finance shelves, trying to decide which book to buy, choose this one.

accounts receivable: Money owed to a company for goods and services it has sold. Payment is expected within one year. This money is listed as a current asset on the company's balance sheet.

accounts receivable turnover: The ratio of sales to accounts receivable. It can be a useful warning of credit or collection problems with a firm's customers. The AR turnover ratio is sometimes expressed in days.

alternative energy: Energy from sources other than the traditional oil, gas, and coal.

Alternative Investment Market (AIM): Created in 1995, a secondary market of the London Stock Exchange to serve small and midsize companies.

amortization: The process of gradually reducing a debt through install-ment payments of principal and interest, versus paying off the debt all at once.

anticipation approach: A stock valuation approach that places primary emphasis on anticipated market performance and assumes that the present market price is an appropriate reflection of the present situ-ation of a stock, including the general-consensus view of its future.

arbitrage: The business of taking advantage of the difference in prices of a security traded on two or more stock exchanges, by buying in one and selling in another.

assets: Items of value owned by an individual or corporation. Assets that can be quickly converted into cash are considered *liquid assets*. These include bank accounts, stocks, bonds, and mutual funds. Less liquid assets include real estate, personal property, and debts owed to an individual by others.

balance sheet: A financial statement showing the assets, liabilities, and net worth of a business as of a specific date.

bear: One who believes the price of stocks will go down. The opposite of *bull*.

bid: The highest declared price a buyer is willing to pay for a security at a particular time.

biopharmaceutical: The application of biotechnological research to the development of pharmaceutical products that improve human health, animal health, and agriculture.

biotechnology: The industrial application of living organisms and/or biological techniques developed through basic research. Biotechnology products include pharmaceutical compounds and research materials.

blog (weblog): A publication of personal thoughts on a Web site in reverse chronological order. The content and quality vary greatly, depending on the purpose, talent, and ego of the author. Many bloggers view such writing as an online diary with an audience. Weblogs began in the mid-1990s with the advent of free Web publishing tools.

blogosphere: The universe of blogs found throughout the World Wide Web.

blue chip: Active, leading, well-seasoned, nationally known ordinary (common) stocks, usually with long dividend records in good times and bad, and strong investment qualities.

book value: An accounting measure describing the net worth of common equity according to a firm's balance sheet.

branding: A company's or product's identity established through reputation, image, and quality.

bull: An investor who is buying because he or she feels prices will go up in that stock or that in general, market prices will rise. The opposite of *bear*.

capital market: Financial market where securities with a maturity greater than one year are traded.

capital turnover: A measure of company activity that serves as an early sign that something within the company is changing. Capital turnover = sales × (tangible assets − short-term accrued payments).

cash flow: The amount of cash a company generates and uses during a period, calculated by adding noncash charges (such as depreciation) to net income after taxes. Cash flow can be used as an indication of a company's financial strength.

cash flow per share: A measure of a firm's financial strength, calculated as cash flow from operations minus preferred stock dividends, divided by the number of common shares outstanding. Cash flow per share = (cash flow − preferred dividends)/common shares outstanding).

cleantech: See *greentech*.

collective intelligence: The capability of society to tap the knowledge and ideas from all parties connected to the World Wide Web and collaborate to decide their own future in a complex context.

common shares outstanding: Stock currently held by investors, including restricted shares owned by the company's officers and insiders as well as those held by the public. Shares that have been repurchased by the company are not considered outstanding stock.

common stock: Equities, or equity securities, issued as ownership shares in a publicly held corporation. Shareholders have voting rights and may receive dividends based on their proportionate ownership.

compound annual growth rate (CAGR): The average annual rate of growth of an investment when dividends or interest gains are reinvested. CAGR = (current value/initial value) ^ (1/(current year − initial year)) −1.

consolidation: Industries rolling up from many small companies into only a few big ones.

Consumer Confidence Index (CCI): A survey by the Conference Board that measures how optimistic or pessimistic consumers are with respect to the economy in the near future. A high measure implies higher spending and stimulation of the economy.

consumer confidence trends: A collection of measures used by the financial world to gauge consumer sentiment, and its likely impact on the economy. The most prominent consumer confidence survey is published monthly by the University of Michigan.

consumer price index (CPI): A measure of the average amount (price) paid for a market basket of goods and services by a typical American consumer in comparison to the average paid for the same basket in an earlier base year.

consumer savings: An alternative use of money that increases proportionally with interest rates and consumer confidence.

convergence: Industries and disciplines merging to create new products and disciplines.

current ratio: Current assets, including cash, accounts receivable, and inventory, divided by current liabilities, including all short-term debt. A ratio at or above 1 implies liquidity. Current ratio = total assets/total liabilities.

current yield: The annual income from an investment expressed as a percentage of the investment's current value.

deflation: The opposite of inflation, deflation is a gradual drop in the cost of goods and services, usually caused by a surplus of goods and a shortage of cash. Although deflation seems to increase your buying power in its early stages, it is generally considered a negative economic trend because it is typically accompanied by rising unemployment, falling production, and limited investment.

demographics: Factors among individuals such as age, race, educational level, employment status, and economic standard of living.

depreciation: Decrease in the value of an asset from wear and tear and the passage of time. Depreciation on business equipment is generally deductible for tax purposes.

depreciation and amortization (D&A): A noncash charge that represents a reduction in the value of fixed assets due to wear, age, or obsolescence. This figure also includes amortization of leased property, intangibles, goodwill, and depletion. This number is an add-back to the statement of cash flows.

derivative markets: Markets such as futures and option markets that are developed to satisfy specific needs arising in traditional markets. These markets provide the same basic functions as forward markets, but trading usually takes place on standardized contracts.

dividend yield: The return on investment that an investor will receive as dividends or interest. This is expressed as a percentage of the current market price of the security or, if the investor already owns the security, of the price he paid.

dividends: Cash or stock payments from a company's profits distributed to stockholders. An equal amount is paid for each share of stock owned.

diworsification: a term coined by Peter Lynch to represent a diversification strategy that reduces return.

double play: The combination of high earnings growth and an expanding P/E multiple. Also defined as Heaven on Earth for a growth investor.

due diligence: A thorough investigation of a company that is preparing to go public. It is undertaken by the potential investor's underwriter and accounting firm.

earnings: The net income of a company during a specific period. Generally, but not necessarily, refers to after-tax income.

earnings yield: The earnings per share for the most recent 12 months divided by market price per share.

EBIT (earnings before interest and taxes): A financial measure defined as revenues less cost of goods sold and selling, general, and administrative expenses. In other words, operating and nonoperating profit before the deduction of interest and income taxes.

EBITDA (earnings before interest, taxes, depreciation, and amortization): The measure of a company's earnings before interest, taxes, depreciation, and amortization. EBITDA enables an apple-to-apple comparison between those companies that have debt and those that do not, as well as those companies that fall within different tax brackets. This will allow you to look at the operating earnings of a company before the expenses of interest and taxes.

economic moat: A term coined by Warren Buffett to describe the competitive advantage that one company may have over others in the same industry.

EPS (earnings per share): A company's net income per share of common stock outstanding. EPS = (net income − dividends)/total shares outstanding

equity: The ownership interest in a company of holders of its ordinary and preferred stock.

FIFO (first in, first out): An accounting method based on an assumption regarding the flow of goods that older stock is disposed of first, in accordance with good merchandising policy. The opposite of *LIFO*.

five bagger: A term coined by Peter Lynch to represent an undertaking in which investors receive five times their original investment.

follow-on offering: An offering of additional common stock after the initial public offering.

globalization: The evolution of a worldwide economy. Interdependence between countries is increasing with improvements in communications, technology, and transportation.

greentech: Any technology aimed at improving the well-being of the overall environment.

Gross Domestic Product (GDP): The total value of goods and services produced by a nation in one year.

gross margin: Profit margin before operating expenses are deducted. Gross margin = gross profit/sales.

Gross National Product (GNP): The value (in U.S. dollars) of a country's final output of goods and services in a year. The value of GNP can be calculated by adding up the amount of money spent on a country's final output of goods and services, or by totaling the income of all citizens of a country, including the income from factors of production used abroad.

growth company: A company with rates of EPS and revenue growth sufficient to be of interest to growth investors. Microcap: revenue 25%, EPS 30%; small cap: rev. 20%, EPS 25%; midcap: rev. 15%, EPS 20%; large cap: rev. 10%, EPS 15% per year.

hedge fund: A private, unregulated investment fund for wealthy investors (minimum investments typically begin at US$1 million) specializing in high-risk, short-term speculation on stocks, bonds, currencies, stock options, and derivatives.

homesourcing: Hiring people to work from home in the same way that outsourcers hire people to work from other countries.

human capital: The value of people as an asset to a company or organization in that they contribute to its performance and growth, similar to the way money and machinery do.

hurdle rate: The required rate of return that will get a company or individual "over the hurdle" to invest their money.

in the money: An option whose exercise would produce profits. *Out of the money* describes an option where exercises would not be profitable.

inflation: An increase in the cost of goods and services, most often measured by the consumer price index. When too much money chases too few goods, inflation is the result. Economic growth often causes moderate inflation by increasing consumer spending at a faster rate than the production of goods and services.

initial public offering (IPO): When a company raises money by offering stock to the public in exchange for ownership in the company.

Internet: Media, commerce, education, social life, work, and leisure move to interconnected computers from traditional forms.

IPO: See *initial public offering.*

intrinsic value (of a firm): The value that is justified by assets, earnings, dividends, definite prospects, and the factor of management.

intrinsic value (of an option): Stock price minus exercise price, or the profit that could be attained by immediate exercise of an in-the-money option.

intrinsic value approach: The attempt to value a stock independent of its current market price. This approach is a normative concept that seeks to determine what a stock is worth; that is, the price at which it should sell if properly priced in a normal market.

inventory turnover: Ratio of annual sales to inventory. It shows how many times the inventory of a firm is sold and replaced during an accounting period. Inventory turnover = annual sales/year-end inventory.

knowledge economy: Since World War II, American society has been shifting from an industrial-based economy to a service-based economy in which the educated are kings.

large cap: A publicly traded company with a market capitalization greater than $5 billion.

leveraged buyouts: The purchase of shares, usually by the management of a company, using its own assets as collateral for loans provided by banks or insurance companies.

LIBOR (London interbank offered rate): Often used as a basis for pricing Euroloans, LIBOR represents the interest rate at which first-class banks in London are prepared to offer dollar deposits to other first-class banks. There are a number of similar rates, such as HIBOR (Hong Kong), SIBOR (Singapore), and TIBOR (Toronto).

LIFO (last in, first out): An assumption that the last inventory received will be the first sold. It is a more conservative model than *FIFO* (first in, first out) and lowers earnings by raising the cost of sales.

liquidity ratio: The ratio of the dollar volume of a security's trading to the price of the security. The higher the currency volume, the greater the liquidity of the security.

long position: A purchase position in a security. It signifies ownership of a security.

margin: The difference between the cost and selling price of a product or service.

margin of safety: A term popularized by Benjamin Graham. When an investor will invest only in securities selling at a market price significantly below what the investor believes is the security's intrinsic value, the difference between intrinsic value and price is the investor's margin of safety.

market cap: The value of a company in the stock market as measured by the total dollar value of its common shares outstanding (i.e., stock price multiplied by number of shares outstanding). Market cap = stock price × common shares outstanding.

market maker: A member firm that gives two-way quotations for a particular security and that is under an obligation to buy and sell it subject to certain conditions such as overall exposure and spread.

market share: The percentage of a market that a company dominates. The ratio of market cap to overall market size. Market share = market cap/market size.

Metcalf's Law: Each new member, supplier, and user of a network adds exponential value.

microcap: A publicly traded company with a market capitalization between $50 and $250 million.

midcap: A publicly traded company with a market capitalization between $1 and $5 billion.

Moore's Law: The theory that processing power will double every 18 months, and at half the cost.

mutual fund: Fund operated by an investment company that raises money from shareholders and invests it in stocks, bonds, options, commodities, or money market securities. These funds offer investors the advantages of diversification and professional management.

nanocap: A publicly traded company with a market capitalization below $50 million.

nanotechnology: Technology development at the atomic, molecular, or macromolecular range of approximately 1 to 100 nanometers in order to create and use structures, devices, and systems that have novel properties.

NASDAQ Exchange: A computerized system established by the National Association of Securities Dealers (NASD) to facilitate trading by providing broker/dealers with current bid and ask price quotes on over-the-counter stocks and some listed stocks. Unlike the AMEX and NYSE, the NASDAQ does not have a physical trading floor that brings together buyers and sellers. Instead, all trading on NASDAQ is done over a network of computers and telephones. Also, the NASDAQ does not employ market specialists to buy unfilled orders as the NYSE does.

negatrend: A secular shift in society, the market, and/or politics that will result in a shrinking market opportunity.

nominal GDP: The market value of goods and services produced over time including the income of foreign corporations and foreign residents working in the United States, but excluding the income of U.S. residents and corporations overseas. Nominal GDP is reported as is, without adjusting for inflation.

NTM EPS: The next 12 months of a company's forecasted per-share earnings.

NYSE (New York Stock Exchange): The oldest and largest stock exchange in the United States. Located on Wall Street in New York City, the NYSE is responsible for setting policy, supervising member activities, listing securities, overseeing the transfer of member seats, and evaluating applicants. It traces its origins back to 1792, when a group of brokers met under a tree at the tip of Manhattan and signed an agreement to trade securities. Unlike some of the newer exchanges, the NYSE still uses a large trading floor in order to conduct its transactions. Here, representatives of buyers and sellers—professionals known as brokers—meet and shout out prices at one another in order to strike a deal. Among the exchanges, the NYSE has the most stringent set of requirements for the companies whose stocks it lists, and even meeting these requirements is not a guarantee that the NYSE will list a company.

on-demand: The ability to receive goods and/or services whenever and wherever they are asked for.

open-source: A philosophy of software distribution that allows anyone to read and modify the program's source code. Because anyone can modify the source code, bug fixes, improvements, and implementation of new specific features occur rapidly.

operating margin: Ratio providing information about a firm's profitability from the operations of its core business without regard to investment policy, financing policy, or tax position. Operating margin = operating income/sales.

outsourcing: As employing American citizens becomes increasingly expensive relative to the rest of the world, U.S. employers look abroad.

P/E/G ratio: A valuation ratio of a company's current share price compared to its earnings per share taking growth into account. A general Wall Street rule of thumb is that if a stock's P/E/G ratio equals 1, it is fairly valued; less than 1, it is inexpensive; and if more than 1, it is expensive. P/E/G = market value per share (price)/earnings per share/3- to 5-year growth rate.

Philadelphia SOX Index: A sector index created by the Philadelphia Stock Exchange. It consists of 18 stocks, 14 of which are chip manufacturers such as Intel and National Semiconductor. The remaining four companies provide capital equipment to those manufacturers and include Applied Materials and KLA Tencor.

phishing: Electronic communication scam in which people are fraudulently urged to give their credit card or account information to a third party.

podcasting: Making audio files (most commonly in MP3 format) available online in a way that allows software to automatically download the files for listening at the user's convenience.

PPI (producer price index): A monthly index that measures the level of prices for all goods produced and imported for sale in the primary marketplace. Increase in the PPI tends to lead other measures of inflation.

price-to-earnings ratio (P/E): A valuation ratio of a company's current share price compared to its per-share earnings. This measure is used by investment experts to compare the relative merits of a number of securities. Price-to-earnings ratio = stock price/earnings per share.

private equity: Equity securities of private companies. They are generally illiquid and thus thought of as long-term investments. Investors in private securities generally receive their return through one of three ways: an initial public offering, a sale or merger, or a recapitalization.

private placement memoradum (PPM): A document to outline investment attributes and risk for a private investment.

prospectus: Document containing an invitation to invest. The document explains the workings of the company, provides financial details of the project, and contains the application form for investment.

pure play: An idea, company, or investment whose success is highly correlated to a specific theme or overarching trend.

quick assets: Assets that can be easily converted into cash or are already in cash form. Calculated as current assets minus inventories. Quick assets = current assets – inventories.

quick ratio: A measure of liquidity similar to the current ratio except that the current ratio includes inventory. Quick ratio = (cash + receivables)/liabilities.

random walk theory: Theory that a stock's past price action is no guide to future prices because prices move randomly, not in a pattern. Random walk theoreticians would sneer at the idea that because a stock has been moving up during the past few weeks, it is likely to continue moving up.

real GDP: The market value of goods and services produced over time including the income of foreign corporations and foreign residents working in the United States, but excluding the income of U.S. residents and corporations overseas. Real GDP is measured in relation to a baseline such as the CPI (see *consumer price index*) to account for changes due to inflation.

reality media: The concept of user-generated content through an open forum where people can post and share ideas, thoughts, music, and videos.

relative value: As measured in terms of risk, liquidity, and return, the attractiveness of one instrument relative to another or, for a given instrument, of one maturity relative to another.

relative value approach: An approach to investing in which analysts more or less accept the prevailing level for the general market and seek to determine the relative value of a stock in terms of it.

research and development (R&D): Money spent by companies to invest in the future are costs that must be charged to current expenses on a company's balance sheet. There is no consistent relationship between products, money spent, and the value of the discovery process, but typically growth companies spend a higher percentage of revenue on R&D.

return on equity (ROE): An accounting ratio of net profits divided by equity, which indicates a company's profitability. Return on equity = net income/shareholders' equity.

return on invested capital (ROIC): A measure, usually expressed as a percentage, that gauges the performance of a company. When the ROIC is greater than the cost of capital (usually measured as weighted average cost of capital), the company is creating value. When it is less than the cost of capital, value is destroyed. ROIC = net operating profits after tax/total investment.

risk aversion: Amount of risk an investor is unwilling to take on an investment.

RSS (really simple syndication or rich site summary): An XML-based format for content distribution. RSS feeds can be used for news readers and weblogs (blogs). These feeds include headlines, summaries, and links back to your content.

Russell 2000 Index: This index consists of 2,000 small-cap stocks. These stocks are selected to act as an unbiased barometer of small-cap investment.

S&P 400 Index: A 400-security index intended to cover the midcap range of U.S. stocks.

S&P 500 Index: This index consists of 500 large-cap stocks. These stocks are selected to act as a leading indicator of U.S. equities.

S&P 600 Index: A 600-security index intended to cover the small-cap range of U.S. stocks.

same-store sales (comparative-store sales): Sales from stores open for a year or more.

secondary market: The market for previously issued securities or financial instruments.

secondary offering: A company's selling of additional shares of stock to the public after its initial public offering.

selling, general, and administrative expenses (SG&A): Reported expenses that may or may not include R&D, depending on the nature of the company and the magnitude of R&D as a factor in the total expense composition.

selling short: A maneuver in which an investor sells securities he or she does not own, and is required to buy them back later (hopefully at a lower price).

sensitivity analysis: Evaluating the impact of different scenarios on a company's operating performance. For example, analyzing the impact of 10% higher revenue growth or 1% higher gross margins on earnings per share. (See "Lemonade Stand Discounted Cash Flow Model," page 337.)

small cap: A publicly traded company with a market capitalization between $250 million and $1 billion.

stagflation: The combination of sluggish economic growth, high unemployment, and high inflation.

stagnation: A period of low-volume trading on the securities market.

ten bagger: A term coined by Peter Lynch to represent an undertaking in which investors receive 10 times their original investment.

top-down view: Looking at the big picture and systematically applying the resulting conclusions to more specific situations.

total debt service: The ratio of total debt accrued in a time period to total income. A favorable ratio is generally less than 40%. Total debt service = total debt/total income.

trade deficit balance: The ratio or difference between a country's imports and exports. Trade deficit balance = imports – exports or = imports/exports.

turn: The number of times a company's inventory is sold during the year.

unemployment rate: The percentage of people who have been actively searching but unable to find work over an extended period of time. The unemployment rate is the percentage of unemployed within the total workforce.

venture capitalist (VC): An investor who provides capital to either start-up ventures or small companies that wish to expand but do not have access to public funding.

visibility (of earnings or revenue): The extent to which future projections are predictable and plausible.

VoIP (Voice over Internet Protocol): A technology for transmitting ordinary telephone calls over the Internet using packet-linked routes. Also called *IP telephony.*

Web 2.0: The era in which the Internet is going to emerge as the fundamental global platform for communications, commerce, information, services, and product development. This second wave of the Internet will truly connect the world economy.

wiki: The Hawaiian word for "quick." Wiki sites are Web sites designed for open communication among users, who can make additions or edit as they wish.

Wikipedia: An online encyclopedia open for writing and editing by anyone who has an interest in a subject. There are more than a million articles in English alone, with articles also available in more than 50 other languages.

ACKNOWLEDGMENTS

I'M A BIT EMBARRASSED about seeing my name alone on the cover of this book because, in fact, it "took a village" to produce *Finding the Next Starbucks*.

First and foremost, I want to thank my research assistant Sarah Hopping, who has worked tirelessly pulling this all together and challenging me when I didn't make any sense (while still competing as a nationally ranked track athlete in her spare time!).

My friends and partners at ThinkEquity contributed most of the intellectual capital for the book. In particular, I would like to acknowledge my co-founder, Deborah Quazzo (who rightly points out that many of the best ideas were hers), our director of research Peter Coleman, Ryan Mahoney, Kirsten Edwards, Mike Burton, Nicole Miller, Julie Welter, Suresh Balaraman, Balazs Veress, Nico Herden, Pat Dillingham, Stewart Barry, Jordan Wolfe, Katie Soffey, Mike Armstrong, Ranjini Chandirakanthan, Michael Huang, Michael Zhang, Paul Combs, Ed Weller, David Edwards, Stuart Pulvirent, and Mat Johnson, who all took a special interest in this project.

I'm grateful to those who read all or part of the manuscript and offered suggestions to improve it: Peter Lynch, Mark Moe, Tom Moe, Marcia Massee, John Cogan, and Heather Weir.

I was very fortunate to have been granted interviews by some of the leading minds in the investment and business world, many of whom I've gotten to know well over the years, namely Howard Schultz, Michael Milken, Richard Driehaus, Joe McNay, Vinod Khosla, Randy Komisar, Drew Cupps, Mark Waterhouse, David Spreng, Cliff Greenberg, Bryant Kiehl, Bill Joy, Bill Sahlman, Duncan Byatt, Tony Perkins, Geoff Yang, Mark Olson, Charlie Harris, Tim Draper, Steve Jurvetson, Bruce Dunlevie, Jack Laporte, Dan Levitan, Bob Grady, Marc Benioff, Promod Haque, Sam Colella, Ira Ehrenpreis, and Pip Coburn.

A special thank-you goes to interviewee Dick Perkins, who taught me what a stock was back in Minneapolis. I also give a special thanks to interviewees "Coach" Bill Campbell, Ed Mathias, and Ron Conway (who double as invaluable Advisory Board members at ThinkEquity) and to my other coach, Lou Holtz, who taught me more about business through football than could be imagined.

In particular, I want to acknowledge the incredible support I got for the book from the loves of my life: Bonnie, Maggie, and Caroline. Truly, I've been blessed.

Last but certainly not least, I want to thank my publisher, Adrian Zackheim, who thought I had something to write about. I hope he is right.

To all, a heartfelt thank-you!

INDEX

Page numbers in *italics* refer to graphs and charts.